Living Abundantly
Studies in Ephesians

by Theodore H. Epp
Director
Back to the Bible Broadcast

A
BACK TO THE BIBLE
PUBLICATION

Back to the Bible
Lincoln, Nebraska 68501

13,000 printed to date—1983
(5-1975—2.5M—83)
ISBN 0-8474-1228-8

Printed in the United States of America

Foreword

The wealth of the Book of Ephesians is indicated by the captions expositors have given to it. One expositor has called it "The Grand Canyon of the Scripture," thereby emphasizing its grandeur and splendor and the spiritual depths to which it goes. Another has called it "The Pike's Peak of the Scriptures," emphasizing the height the book attains as it tells believers of their position in Christ.

The Book of Ephesians is especially important to Theodore Epp for two reasons. First, it was when he was a young man that, on hearing an exposition of this book, he realized he didn't possess the riches in Christ that had been described. Upon further thought he realized that even though he had grown up in a Christian home, he did not have a personal relationship with Christ. He then placed his trust in Christ, receiving Him as his Saviour. Second, early in his ministry he was impressed with the truth of Romans 10:17: "So then faith cometh by hearing, and hearing by the Word of God." As a young minister, Theodore Epp realized that if believers were to have their faith strengthened, the Word of God must be clearly expounded to them. This particularly includes the Book of Ephesians, which tells what a believer really is and has in Christ.

The main burden expressed in *Living Abundantly* is that believers might see the need—and the possibility—of living abundantly. Jesus said, "I am come that they might have life, and that they might have it more abundantly" (John 10:10). This volume reveals that we live abundantly as we recognize and appropriate the resources we have in Christ.

—The Publishers

Contents

Chapter 1

Living Abundantly

The Book of Ephesians is especially significant to the believer because it reveals what he possesses because he is "in Christ." Throughout this study much will be said about the expression "in Christ" as we examine resources that belong to every believer.

To properly understand the Book of Ephesians, one must understand that every believer is involved in spiritual conflict and that this conflict will last as long as the believer is on earth. To miss this point is to miss the significance of the Book of Ephesians, because it is the believer's spiritual conflict that makes his resources in Christ so important.

A soldier's success in battle depends on the resources available to him. If all the resources he has are what he is able to carry with him, he will soon be defeated. For him to have success in battle, the resources of the country he represents must be available to him while he is fighting, and he must use them to their full potential.

So, too, if the Christian is to have victory in his spiritual battles, he must make full use of the resources which he has in Christ. The Book of Ephesians reveals the intensity of the spiritual battle and shows the resources that every believer has in Christ.

An Old Testament counterpart to Ephesians is the Book of Joshua. The Book of Joshua tells how God had promised the land to the Israelites—which made it potentially theirs—but they had to go into the land to claim it for themselves. It was not enough for them to realize that God was able to give them the land; they had to move ahead by faith to actually take what God had promised. God told

7

Joshua, "Every place that the sole of your foot shall tread upon, that have I given unto you, as I said unto Moses" (1:3). God gave it, but the Israelites had to take it.

God desires to do a tremendous work in and through each believer. Paul, who wrote the Book of Ephesians, said, "For we are his workmanship, created in Christ Jesus unto good works, which God hath before ordained that we should walk in them" (Eph. 2:10). Another translation states it this way: "For He has made us what we are, because He has created us through our union with Christ Jesus for doing good deeds which He beforehand planned for us to do" (Williams). So God wants to accomplish much through the believer but is able to do this only as the believer makes use of his resources in Christ.

Because Satan and his emissaries attack every Christian, it is imperative that all believers know what their standing, or position, is in Christ. To know one's standing is to know one's resources. Therefore, Paul prayed, "That the God of our Lord Jesus Christ, the Father of glory, may give unto you the spirit of wisdom and revelation in the knowledge of him: the eyes of your understanding being enlightened; that ye may know what is the hope of his calling, and what the riches of the glory of his inheritance in the saints, and what is the exceeding greatness of his power to us-ward who believe, according to the working of his mighty power" (1:17-19).

The believer needs to realize that when he puts to use what God has made available, no spiritual enemy can have victory over him. Realizing this, Paul exclaimed, "What shall we then say to these things? If God be for us, who can be against us? He that spared not his own Son, but delivered him up for us all, how shall he not with him also freely give us all things? Who shall lay anything to the charge of God's elect? It is God that justifieth. Who is he that condemneth? It is Christ that died, yea rather, that is risen again, who is even at the right hand of God, who also maketh intercession for us" (Rom. 8:31-34).

Abundant Life

In order to understand the significance of the Book of Ephesians, it is also imperative to keep in mind the kind of life Christ intends for every believer. When a person acknowledges his sin and accepts Jesus Christ as his personal Saviour, he receives forgiveness of sin and comes into possession of eternal life. Christ intends the believer to have more than eternal life; He wants the believer to have abundant life. This was the purpose of Jesus' coming to earth. He said, "I am come that they might have life, and that they might have it more abundantly" (John 10:10). Every person who receives Jesus Christ as Saviour has eternal life, but not every believer has entered into an abundant, or overflowing, life. That is, not every believer has the joy that comes from knowing what he has in Christ and living accordingly.

Although not referred to by this terminology, the abundant life is spoken of in Colossians 2:6: "As ye have therefore received Christ Jesus the Lord, so walk ye in him." A person becomes a believer as he places his faith in Christ alone for salvation; he has abundant life as he exercises his faith in Christ in the routine of daily living.

Eternal life is God-produced; it is the result of the second birth. A person experiences this birth by receiving Christ as Saviour, at which time he comes into possession of this God-produced life. However, the abundant life has to do with the way a person lives *after* he has been born again. The way a person lives is referred to in the Scriptures as his "walk." Thus, a person comes into possession of eternal life when he places his faith in Christ alone and experiences a spiritual birth; a believer has abundant life as he exercises his faith in Christ for his daily walk.

Eternal life is based on the finished work of Christ for redemption; the abundant life is based on the present work of Christ through the Holy Spirit's operating in the believer's life. Because the work of redemption has been finished, nothing the believer does adds to this aspect of his life. However, the abundant life is to be a present experience which the believer has as he yields to the Holy Spirit. As such, the abundant life depends on the believer's continuous faith as he walks daily with Christ. Just as a person becomes a Christian by placing his faith in Christ alone as Saviour, so a believer has abundant life as he lives by faith. The Bible says, "The just shall live by faith" (Rom. 1:17).

Eternal life is procured by the death, burial and resurrection of Jesus Christ. By His death Jesus paid the penalty for sin; by His burial He took sin away; by His resurrection He lives in the believer. This is all involved in the new birth. On the other hand, the abundant life is procured for the believer through the living, ascended Christ, who is seated at the right hand of the Father. The believer who lives on the basis of what he possesses in Christ has an abundant life. He realizes the indwelling Christ is able to meet any need.

Eternal life is objective in the sense that a person obtains it by placing faith in the fact of Christ's shed blood for the remission of sins. The abundant life is subjective in that it is a personal response to what a believer has in Christ. The one who knows that Christ is able to meet every need and who lives accordingly has the abundant life.

Eternal life is the same for all believers regardless of their sinful past. It does not matter whether the person was guilty of gross sin, as society measures sin, or whether he was a person of high moral standards. All who receive Christ have eternal life. However, not all believers have abundant life. The abundant life varies in believers according to their individual responses to Jesus Christ.

In the physical realm, it is one thing to have life but it is quite another to enjoy the treasure of life and to see and take advantage of the opportunities of each day. So in the spiritual realm, the person who knows Jesus Christ as Saviour has eternal life, but only the one who knows what he has in Christ and lives accordingly is living the abundant life. Unless the distinctions between eternal life and abundant life are recognized, there will be much confusion in the believer's life. If a believer is trying to add to his eternal life or retain it by what he does, he will be frustrated because he does not understand what the Scriptures say concerning eternal life. Once he realizes it is a completed work in his behalf, he will be able to turn his attention toward living the Christian life by faith, which is the abundant life. His experiencing a lapse of faith in the Christian life does not mean that he loses his eternal life but that he is no longer living the abundant life. This is another way of saying that sin in the believer's life does not break his union with God but it breaks his communion. The believer who confesses his known sin and walks in dependence on the Holy Spirit experiences the abundant life.

The Book of Ephesians clearly reveals not only the eternal life that each believer has but also the abundant life that it is possible for every believer to live. Chapters 1-3 reveal the believer's position in Christ, and chapters 4-6 challenge the believer to walk in Christ.

The believer's position is emphasized in these words: "Blessed be the God and Father of our Lord Jesus Christ, who hath blessed us with all spiritual blessings in heavenly places in Christ" (1:3). The believer's walk in Christ is emphasized in these words: "I therefore, the prisoner of the Lord, beseech you that ye walk worthy of the vocation wherewith ye are called" (4:1).

In beginning this inspired letter, the Apostle Paul gave a twofold salutation: (1) "to the saints which are at Ephesus," and (2) "to the faithful in Christ Jesus" (v. 1). A "saint" is one who has received Jesus Christ as Saviour. The position of such a person is revealed in the first three chapters of Ephesians. The last three chapters deal specifically with the second part of the twofold salutation, "to the faithful in Christ Jesus," because it emphasizes the abundant life.

The Church

The word "church" is used to mean various things. It is used to refer to a building; to a group of people who constitute a local assembly of believers; and to the Body of Christ, which is composed of all who receive Him as Saviour during this present age. The Bible has much to say about this latter group. Ephesians 1:22,23 reveals that the Father "hath put all things under his [the Son's] feet, and gave him to be head over all things to the church, which is his body, the fulness of him that filleth all in all." First Corinthians 12 reveals that each believer is a member of the Body of Christ. This is true regardless of the local church in which he worships. The present age—from the Day of Pentecost to the Rapture of the Church—is commonly designated as "the Church Age."

The Church, as the Body of Christ, was not revealed or anticipated in the Old Testament. That which believers looked forward to in the Old Testament was the First Coming of the Messiah to suffer for sin and His Second Coming to earth to establish the kingdom of God. As the writers of the Old Testament Scriptures looked ahead to these two events they were like a person looking across mountain peaks. Such a person is able to see the tops of the mountains. As a result, Old Testament believers knew the teaching of the Scriptures about the First and Second Comings of Christ but did not know (because the Old Testament Scriptures did not reveal it) what was to happen between these two events.

Concerning salvation during the Church Age, Peter said, "Of which salvation the prophets have inquired and searched diligently, who prophesied of the grace that should come unto you: searching what, or what manner of time the Spirit of Christ which was in them did signify, when it testified beforehand the sufferings of Christ, and the glory that should follow" (I Pet. 1:10,11). The suffering of Christ was revealed in such passages as Isaiah 53 and Psalm 22. The glory that followed is referred to in such a passage as Psalm 24. But no passage in the Old Testament revealed truth concerning the Church Age, which would exist between these two events.

The Old Testament portrays Christ not only as coming King but as Saviour. Zechariah 9:9 says, "Rejoice greatly, O daughter of Zion; shout, O daughter of Jerusalem: behold, thy King cometh unto thee: he is just, and having salvation; lowly, and riding upon an ass, and upon a colt the foal of an ass." Thus the Old Testament Scriptures were clear that the coming Messiah would provide salvation.

The Gospel of Matthew records the fulfillment of Zechariah's prophecy and the reaction of the people. "And when they had approached Jerusalem and had come to Bethphage, to the Mount of Olives, then Jesus sent two disciples, saying to them, 'Go into the village opposite you, and immediately you will find a donkey tied there and a colt with her; untie them, and bring them to Me. And if anyone says something to you, you shall say, "The Lord has need of them;" and immediately he will send them.' Now this took place that what was spoken through the prophet might be fulfilled, saying, 'Say to the daughter of Zion, Behold your King is coming to you, gentle and mounted upon a donkey, even upon a colt, the foal of a beast of burden.' And the disciples went and did just as Jesus had directed them, and brought the donkey and the colt, and laid on them their garments; on which He sat. And most of the multitude spread their garments in the road, and others were cutting branches from the trees, and spreading them in the road. And the multitudes going before Him, and those who followed after were crying out, saying, 'Hosanna to the Son of David; blessed is He who comes in the name of the Lord; hosanna in the highest!' " (21:1-9, NASB).

The common people seemingly accepted Him as a king but saw no need of Him as a Saviour. Israel's religious leaders rejected Him even as King. Matthew also records, "And when He had entered Jerusalem, all the city was stirred, saying, 'Who is this?' And the multitudes were saying, 'This is the prophet Jesus, from Nazareth in Galilee' " (vv. 10,11, NASB). The response of the religious leaders is seen in verses 15-17: "But when the chief priests and the scribes saw the wonderful things that He had done, and the children who were crying out in the temple and saying, 'Hosanna to the Son of David,' they became indignant, and said to Him, 'Do You hear what these are saying?' And Jesus said to them, 'Yes; have you never read, "Out of the mouth of infants and nursing babes Thou hast prepared praise for Thyself"?' And He left them and went out of the city to Bethany, and lodged there" (NASB). Israel's leaders rejected Him as the Messiah. It was at the time of this rejection, as Luke records in his Gospel, that the Lord Jesus Christ wept over Jerusalem. "And when He approached, He saw the city and wept over it, saying, 'If you had known in this day, even you, the things which make for peace! But now they have been hidden from your eyes. For the days shall come upon you when your enemies will throw up a bank before you, and surround you, and hem you in on every side, and will level you to the ground and your children within you, and they will not leave in you one stone upon another, because you did not recognize the time of your visitation' " (19:41-44, NASB).

It is understandable that in the midst of the people's confusion the disciples did not recognize that the Church was going to be brought into existence after Christ's rejection by Israel.

Prophecy of the Church

The first direct prophecy of the Church was given by Christ Himself. When He asked His disciples to give their opinions as to who He was, Peter said, "Thou art the Christ, the Son of the living God" (Matt. 16:16). In reply to Peter's statement, Jesus said, "Thou art Peter, and upon this rock I will build my church; and the gates of hell shall not prevail against it" (v. 18). It is important to notice that Peter was not the rock to whom Christ referred. This is evident from the Greek New Testament. The word for "Peter" is *petros*, which was used in referring to a stone, but the word for rock is *petra*, which was used in referring to a massive rock. The foundation of the Church was not Peter but "Christ, the Son of the living God" (v. 16).

Observe what we learn about the Church from Christ's prophetical statement in verse 18. First, it was to be His work—"I will build." Second, it was to be His Church—"my church." Third, it was to be a progressive work—"I will build." Fourth, there was to be stability in the Church—"the gates of hell shall not prevail against it."

The Lord Jesus Christ gave this prophecy concerning the Church, but He did not give further details concerning it. As a result, the disciples did not understand how the Church Age fit into the program of God. In fact, it is apparent that just before Jesus returned to heaven the disciples were still looking for the kingdom of God to be established on earth. They asked Him, "Lord, is it at this time You are restoring the kingdom to Israel?" (Acts 1:6, NASB). The disciples did not understand that after the crucifixion and resurrection of Christ, the Church Age would begin.

Detailed revelation concerning the Church was later given to the apostles, particularly to the Apostle Paul, and it is especially set forth in the Book of Ephesians. Paul told the Ephesian believers, "If ye have heard of the dispensation of the grace of God which was given me to you-ward: how that by revelation he made known unto me the mystery; . . . that the Gentiles should be fellowheirs, and of the same body, and partakers of his promise in Christ by the gospel" (Eph. 3:2,3,6). A "mystery" in Scripture is something revealed which was previously hidden. Details concerning the Church Age were previously undisclosed, but now they were revealed.

Throughout the Old Testament, God was working with the Jews. They were a special earthly people through whom He worked. The mystery now revealed by Paul was not that Gentiles could also have salvation, because this was true even in Old Testament times. The mystery was that the believing Jew and the believing Gentile were being formed into one body called the Church, which is also referred to as "the Bride of Christ." Great cultural barriers separated the Jews and the Gentiles, but the revelation concerning the Church is that when a Jew and a Gentile receive Christ as Saviour, they become one in Him. This is a level of fellowship previously unknown to Jews and Gentiles.

Those living during Old Testament times were saved by grace just as were those living during New Testament times. However, those saved during Old Testament times did not become members of the Body of Christ, the Church. The Church Age did not begin until the Day of Pentecost, when the Holy Spirit descended and baptized believers into the Body of Christ.

Truth concerning the Body of Christ was revealed before Ephesians was written but it is Ephesians that emphasizes that the believing Jew and Gentile are one in Christ. From I Corinthians 12:13 we learn that it is the baptism of the Holy Spirit that places a person into the Body of Christ. "For by one Spirit are we all baptized into one body, whether we be Jews or Gentiles, whether we be bond or free; and have been all made to drink into one Spirit."

Paul's Letters

Paul's epistles, or letters, deal with both the universal Church—of which every believer is a member—and the local church.

Paul's letters have been arranged in the Bible in a way that shows progression in the believer's life and in the church.

Although not an inspired arrangement, obviously it was superintended by the Holy Spirit.

The first group of Paul's letters—Romans, I and II Corinthians and Galatians—reveals truths that have to do with salvation. They are key books to study in order to learn what it means to be justified, sanctified and liberated from all forms of legalism. Because of an emphasis on salvation, these letters focus attention on the cross of Christ where Christ provided all things for the believer.

The next three epistles—Ephesians, Philippians and Colossians—reveal truths to the believer concerning his indissoluble oneness with the Son of God as a chosen member of His mystical Body, the Church. These letters tell of the believer's completeness in Christ and show that the believer has an exalted position with Christ. They focus attention on the ascended Christ, and they emphasize the need for the believer to be in fellowship with Christ so that the spiritual unity will be evident to others.

The next two epistles—I and II Thessalonians—reveal the consummation of the Church Age. Believers in Christ will be caught up from the earth when the Lord Jesus descends from heaven. All believers in Christ during the present age are part of the universal Church, which is referred to as "the Bride of Christ." These two epistles look forward in hope to the soon coming of the Bridegroom for the Bride, the Church.

Paul's other letters were written to individuals—Timothy, Titus and Philemon. Timothy and Titus were young pastors and Paul's letters to them had much to do with the local church and its organization. Philemon was a personal friend whom Paul wrote and urged to welcome back a runaway slave who had found Christ.

Comparisons

In focusing attention on Ephesians it is helpful to compare this letter with Paul's other epistles. For instance, many of his letters deal with the church as an organization, whereas Ephesians treats the Church more as an organism—the living Body of Christ. Whereas most of Paul's letters emphasize the local church, Ephesians emphasizes the universal Church.

The Book of Romans presents Christ as crucified and risen and reveals that the believer has been crucified and has risen with Him. In Ephesians, Paul tells of the ascended position that the believer has in Christ.

Ephesians and Colossians are closely associated in their emphasis. Both letters were written by Paul during one of his imprisonments. Ephesians emphasizes the Body of Christ, which is the Church; Colossians emphasizes the Head of the Body, Jesus Christ. Ephesians reveals the believer's position in Christ as part of His Body; Colossians reveals the believer's completeness in Christ, who is the Head of the Body. Ephesians reveals the believer's position in Christ more clearly than any other epistle; Colossians presents Christ as the Head of the Body more clearly than any other epistle.

Ephesians reaches the highest peak in relating the believer's position in Christ while at the same time emphasizing the walk, or life, of the believer who is engaged in spiritual warfare against the forces of evil. The Body of Christ is what believers *are;* walking, or living, in a manner glorifying to the Lord is what believers are to *do.*

Ephesians contains the highest Church truth but nothing about church order. As has been said, the Church in focus in Ephesians is the universal Church, not the local church. Ephesians emphasizes those believers everywhere in contrast to believers in one locality.

A Glimpse Ahead

Before beginning a detailed examination of the verses of Ephesians, it is important to have a glimpse at the entire book by considering its extent, content, central teaching, central thought, key words, and the truth that will be emphasized throughout this study.

First, the extent, or scope, of Ephesians. All believers are seen as the mystical Body of Christ, the Church. Ephesians tells of the heavenly calling of the Church—its position in Christ—and describes the earthly conduct of the Church—how believers are to act because of their position in Christ. The letter also tells of the spiritual conflict; especially the satanic warfare against the believer.

Second, the content of Ephesians. This is closely related to the extent of the book. The content of Ephesians reveals the wealth, walk and warfare of the believer. The wealth of the believer is that he is "in Christ." The walk of the believer emphasizes Christ in the believer living His life through the believer. The warfare of the believer is Christ in union with the believer against the forces of Satan and his host.

Third, the central teaching of Ephesians. This letter reveals the eternal calling and character of the Church. This is seen in that believers are referred to as chosen in Christ "before the foundation of the world" (1:4). Believers are also seen as those through whom Christ wishes to display His grace and glory in eternity to come (2:7). From this it is seen that the teaching of Ephesians relates the believer to eternity past as well as to eternity future.

Included in the central teaching of Ephesians is the temporal conduct of the Church—its behavior on earth—especially in relation to spiritual warfare and the victory that is possible for every believer.

Fourth, the central thought of Ephesians. Throughout the book it will be evident that Christ is the fullness of the Church; that is, the Church is not complete without Him.

The Church is also seen in Ephesians as the fullness of Christ; that is, without the Church He is not complete as He desires to be. As people receive Christ as Saviour, they become members of the Body of Christ. His mystical Body will not be complete until the last individual to receive Him as Saviour has done so and the Church has been caught up to heaven. Christ makes the Church complete inasmuch as He fills, or indwells, every member; the Church makes Christ complete in that it comprises His mystical Body.

Fifth, the key words in Ephesians. These words are "in Christ." This phrase, in its various forms, is found over 90 times in Ephesians. The significance of these words in Ephesians is that a believer is "made one with" Christ.

Becoming one with Christ is similar in meaning to what happens to copper and zinc when they are combined—they become an alloy known as brass which is neither copper nor zinc. In such a state, the copper is "made one with" zinc and the zinc is "made one with" copper so that together they constitute brass.

As the believer lives according to the spiritual union he has with Christ, he will discover that Christ will work mightily in and through him. As the believer does this, he will have what is commonly referred to as "the abiding life." Christ said, "Abide in me, and I in you. As the branch cannot bear fruit of itself, except it abide in the vine; no more can ye, except ye abide in me" (John 15:4).

Sixth, the truth of Ephesians, which will be especially emphasized in this study. This truth is that the believer has resources in Christ. It is imperative that each believer realize what is deposited in his account in the bank of heaven. The believer's riches are in Christ because of all that Christ has accomplished for the believer. These riches can be drawn upon according to the believer's need and according to his faith in Christ. It is important to know that the spiritual resources are more than enough to cover all past debts (1:7), present liabilities (3:16), and future needs (v. 8).

The Book of Ephesians reveals that God has overwhelming reserves for the believer. The believer has available to him the fullness of God (3:19), the fullness of Christ (4:13), and the fullness of the Holy Spirit (5:18).

The Book of Ephesians can be divided into three main divisions: (1) Doctrine—The believer's heavenly calling (the believer in Christ) (1:1—3:21); (2) Practice—The believer's earthly conduct (Christ in the believer) (4:1—6:9); (3) Conflict—The believer's spiritual conflict (Christ through the believer) (6:10-20). The more detailed outline that follows will be the guide for this study.

Study Outline for the Book of Ephesians

I. DOCTRINE—The believer's **heavenly calling** (the believer in Christ) (1:1—3:21)

   A. Praise for the believer's spiritual treasures (1:3-14)

   B. Prayer for the believer's spiritual apprehension (1:15-23)

   C. Man made new by the grace of God (2:1-10)

   D. Jew and Gentile made one by the blood of Christ (2:11-22)

   E. God's eternal mystery of the Church revealed (3:1-12)

   F. Prayer for realization and appropriation of God's fullness (3:13-21)

II. PRACTICE—The believer's **earthly conduct** (Christ in the believer) (4:1—6:9)

   A. The conduct of the Church united (4:1-16)

   B. The conduct of the believer individually as a new man (4:17-32)

   C. The conduct of the believer in relation to the outside world (5:1-14)

   D. The Spirit-filled inner life of the believer (5:15-21)

   E. The believer's married life—illustrating Christ's relationship to the Church (5:22-33)

   F. The domestic life of the believer regarding children, parents, servants and masters (6:1-9)

III. CONFLICT—The believer's **spiritual conflict** (Christ through the believer) (6:10-20)

Chapter 2

Paul's Greeting

(Eph. 1:1,2)

The salutation of Paul's letter to the Ephesians begins with these words: "Paul, an apostle of Jesus Christ by the will of God, to the saints which are at Ephesus, and to the faithful in Christ Jesus" (v. 1).

In New Testament times it was customary for the writer to place his name at the beginning of a letter rather than at the end of it as we do today. Often, a descriptive phrase about the writer was given so the readers would know his qualifications for writing on a particular subject.

The very first word in Paul's letter to the Ephesians was his own name—Paul. The meaning of this name is significant. People today name their children without being too concerned about the meaning of the names. This was not so in Bible times, for the names given then reflected the aspirations the parents had for their children.

Two Names

The writer of Ephesians had two names—Saul and Paul. Saul is a Hebrew name and Paul is a Greek name. Some Bible interpreters maintain that Paul had always had both names because it was the custom for Jews living in a Greek culture to have both a Hebrew, or Jewish, name and a Greek one. Others maintain that Paul's name was Saul before his conversion and that afterwards he was given the name Paul. The Hebrew name Saul means "asked" and as such probably implies greatness. Because he was great, his counsel was sought, or asked, by many.

21

"Saul" was an important name in Israel's history. The first king bore this name, so those who bore it later were probably looked upon as having potential greatness. Certainly, before Paul became a Christian he had attained great standing because of his religious life as an Israelite.

The first time the Bible mentions Paul it refers to him as "Saul." Referring to the time when Stephen was being stoned by the Israelites for the message of God he had preached to them, the Bible says, "Saul was consenting unto his death" (Acts 8:1). The passage continues, "And at that time there was a great persecution against the church which was at Jerusalem; and they were all scattered abroad throughout the regions of Judaea and Samaria, except the apostles. And devout men carried Stephen to his burial, and made great lamentation over him. As for Saul, he made havock of the church, entering into every house, and haling men and women committed them to prison" (vv. 1-3).

Acts 9:1,2 says, "And Saul, yet breathing out threatenings and slaughter against the disciples of the Lord, went unto the high priest, and desired of him letters to Damascus to the synagogues, that if he found any of this way, whether they were men or women, he might bring them bound unto Jerusalem." As he was on his way to Damascus, the Lord suddenly appeared to Saul and he came to know Jesus Christ as his personal Saviour.

The name "Paul" is first recorded in Acts 13:9: "Then Saul, (who also is called Paul,) filled with the Holy Ghost, set his eyes on him." This incident took place after Paul had come to know Jesus Christ as his Saviour, for he was confronting Elymas the sorcerer, who was seeking to turn away a person from the faith.

The name "Paul" means "little." From this point forward in the New Testament, this is the name by which this choice servant of God was known. He was known as "Paul, the little one" in the Lord's service.

Paul's own testimony is recorded in Philippians 3:4-7: "Though I might also have confidence in the flesh. If any other man thinketh that he hath whereof he might trust in the flesh, I more: circumcised the eighth day, of the stock of Israel, of the tribe of Benjamin, an Hebrew of the Hebrews; as touching the law, a Pharisee; concerning zeal, persecuting the church; touching the righteousness which is in the law, blameless. But what things were gain to me, those I counted loss for Christ." Many believers are too important in their own eyes for God to use. Paul was used by God because he was small in his own eyes. This reveals the struggle of the Christian life. The believer must determine whether he is going to rely on himself or whether he is going to rely on God.

An Apostle

In writing to the Ephesians, Paul described himself as "an apostle of Jesus Christ by the will of God" (1:1). The word "apostle" refers to "one sent on a mission"—one commissioned to do something as another's representative. In the technical sense, it refers to the 12 men chosen by the Lord while He was on earth. Paul's apostleship was on this level because the Lord appeared to him from heaven. In the general sense, every believer is an apostle because he is sent on a mission for Jesus Christ.

Paul referred to believers as "ambassadors for Christ" (II Cor. 5:20). Verses 18 and 19 reveal that to believers has been committed the "ministry of reconciliation" and the "word of reconciliation." It is the responsibility of every believer to be an ambassador to take the Good News to unbelievers. The Good News is that Christ has paid the penalty for their sin and that they can be delivered from condemnation by receiving Him as Saviour.

From other letters written by Paul we learn that he was an apostle to the Gentiles. Paul wrote: "For I speak to you Gentiles, inasmuch as I am the apostle of the Gentiles, I magnify mine office" (Rom. 11:13). Paul was pleased to be an apostle of the Gentiles, those whom he had previously considered to be outcasts. Paul was no longer great in his own eyes; he saw himself as God's ambassador to take the gospel to everyone, especially the Gentiles. God has a plan for every person, and his plan for Paul was that he would be an apostle to the Gentiles. Ephesians 3, which we will later consider in detail, tells of the message Paul was given for the Gentiles.

Paul told the Ephesians that he was an apostle of Jesus Christ "by the will of God" (1:1). He was not a self-appointed apostle, nor was he elected by the majority—he was appointed by God. Concerning his apostleship, he emphasized to the Galatians, "An apostle, (not of men, neither by man, but by Jesus Christ, and God the Father, who raised him from the dead;)" (1:1). Further emphasizing his apostleship from God, Paul said, "God . . . separated me from my mother's womb, and called me by his grace, to reveal his Son in me, that I might preach him among the heathen [Gentiles]" (vv. 15,16). Paul was especially chosen by God for a special purpose. When God sent Ananias to Paul after Paul was blinded by light on the road to Damascus, the Lord told Ananias, "He is a chosen vessel unto me, to bear my name before the Gentiles, and kings, and the children of Israel" (Acts 9:15). Concerning all believers, the Lord Jesus Christ said, "Ye have not chosen me, but I have chosen you, and ordained you, that ye should go and bring forth fruit" (John 15:16).

When declaring his appointed message, Paul referred to himself as an "apostle of Jesus Christ." However, when appealing to believers to walk worthy of God's call, he referred to himself as a "prisoner of the Lord." A prisoner is one who lives under another's control. Because Paul lived in this manner, he knew the life he was speaking of when he told the Ephesians, "I therefore, the prisoner of the Lord, beseech you that ye walk worthy of the vocation wherewith ye are called" (4:1).

Saints

Having introduced himself as the writer of the letter, Paul specified those whom he was addressing. He wrote: "To the saints which are at Ephesus, and to the faithful in Christ Jesus" (Eph. 1:1). The word "saint" has been grossly misused and misunderstood. Some use it to refer to a venerated individual; others use it in referring to some Christian—"Isn't he a saint?"

The Greek word that is translated "saint" was commonly used in New Testament times. In fact, the pagan Greeks used it to refer to something or someone "devoted to the gods." It is lifted to a new level as it is used in the New Testament to refer to something or someone separated, or set apart, unto the true God. From the basic Greek word many terms are derived such as sanctify, holy, holiness, to hallow.

Inasmuch as the basic word refers to something or someone set apart for God, it is used in the New Testament to refer to the act of the Holy Spirit setting a person apart for God. When a person receives Jesus Christ as Saviour, he is taken out of the first Adam and placed in the last Adam—"in Christ Jesus." This is a once-and-for-all act which is accomplished at the time of salvation. The individual has a perfect position in Christ, known as "positional sanctification." Because his conduct on earth fluctuates, it is necessary for him to experience the process of sanctification, which lasts a lifetime. This latter is known as "progressive sanctification" because it has to do with a person's spiritual life after he is saved. The first three chapters of Ephesians emphasize positional sanctification—what a person is in Christ; the last three chapters emphasize progressive sanctification—the process through which the believer passes to make him more like Christ.

It is progressive sanctification that is the subject of Romans 8:28,29: "We know that all things work together for good to them that love God, to them who are the called according to his purpose. For whom he did foreknow, he also did predestinate to be conformed to the image of his Son, that he might be the firstborn among many brethren." Notice the purpose of progressive sanctification—that the individual be "conformed to the image of his Son."

Every person who has received Jesus Christ as Saviour is set apart to God positionally. As such, the individual is set apart to worship and to serve God. This position is unchangeable. A person becomes a "saint" in the scriptural use of the term the moment he receives Christ as Saviour, and nothing can change that position. As to his earthly conduct, a believer does not always live like a saint; that is, he does not always walk according to his position in Christ.

A saint is what each believer is because of the finished work of Christ. The individual's part is to receive Jesus Christ by faith; God's part is already finished and is applied to the person the moment he believes. The believer's behavior does not change his position—it neither adds to it nor subtracts from it.

A person born into a family is a member of the family by birth. Nothing changes that relationship. He may not act like a member of the family, but he is such regardless of the way he acts. So an individual becomes a member of God's family by receiving Jesus Christ as Saviour. At the moment of salvation the individual receives a perfect position in Christ and remains a child of God by birth whether or not his behavior measures up to God's standards. However, this does not mean that an individual who is truly born again will want to live in sin. At the time of salvation the individual is given a new nature. Therefore, his basic desire is to please Christ even though he occasionally experiences pitfalls in his Christian life.

The set-apart position a believer has in Christ demands a life separated from everything in this world that interferes with his worship and service. Paul emphasized this truth when he wrote: "I therefore, the prisoner of the Lord, entreat you to walk in a manner worthy of the calling with which you have been called" (Eph. 4:1, NASB). The Ephesian believers had been called to a perfect position in Christ and they were to walk accordingly.

After enumerating in the Book of Romans evidences of the wonderful grace of God, Paul wrote: "I urge you therefore, brethren, by the mercies of God, to present your bodies a living and holy sacrifice, acceptable to God, which is your spiritual service of worship. And do not be conformed to this world, but be transformed by the renewing of your mind, that you may prove what the will of God is, that which is good and acceptable and perfect" (12:1,2, NASB).

Sanctification indicates ownership—because believers have been bought by Jesus Christ, they are set apart for Him. Paul told the believers at Corinth: "What! know ye not that your body is the temple of the Holy Ghost [Spirit] which is in you, which ye have of God, and ye are not your own? For ye are bought with a price: therefore glorify God in your body, and in your spirit, which are God's" (I Cor. 6:19,20).

Paul's second letter to the Corinthians also instructs believers as to what they should do because of their relationship with the Lord. Paul told the Corinthian believers, "Be ye not unequally yoked together with unbelievers"

(6:14). Instead, the believer is to heed the words, "Wherefore come out from among them, and be ye separate" (v. 17).

Because Paul's letter was written "to the saints which are at Ephesus," it was addressed to every person in Ephesus who had received Christ as Saviour. By inspiration, this letter also applies to every person who has become a believer in Christ since Paul wrote the letter. In fact, the words "at Ephesus" are thought by some not to have appeared in Paul's original letter. As such, it would have been a letter to have been circulated among many groups of Christians. It is certainly applicable to all believers.

Paul completed his greeting by saying, "and to the faithful in Christ Jesus." The words "in Christ Jesus" show he is addressing believers, not unbelievers.

Grace and Peace

Having designated those to whom he was writing, Paul said, "Grace be to you, and peace, from God our Father, and from the Lord Jesus Christ" (v. 2). The grace Paul referred to was not the saving grace of God but God's grace manifested to the believer after salvation. The saving grace of God is mentioned in II Corinthians 8:9: "For ye know the grace of our Lord Jesus Christ, that, though he was rich, yet for your sakes he became poor, that ye through his poverty might be rich." In Ephesians, Paul was addressing those who had already experienced saving grace, so his emphasis was on God's grace for daily living. The main purpose of Ephesians is to inform believers of what they have in Christ and then to exhort them to live accordingly.

It is the grace of God in living that believers need to realize. This grace is mentioned in II Corinthians 9:8: "God is able to make all grace abound toward you; that ye, always having all sufficiency in all things, may abound to every good work." Romans 5:1,2 reveals that believers have access to the grace of God by faith: "Therefore being justified by faith, we have peace with God through our Lord Jesus Christ: by whom also we have access by faith into this grace wherein we stand, and rejoice in hope of the glory of God." Having received Jesus Christ as Saviour, believers have access to God's grace for daily living. God's grace is as a bank account for the believer to write checks on. The believer derives benefits as he exercises faith.

In Paul's salutation to the Ephesians he also mentioned "peace." Here again, it is not the peace related specifically to salvation but peace in daily living. At the time of salvation, a person becomes at peace *with* God. However, the believer also needs to have the peace *of* God. Romans 5:1 reveals that a person has peace with God when he is saved: "Therefore being justified by faith, we have peace with God through our Lord Jesus Christ." However, many who have peace with God do not have the peace of God in their daily experience. This is an inner peace that is possible for every believer but not always possessed by every believer. Paul mentioned the peace of God in writing to the Colossians: "Let the peace of God rule in your hearts" (3:15). Philippians 4:6,7 also tells of the peace of God: "Be careful [anxious] for nothing; but in every thing by prayer and supplication with thanksgiving let your requests be made known unto God. And the peace of God, which passeth all understanding, shall keep your hearts and minds through Christ Jesus."

Jesus spoke of this inner peace when He said, "Peace I leave with you, my peace I give unto you: not as the world giveth, give I unto you. Let not your heart be troubled, neither let it be afraid" (John 14:27). Notice that Jesus said He was leaving "my peace." When believers claim this peace for their lives, they will not be troubled or afraid because they will possess the peace of One who is never troubled or afraid.

Peace is a fruit of the Spirit (Gal. 5:22). As the believer walks in dependence on the Holy Spirit, this fruit will be evident in his life.

In Ephesians 1:2, Paul stated that the grace and peace was "from God our Father, and from the Lord Jesus Christ." Paul carefully distinguished between the Father and the Son, and it is important to observe this distinction throughout the Book of Ephesians. Paul's emphasis was that all that the Father has for the believer is available in the Son, Jesus Christ.

Although the Father and the Son are equal, they have different relationships with the believer. Notice that Paul said, "God our Father." This designation reveals the concern of God for the believer. Paul referred to the Son as "the Lord Jesus Christ." The title "Lord" reveals mastership, or headship. Jesus Christ is the Head of the Body, the Church, and every believer is to serve Him as Master.

Chapter 3

Praise for Spiritual Treasures
(Eph. 1:3)

In verses 3-14, Paul praises God for the spiritual treasures each believer has because of his relationship with Jesus Christ. Paul was so taken up with the riches in Christ Jesus that he wrote on and on about the same things. In fact, verses 3-14 are just one sentence in the original language.

Paul began his statement, "Blessed be the God and Father of our Lord Jesus Christ, who hath blessed us with all spiritual blessings in heavenly places in Christ" (v. 3). The word "bless," and its various forms, has almost lost its meaning in contemporary language. Perhaps this is both from overuse and misuse. The word translated "blessed" in verse 3 is the word from which the English word "eulogize" is derived. Another word is also translated "bless" in the Beatitudes of Matthew's Gospel. The word used there means "happy." In Ephesians, however, Paul was eulogizing God because of all the blessings He has made available to the believer in Christ Jesus.

We bless God by praising Him, whereas He blesses us by showering His benefits upon us. The logical question is, How can we qualify for these benefits? The answer is seen in verse 3: "Blessed be the God and Father of our Lord Jesus Christ, who hath blessed us with all spiritual blessings in heavenly places in Christ."

Paul was writing to believers; thus, he said, "Our Lord Jesus Christ." Ephesians was directed to Christians and therefore is, in a sense, a family letter because it tells what the Heavenly Father has provided for His children everywhere.

One qualifies for the benefits of God by receiving Jesus Christ as personal Saviour. When Paul said that God has blessed "us," he was referring to all believers. Every person who has received Christ as Saviour can rejoice in this verse because it reveals that God has provided all that he needs, and more, in the Person of Jesus Christ.

As to when God blesses His own with these benefits, notice that the expression is in the past tense—"[God] hath blessed us." Through what God has accomplished in the past, He has bequeathed to the believer unsearchable riches. This makes it an even greater shame when the believer lives as a spiritual pauper. Every person who has received Christ as Saviour is spiritually rich. Paul said of the Lord Jesus Christ, "Though he was rich, yet for your sakes he became poor, that ye through his poverty might be rich" (II Cor. 8:9).

When believers do not walk according to their position in Christ—that is, when believers do not appropriate the riches of Christ—the result is spiritual immaturity. This is seen from the Book of Hebrews, where believers were told, "For though by this time you ought to be teachers, you have need again for some one to teach you the elementary principles of the oracles of God, and you have come to need milk and not solid food. For every one who partakes only of milk is not accustomed to the word of righteousness, for he is a babe. But solid food is for the mature, who because of practice have their senses trained to discern good and evil" (5:12-14, NASB). The believer is to appropriate the riches he has in Christ. Particularly, God has revealed in the Bible truths and principles that, when applied to daily living, produce maturity in the believer.

That God has already provided all that the believer needs becomes apparent as one observes the past tense used in Ephesians 1:3-14. Every believer would do well to read through these verses and underline the verbs that are in the past tense, which appear in almost every verse. In days ahead, this would serve as a reminder of the resources he possesses in Jesus Christ.

Spiritual Blessings

Verse 3 not only tells us that God has blessed us but it also tells with what He has blessed us—"with all spiritual blessings." Notice they are "spiritual" blessings.

Certain benefits of God are available to all mankind, whereas other benefits are available only to His children—those who have received Jesus Christ as Saviour. God's benefits to mankind in general are seen in Matthew 5:45: "For he maketh his sun to rise on the evil and on the good, and sendeth rain on the just and on the unjust." These are physical benefits that God sends to the whole earth and individuals benefit whether they are believers or not. These benefits are in the natural realm.

However, the believer has benefits in the spiritual realm that the unbeliever does not possess. The believer lives on a higher level—he lives in a spiritual sphere and has had provided for him all that he needs. Colossians 1:13 says that God "hath delivered us from the power of darkness, and hath translated us into the kingdom of his dear Son." The one who has received Christ as Saviour has a heaven-born nature so he needs heaven-sent supplies to spiritually nourish and develop him. All such spiritual supplies are provided for the believer in Christ.

The individual who has received Christ as Saviour has been united to Christ, but he is traveling through a world which has an ungodly, hostile atmosphere. Thus, the believer needs a spiritual atmosphere in which to breathe. Just as astronauts have to take along their own atmosphere when they go to the moon, the believer needs spiritual atmosphere to sustain his spiritual life while on earth. The believer needs spiritual food, spiritual companions, spiritual exercise, spiritual strength and spiritual weapons.

God has blessed believers with "all" spiritual blessings (Eph. 1:3). Many of these are mentioned in Paul's letter to the Ephesians and we will be examining them in detail in our study.

God has withheld nothing in providing benefits for the believer—all spiritual blessings are available. God has not just given "out of" His riches but He has provided for the believer "according to" His riches. This truth is emphasized often throughout Ephesians. Concerning Christ, Paul said, "In whom we have redemption through his blood, the forgiveness of sins, according to the riches of his grace" (1:7). That God has provided for the believer according to His riches is also revealed in Paul's other writings, such as Philippians 4:19: "But my God shall supply all your need according to his riches in glory by Christ Jesus."

There is not a single benefit that God wants to provide for the believer that He is unable to provide. Every blessing that is needed for the spirit, soul and body; every blessing that is needed for past, present and future; every blessing that is needed for salvation, sanctification and service; and every blessing that is needed for time and eternity has been provided in Christ for the believer. As is seen from II Corinthians 9:8, God is able to make His grace overflow to the believer so that the believer has everything he needs to meet any spiritual problem.

'In Heavenly Places'

Ephesians 1:3 reveals that God has blessed believers with all spiritual benefits "in heavenly places." In the King James Version, the word "places" is in italics, which indicates the word was added by the translators because they thought it was needed to convey the meaning of the original language. However, the word translated "in heavenly" can mean "in the heavenly sphere." As such, it would not necessarily refer to heaven itself but to the sphere in which a believer lives because he is identified with Jesus Christ. The believer is a "heavenly" individual because he has a nature that has come from heaven. Living "in the heavenlies" is living spiritually on a heavenly level while living physically on earth. Because all believers are in Christ, all believers are in this spiritual realm even though living on earth.

The one who has received Christ as Saviour and therefore has a nature from heaven is to have his mind on the things of heaven. Paul wrote: "If [since] ye then be risen with Christ, seek those things which are above, where Christ sitteth on the right hand of God. Set your affection on things above, not on things on the earth. For ye are dead, and your life is hid with Christ in God" (Col. 3:1-3). The person who has received

Christ as Saviour has taken part in the death of Christ and has also become a sharer in the life of Christ. Having died with Christ, the believer is to be living in a way that pleases Him.

As Paul wrote his letter to the Ephesians he was in a Roman prison, but he was living in the heavenlies because of his union with Christ. It is obvious that Paul had his mind set on heavenly things as he wrote by inspiration of God. Philippians and Colossians were also written during this time, and the reader sees nothing of despair and gloom in these letters. Paul realized he was living in a heavenly realm even though he was in a Roman prison, and what he wrote brought glory to Christ. Every believer has the spiritual resources available to him that Paul had. Even while on earth, it is possible for the believer to enjoy the benefits of God that will be fully enjoyed in heaven.

'In Christ'

In Ephesians 1:3 the significant words "in Christ" appear. Verse 1 refers to the faithful "in Christ Jesus." The expression "in Christ" and its equivalents, such as "in him" and "in whom," appear over 130 times in the New Testament. The words "in Christ" are the master key which gives access to all spiritual blessings in the heavenly realm. These two short words are the most important words ever written to express the mutual relationship of the believer and Christ.

The expression "in Christ" means far more than partnership with Christ; it actually means that the individual believer is a member of Christ's Body, the Church. Paul told the Corinthian believers, "Now ye are the body of Christ, and members in particular" (I Cor. 12:27). As part of His Body, the believer glorifies Christ as he does the will of Christ, who is the Head of the Body. Just as in a physical body the desires of the head are carried out through the body, so in the mystical Body the desires of Christ, the Head, are carried out through the Body, the believers.

The person who receives Christ does not lose his identity even though he is part of the Body of Christ. The individual still has a distinct personality, but it will be drastically affected because of the person's being in Christ and living in the heavenly sphere.

The believer's resources—all spiritual blessings—are "in Christ." Christ is the life of the believer and thus provides for him all that he needs. Before salvation the individual was in Adam, but after salvation he is in Christ. In Adam the individual possessed only a sinful nature, but in Christ he possesses a divine nature. The divine nature of the believer causes him to want to do the will of God.

Apart from Christ, a person has no relationship to God and God has no relationship to him. Before a person receives Christ, he is unable to benefit from the spiritual blessings God has provided. Only after a person becomes "in Christ" are all the resources of God available to him. God's wealth for the believer is deposited in Christ, and it is only when a person receives Christ that this spiritual wealth becomes available to him.

Without Christ a person is spiritually dead but in Christ he is spiritually alive. Those in Christ inherit the blessings of God because they are joint heirs with Jesus Christ (Rom. 8:17).

Without Christ one has no spiritual strength, but in Christ he is able to achieve any spiritual victory. However, even the believer must rely on spiritual provisions if he is to experience spiritual victories. Jesus told believers, "I am the vine, ye are the branches: He that abideth in me, and I in him, the same bringeth forth much fruit: for without me ye can do nothing." Because Paul knew his spiritual resources, he said, "I can do all things through Christ which strengtheneth me" (Phil. 4:13).

In Christ a person has position—where He is, the believer is; privilege—what He is, the believer is; possession—what He has, the believer shares. The two words "in Christ" open up all the treasures of Ephesians for the believer.

Ephesians 1:3 and Joshua 1:3 provide a significant comparison. Ephesians 1:3 emphasizes God's responsibility. All the resources of God are made available to the believer. Joshua 1:3 emphasizes the believer's responsibility. God had promised the land of Canaan to the Israelites but He told Joshua, "Every place that the sole of your foot shall tread upon, that have I given unto you, as I said unto Moses."

Although God had given the land to the Israelites, the people were responsible to take the land. God was telling Joshua, "It's already yours but you have to go in and take it." So also, present-day believers possess all spiritual blessings in Christ but it is necessary for them to appropriate these blessings. God never forces His benefits on anyone, but He never withholds His blessings from anyone who will take Him at His word. All that follows in the Book of Ephesians is meaningless to believers unless they claim it because of their position in Christ.

Between Eternity Past and Future

Ephesians 1:4 continues the thought of verse 3: "According as he hath chosen us in him before the foundation of the world, that we should be holy and without blame before him in love." Notice especially the time element in verse 4—"before the foundation of the world." From the human standpoint, this time element can be referred to as eternity past.

Another time element is mentioned in verse 10: "That in the dispensation of the fulness of times he might gather together in one all things in Christ." This refers to eternity future. The same time is referred to in 2:7: "In order that in the ages to come He might show the surpassing riches of His grace and kindness toward us in Christ Jesus" (NASB). An examination of the time elements mentioned in the above verses reveals that God's plan is an eternal one. Also, we see that the Church, composed of individual believers of the present age, was in the plan and purpose of God from all eternity and that He has a purpose for the Church throughout all eternity.

Thus, the Book of Ephesians reaches from eternity past to eternity future and places special attention on the present. Because man has a finite, or limited, mind, it is difficult for him to think in terms of eternity. When Moses recorded God's inspired message about creation, he said, "In the beginning God created" (Gen. 1:1). Moses was permitted to see as far back as the beginning of creation. In the New Testament the Apostle John was enabled to see even farther back into eternity: "In the beginning was the Word, and the

Word was with God, and the Word was God. The same was in the beginning with God" (John 1:1,2). Just as John went beyond any other writer in looking to eternity past, he went beyond any other writer in looking to eternity future. In the Book of the Revelation he recorded many truths concerning the future eternal state.

No matter how far one is able to see, there is a point beyond which he cannot see. It is like watching an airplane in flight; it reaches the point where it vanishes from sight. So regardless of how far one looks into eternity past or into eternity future he reaches a point beyond which he cannot go in his understanding. When the Bible says, "From everlasting to everlasting, thou art God" (Ps. 90:2), it is almost the same as saying, "From the vanishing point in the past, and beyond, to the vanishing point in the future, and beyond, thou art God."

From Ephesians we learn that the Church was planned by God from eternity past—it was not an afterthought. Every believer can be assured that he was chosen in Christ "before the foundation of the world." The Body of Christ is the universal Church because it is made up of believers of the present age from the entire world. The local church is to be composed of believers meeting in a certain locality. Some view the assembly of believers with despair and say the church has failed. But even though some local churches may be slack in their ministry for Christ, the universal Church will not fail. Christ said, "I will build my church; and the gates of hell shall not prevail against it" (Matt. 16:18). So individual churches, or even a denomination, may fail, but the Church of Jesus Christ—His Body—will not fail. What God purposes, He accomplishes; what He plans, He fulfills.

When a person is born into the family of God by receiving Christ as Saviour, he is brought in line with God's eternal plan. Of course, it must be emphasized that one enters the family of God by choice. Even John 3:16 says, "That whosoever believeth in him," which emphasizes that people must choose whether to believe in Christ or not. Verse 18 says, "He that believeth on him is not condemned: but he that believeth not is condemned already, because he hath not believed in the name of the only begotten Son of God." In His long-suffering, God continues to wait for people to receive Christ. Peter wrote: "The Lord is not slack concerning his promise, as some men count slackness; but is longsuffering to us-ward, not willing that any should perish, but that all should come to repentance" (II Pet. 3:9).

The eternal power of God is now constructing the Church, the Body of Christ; that is, He is perfecting, or maturing, believers by His eternal power. God's plan for the Church is that it might be with Him throughout eternity. In the ages to come God's grace will be seen in the Church He has redeemed and it will be a testimony of the infinite wisdom of God.

Thus, the Book of Ephesians is the meeting point between eternity past and eternity future and deals in particular with the believer living in the present age.

Chapter 4

The Father's Redemptive Work
(Eph. 1:4-6)

Verses 4-14 reveal eight truths about the believer. Each member of the Godhead is responsible for some of these elements. Through the Father, the believer is chosen, predestinated, and accepted in the Son. Through the Son, the believer has redemption, forgiveness, and an inheritance. Through the Holy Spirit, the believer has been made alive and has been sealed. We now turn our attention to the Father's redemptive work.

Chosen

One of the Father's activities is revealed in verse 4: "He hath chosen us in him before the foundation of the world, that we should be holy and without blame before him in love."

The Father has chosen believers for a specific purpose. The word translated "chosen" means "to pick, to choose." The form of the Greek word for "chosen" in this verse indicates that God has chosen the individual for Himself. The Scriptures view the believer as one whom God has chosen out of the world, once and for all, to be His special treasure.

God's choice of the nation of Israel is comparable to His choice of the individual believer. Israel was chosen from among the nations as God's special, or peculiar, people through whom He desired to accomplish many things.

God's choosing Israel from among the nations did not mean that all the other nations were rejected by Him. Rather, it meant that Israel was chosen for special favor by Him. When organizations advertise for personnel, they sometimes enumerate the fringe benefits available. In order to share in these benefits, the individual must join the organization. So also, God has made salvation available to all and does not coerce any to believe. When individuals receive Christ as Saviour, they find they have been chosen to receive special benefits within the family of God. These benefits have been announced ahead of time but are not available until the unbeliever has come into the family of God.

Israel was chosen for the purpose of making salvation available to all other nations. Through this nation, God produced (1) the Saviour of the world, (2) the Bible, and (3) witnesses to the world. So also, those who receive Jesus Christ as Saviour are chosen to make salvation available to everyone. As the Lord Jesus told believers, "Ye have not chosen me, but I have chosen you, and ordained you, that ye should go and bring forth fruit" (John 15:16). The Apostle Paul also wrote of what the believer is chosen for: "All things are of God, who hath reconciled us to himself by Jesus Christ, and hath given to us the ministry of reconciliation" (II Cor. 5:18). Paul went on to say, "Now then we are ambassadors for Christ, as though God did beseech you by us: we pray you in Christ's stead, be ye reconciled to God" (v. 20). The believer has been chosen by God and entrusted with the gospel as an ambassador for Christ.

Subjects Involved

Notice in Ephesians 1:4 the ones who have been chosen—"us." This refers to believers. It is important to realize that Paul's letter to the Ephesians was written to believers, not to unbelievers.

Many people have difficulty with the matter of God's choosing. There are those who believe that God has chosen some for salvation and others for condemnation. However, I do not believe that this is the meaning of Ephesians 1:4, nor do I find such a choice indicated anywhere else in the Scriptures. The choice involved is not God's choosing some for salvation and some for condemnation but His choosing certain things for the one who already has received Jesus Christ as Saviour. God sovereignly chooses every believer to live intimately and eternally with Him. His choice is absolute and final and is not based on partiality.

Concerning salvation, God gives all sinners equal opportunity to obtain His mercy and be saved according to His grace. Although all sinners deserve the judgment of God, He has made salvation available to all. Paul wrote: "I exhort therefore, that, first of all, supplications, prayers, intercessions, and giving of thanks, be made for all men. For this is good and acceptable in the sight of God our Saviour; who will have all men to be saved, and to come unto the knowledge of the truth" (I Tim. 2:1,3,4). If God wants everyone to be saved it seems obvious that He has not chosen some to be lost. Second Peter 3:9 also emphasizes that God's invitation is open to all: "The Lord is not slack concerning his promise, as some men count slackness; but is long-suffering to us-ward, not willing that any should perish, but that all should come to repentance." No one will be able to stand before God in the future and say it was impossible for him to receive Christ because he was not a chosen one.

The Bible teaches both the sovereignty of God and the free will of man. With our finite minds it is impossible for us to completely understand how these two can be harmonized, but we will understand when we are in the presence of Christ.

Paul's words "chosen us in him" (Eph. 1:4) reveal who is chosen—those who are already believers—and that they are chosen by God for a specific purpose. Paul said, "For we are his workmanship, created in Christ Jesus unto good works, which God hath before ordained that we should walk in them" (2:10). So God long ago chose believers to produce good works which would evidence His creative work.

However, God's concern for the unbeliever is that he receive Christ as Saviour. Jesus Christ came to earth to seek and to save those who were lost. Although the unbeliever deserves judgment, God offers him grace. Paul reminded the Ephesians, "And you hath he quickened [made alive], who were dead in trespasses and sins" (v. 1). Because the Ephesians had put their trust in Christ's redeeming blood, they were now chosen as special objects in whom God desired to work. It is important to remember that those who are lost are lost because they refuse to accept Christ as Saviour—they choose not to be among God's elect. They are those of whom Christ said, "Ye will not come to me, that ye might have life" (John 5:40).

Time of the Choosing

The question arises, When did God do this choosing of the believer for special benefits? Ephesians 1:4 gives the answer: "Before the foundation of the world." Genesis 1:1 says, "In the beginning God created the heaven and the earth." So the choice described in Ephesians 1:4 predates the event in Genesis 1:1. What a marvelous God we have! Even before the world was created He had plans for what He was going to do in and through believers.

The psalmist said, "You saw me before I was born and scheduled each day of my life before I began to breathe. Every day was recorded in your Book!" (139:16, Living Bible). There are no surprises to God; He is omniscient. Acts 15:18 says, "Known unto God are all his works from the beginning of the world." God's blueprint for the Church as well as for individual believers was already drawn before the foundation of the world. As the psalmist considered the omniscience of God, he exclaimed, "Such knowledge is too wonderful for me; it is high, I cannot attain unto it" (139:6). God's choosing the believer before the foundation of the world is more than a finite mind can comprehend.

God's great and complete redemption of man was part of His eternal plan. This meant that Jesus Christ must become man, die for sin, be buried, rise to life again, and then ascend to the Heavenly Father. By His death and burial, Christ provided the payment for sin's penalty, and by His resurrection, He provided life for all who receive Him as Saviour. By His ascension to the Father and His present high priestly work, He makes it possible for every believer to attain full maturity. This work of Christ for the believer, who is a member of His Body, will be consummated when Christ returns to take all believers to be with Himself.

God's Eternal Purpose

God's eternal purpose for those of us who know Jesus Christ is that "we should be holy and without blame before him in love" (Eph. 1:4). Notice again that His purpose was not salvation but holiness. This further clarifies that the choosing work of God was related to believers, not to unbelievers. God's calling for the believer is also seen in I Peter 1:15,16: "But as he which hath called you is holy, so be ye holy in all manner of conversation [behavior]; because it is written, Be ye holy; for I am holy."

Paul was deeply sensitive to God's call. He saw himself in the process of being molded into what God wanted him to be. He wrote: "Not that I have already obtained it, or have already become perfect, but I press on in order that I may lay hold of that for which also I was laid hold of by Christ Jesus. Brethren, I do not regard myself as having laid hold of it yet; but one thing I do: forgetting what lies behind and reaching forward to what lies ahead, I press on toward the goal for the prize of the upward call of God in Christ Jesus" (Phil. 3:12-14, NASB).

So from Ephesians 1:4 and other verses it is evident that individuals are not chosen because they are holy but because they are to be holy. God's purpose is that those who receive His grace for salvation should be partakers of the divine nature, thus becoming capable of communion and fellowship with Him. Peter emphasized how believers share the divine nature when he wrote: "According as his divine power hath given unto us all things that pertain unto life and godliness, through the knowledge of him that hath called us to glory and virtue: whereby are given unto us exceeding great and precious promises: that by these ye might be partakers of the divine nature, having escaped the corruption that is in the world through lust" (II Pet. 1:3,4). Thus, people are saved from condemnation by receiving Christ as Saviour, and at that moment they are given new natures so that Christ might work out His life in them.

Paul told the Ephesians, "That ye put on [literally, have put on] the new man, which after God is created in righteousness and true holiness" (4:24). God works with believers as fathers work with their children. As such, He chastens the believer to bring about the best in him. Hebrews 12:10 says, "For they [earthly fathers] verily for a few days chasten us after their own pleasure; but he for our profit, that we might be partakers of his holiness."

The word translated "holy" in Ephesians 1:4 has the same basic meaning as the word translated "saints" in verse 1. The word emphasizes that the believer has been entirely set apart *to* something or someone. Obviously it implies being set apart *from* something or someone. The believer has been set apart from the secular and is set apart to the sacred. Although this setting apart was completely accomplished for each believer at the moment of salvation as far as his position is concerned, it is not always evident in his practice.

The difference between position and practice is indicated in verse 4: "That we should be holy and without blame before him in love." The word "should" emphasizes practice because by position every believer *is* holy and without blame before God. Each person must first make sure of his salvation and then be sure that he lives in accordance with his position in Christ. God does not intend that there be spiritual birth only; He intends that believers mature in the spiritual life. This is accomplished as the believer is sensitive to the Lord Jesus Christ, who is working within him.

There is much talk today about "working for Christ" but little about "being like Christ." Being like Christ means more than just following Him as a good teacher or example; it refers to the believer's being molded into the image of Jesus Christ. This is accomplished only as the believer yields to the work of the indwelling Christ.

The word "blameless" in Ephesians 1:4 means "without blemish"; that is, free from faultiness." The believer is to live above reproach. This is the potential of every believer because he is in Christ, but it is true of the believer only as he appropriates the resources God has made available to him. The believer possesses a nature that is blameless, and he is to live accordingly.

Paul emphasized the need of believers to live in accordance with their position when he wrote: "Till we all come in the unity of the faith, and of the knowledge of the Son of God, unto a perfect [mature] man, unto the measure of the stature of the fulness of Christ" (4:13). Hebrews 13:21 emphasizes the same truth: "Make you perfect [mature] in every good work to do his will, working in you that which is wellpleasing in his sight, through Jesus Christ." Notice the words "working in you." This is what Christ does in each believer. And the believer may be sure that what God begins, He will accomplish. Philippians 1:6 says, "Being confident of this very thing, that he which hath begun a good work in you will perform it until the day of Jesus Christ."

Believers are to be holy and blameless "before him" (Eph. 1:4). Notice that this verse is not referring to a future time, such as the believer's judgment, but to the present. The believer should allow God to work in his heart so that his practice might measure up to his position—holy and blameless. As the refiner can see his image in the purified gold, so God works with a believer until He sees His image. Each believer's prayer should be, "Search me, O God, and know my heart: try me, and know my thoughts: and see if there be any wicked way in me, and lead me in the way everlasting" (Ps. 139:23,24).

Predestinated

Paul continued telling what God has done for the believer: "Having predestinated us unto the adoption of children by Jesus Christ to himself, according to the good pleasure of his will" (Eph. 1:5). The last two words of verse 4 probably go with verse 5 rather than verse 4. As such, verse 5 would begin, "In love having predestinated us. . . ." This emphasizes that all of God's activity for us was because of His love. When the New Testament was first written it was not divided into verses as we have in our English translations. This explains why words such as "in love" seem to go with either verse and could therefore be placed in the wrong one.

The subject of predestination has caused considerable discussion and difference of opinion among believers. However, as already stressed concerning the matter of being chosen in Christ, predestination has to do with believers, not unbelievers. That is, it is not that God predestinates an unbeliever to salvation; rather, it is that every person who has come to salvation has, as a believer, already been predestinated by God to certain things.

The Greek word for predestinate is actually comprised of two words: *pro*, meaning "before," and *horizo*, meaning "to mark off by boundaries" [the English word "horizon" is derived from this last word]. Hence, when the two Greek words were combined they referred to boundaries, or destinies, that were determined beforehand.

Concerning the believer, God has determined what he should be like. Paul wrote: "For we are his workmanship, created in Christ Jesus unto good works, which God hath before ordained that we should walk in them" (2:10).

Position of Believer

Ephesians 1:5 is specific about what God has pre-destinated us to—"the adoption of children by Jesus Christ to himself." The term "adoption" is used in the New Testament far differently than it is customarily used today. The practice of accepting a child into the home and legally adopting him as a member of the family existed in Old Testament times, but something quite different was meant when Paul referred to adoption.

The word Paul used in referring to adoption literally meant "son-placing." In Paul's day this word was used of the Greek and Roman custom of publicly declaring a son to have full privileges and responsibility as a member of the family. This ceremony usually took place while the son was still a teenager. Until this time the child had been considered a servant, but after the son-placing he was considered to have full privileges and responsibilities in the family. Paul referred to this when he said, "Now I say, That the heir, as long as he is a child, differeth nothing from a servant, though he be lord of all" (Gal. 4:1). Paul stated the truths of spiritual adoption when he said, "And because ye are sons, God has sent forth the Spirit of his Son into your hearts, crying, Abba, Father. Wherefore thou art no more a servant, but a son; and if a son, then an heir of God through Christ" (vv. 6,7).

Thus, when Paul referred to adoption, he was not referring to one's becoming a member of a family but of his being given full privileges and responsibility in the family. As such, spiritual adoption emphasizes position more than relationship. A person becomes a member of God's family by personally receiving Jesus Christ as Saviour—this is relationship. The believer is given all the privileges and responsibilities as a member of God's family—this is position.

Whereas the child of Paul's day had to wait until he was a teenager to be officially placed as a son, there is no waiting period for the believer. At the time of salvation, a person is immediately placed in this position—that of a full-fledged member of God's family. It is this truth that Paul emphasized in Ephesians 1:5: "Having predestinated us unto the adoption of children." God has before determined that everyone who receives Jesus Christ as Saviour will immediately receive a position in the family of God as an adult son.

Even though a believer has the position as God's son, this does not put him on the same level as Jesus Christ, the Son of God. Jesus Christ is the eternal Son, the only begotten of the Father. Hebrews 1:5-13 reveals that Jesus Christ is uniquely the Son of God—no one else holds such a position.

Although no one else can be elevated to the position of Christ, believers are heirs with Him. Paul told believers, "Ye have received the Spirit of adoption, whereby we cry, Abba, Father. The Spirit itself beareth witness with our spirit, that we are the children of God: and if children, then heirs; heirs of God, and joint-heirs with Christ; if so be that we suffer with him, that we may be also glorified together" (Rom. 8:15-17). This is what we possess because we are in Christ. Paul referred to waiting for the time to be with Christ when he said, "Not only this, but also we ourselves, having the first-fruits of the Spirit, even we ourselves groan within ourselves, waiting eagerly for our adoptions as sons, the redemption of our body" (v. 23, NASB). Although we have positionally received the adoption of sons, there is a sense in which it will be fully realized when we are with Christ.

Our position in Christ is far above the position of angels. Angels are "ministering spirits, sent forth to minister for them who shall be heirs of salvation" (Heb. 1:14). We are elevated to a position far above servant; we have a position in God's family as adult sons with all the privileges and responsibilities that go with such a position. Eventually, we will actually be with God in a unique relationship. All of these things are ours because God predestinated us to this adoption. This position is not determined by human merit; it is determined by God for everyone who receives Christ as Saviour.

Because of our position with Christ we will reign with
Him. The Lord Jesus said, "To him that overcometh will I
grant to sit with me in my throne, even as I also overcame,
and am set down with my Father in his throne" (Rev. 3:21).
Those who overcome are those who have received Jesus
Christ as Saviour. First John 5:5 says, "Who is he that
overcometh the world, but he that believeth that Jesus is the
Son of God?"

Positionally, every believer is an overcomer, but his
practice on earth does not always measure up to his position.
There needs to be progressive sanctification in his life for him
to measure up to his positional sanctification. All of this has
been included in God's predestination of the believer, for He
has predestinated the believer to be conformed to the image
of Jesus Christ. This is the very point Paul emphasized in
Romans 8:28-30: "And we know that all things work
together for good to them that love God, to them who are
the called according to his purpose. For whom he did
foreknow, he also did predestinate to be conformed to the
image of his Son, that he might be the firstborn among many
brethren. Moreover whom he did predestinate, them he also
called: and whom he called, them he also justified: and
whom he justified, them he also glorified."

Although God works in our lives to mold us into the
image of Christ, this will not be fully accomplished until we
are with Christ. John referred to the time when we will be
fully like Christ: "Beloved, now are we the sons of God, and
it doth not yet appear what we shall be: but we know that,
when he shall appear, we shall be like him; for we shall see
him as he is" (I John 3:2).

It has already been determined by God that each believer
will be like Jesus Christ. This includes the process of God's
working with the believer on earth and the completed work
of God that will be accomplished at the resurrection. This is
also referred to in Ephesians 1:14, which speaks of the Holy
Spirit, who is "the earnest of our inheritance until the
redemption of the purchased possession, unto the praise of
his glory."

Notice that believers are predestinated to the adoption of
sons "by Jesus Christ" (v. 5). As has been emphasized
previously, all of our riches and position have been made

available to us in Jesus Christ. This includes what we have now and what is kept in store for us for the future.

It is through Christ that we "have access by one spirit unto the Father" (2:18). Also, God has predestinated us to the adoption of sons through Jesus Christ "to himself" (1:5). This reveals that the Father has done this for His own satisfaction—that He might lavish His love on those who are His sons. Observe that it is all done "according to the good pleasure of his will." It pleased God to choose the believer and to determine ahead of time what he should be in Christ. Because God is sovereign, He is able to bring to pass what He has chosen to do. Philippians 1:6 says, "Being confident of this very thing, that he which hath begun a good work in you will perform it until the day of Jesus Christ."

Accepted

Not only has God predestinated believers "according to the good pleasure of his will," but He has also done it "to the praise of the glory of his grace, wherein he hath made us accepted in the beloved" (v. 6). Certainly, those of us who know Christ can praise God for the grace He has freely bestowed upon us in Christ. Paul told believers, "And you hath he quickened [made alive], who were dead in trespasses and sins: wherein in time past ye walked according to the course of this world, according to the prince of the power of the air, the spirit that now worketh in the children of disobedience: among whom also we all had our conversation in times past in the lusts of our flesh, fulfilling the desires of the flesh and of the mind; and were by nature the children of wrath, even as others" (2:1-3).

Paul told these Ephesians that before they came to know Christ, they "were without Christ, being aliens from the commonwealth of Israel, and strangers from the covenants of promise, having no hope, and without God in the world" (v. 12). But what a difference now that they had received Christ! "But now in Christ Jesus ye who sometimes were far off are made nigh by the blood of Christ" (v. 13).

Notice that no reference is made to a person's being accepted in Christ because of what the person has done. The believer does not make himself accepted; God has made him accepted. Observe the past tense in verse 6—God has made the believer accepted in the Beloved.

"In the beloved" is synonymous with "in Christ." The believer has a perfect position in Christ; therefore, the believer is fully accepted in Him.

Because the believer is in Christ, all of Christ's worthiness and righteousness are imputed to him. As Christ is, so is the believer before the Father. No wonder Paul said it is "to the praise of the glory of his grace."

Chapter 5

The Son's Redemptive Work
(Eph. 1:7-12)

The work of Christ in behalf of the believer is seen in the words "redemption" and "forgiveness" (v. 7) and "inheritance" (v. 11).

Redemption

Of Christ, Paul said, "In whom we have redemption through his blood" (v. 7). The words "in whom" emphasize again the spiritual blessings every believer has in Christ. "Redemption" reveals what Christ has accomplished for the believer.

In the New Testament, different Greek words were used to convey the meaning of redemption. A study of these words shows that the believer is viewed as having been purchased out of the marketplace of sin and set free. The purchase and freedom is applied to a person when he receives Christ. The word used by Paul in Ephesians 1:7 emphasizes the deliverance aspect of redemption.

The Greek words used in the New Testament were commonly used concerning slaves, but New Testament writers such as Paul used these words to describe what Christ has done for the individual. Of course, in no illustration should every detail be forced to mean something significant. If this were done with the illustration of the slave market, one would conclude that Christ paid the price to Satan since every person is under Satan's domination before salvation. However, the Bible does not teach that any price was paid to Satan.

Concerning the penalty, it is as if every individual were waiting on death row because of a crime he had committed. Then, the Lord Jesus Christ completely paid the death penalty for the individual by giving His own life. In so doing, Christ released the person from the death penalty.

Before salvation, all are "dead in trespasses and sins" (2:1). By His death, Jesus became the "propitiation [satisfaction] for our sins: and not for our's only, but also for the sins of the whole world" (I John 2:2). Jesus Christ satisfied the righteous demands of the Heavenly Father so that any person could have forgiveness of sins by receiving Christ as his Saviour. In the phrase, "we have redemption" (1:7), the original language emphasizes a present, continuous action. The believer's redemption is an abiding fact from the past, through the present, and into the future. For the one who has just received Christ as Saviour, redemption is his at that moment as completely as it will ever be. Of course, the believer will later be taken from this life to be with the Lord Himself, but his redemption is complete in Christ the moment he believes. Salvation belongs to the believer in such a way that it is never taken from him.

Included in the redemptive work of Christ are freedom from the penalty of sin and freedom from the power of sin. Romans 5:10 includes both aspects when it says, "For if, when we were enemies, we were reconciled to God by the death of his Son, much more, being reconciled, we shall be saved by his life." The death of Jesus Christ paid the penalty for sin, and His living in the believer gives freedom from the power of sin.

Israel provides an Old Testament illustration of this twofold deliverance. When the Israelites were in Egypt they were saved from having their firstborn put to death by their having placed blood on the doorposts (Ex. 12). However, they were still slaves in Egypt and were not delivered from the power of slavery until they crossed the Red Sea (Ex. 14).

Although a person's redemption is complete the moment he receives Christ as Saviour, the Scriptures present different aspects of salvation. First, there is redemption from sin and from slavery to Satan. Second, there is redemption from the power of sin and slavery to the flesh. Third, there is redemption from the location of sin (the earth). A believer is delivered from the location of sin when he goes to be with the Lord.

Paul emphasized that redemption is "through his blood" (Eph. 1:7). The significance of blood is seen throughout the Scriptures. Leviticus 17:11 says, "For the life of the flesh is in the blood: and I have given it to you upon the altar to make an atonement for your souls: for it is the blood that maketh an atonement for the soul." Hebrews 9:22 says, "And almost all things are by the law purged with blood; and without shedding of blood is no remission [forgiveness]." Thus, it was necessary for Christ to shed His blood as the basis for redemption. Isaiah prophesied the kind of death Christ would die when he wrote: "But he was wounded for our transgressions, he was bruised for our iniquities: the chastisement of our peace was upon him; and with his stripes we are healed. All we like sheep have gone astray; we have turned every one to his own way; and the Lord hath laid on him the iniquity of us all" (53:5,6). Peter also referred to the kind of death Christ died when he told the Israelites, "Him, being delivered by the determinate counsel and foreknowledge of God, ye have taken, and by wicked hands have crucified and slain" (Acts 2:23).

Forgiveness

Paul continued describing what believers have in Christ when he told the Ephesians that believers have "the forgiveness of sins, according to the riches of his grace" (1:7). The word translated "forgiveness" means "dismissal, release." Thus, forgiving is releasing sin, letting it go as if it had never been committed. It involves a pardon, a remission, of the penalty. Because of what Jesus Christ did on the cross, the Heavenly Father could release from the penalty of sin all who receive Christ as Saviour.

The Day of Atonement provides an illustration of what is accomplished at the time of salvation (Lev. 16). On the Day of Atonement the priest took two goats. One was given as a sin offering—the shedding of its blood was the picture of redemption. Then, the sins of the people were symbolically placed on the remaining goat and it was sent into the wilderness never to return. The one who has redemption in Christ has had his sins sent away, never to return.

Jeremiah 31:34 records God's words: "I will forgive their iniquity, and I will remember their sin no more." The same truth is stated in Hebrews 8:12: "For I will be merciful to their unrighteousness, and their sins and their iniquities will I remember no more." This thought recurs again in Hebrews 10:17,18: "And their sins and iniquities will I remember no more. Now where remission of these is, there is no more offering for sin."

From Ephesians 1:7 we learn that redemption and forgiveness of sins are "according to the riches of his grace." Notice it is not "out of" but "according to" the riches of His grace. God is infinitely rich and the degree of forgiveness is determined by the "riches of his grace." There is no need that God is not able to satisfy. Because the forgiveness is determined by the plentitude of God's grace, it is complete, unqualified, and unchanging. Because God is infinite, His grace is infinite. What a wonderful God we have!

Inheritance

The third thing the Son has accomplished for the believer is seen in the word "inheritance." Concerning Christ, Ephesians 1:11 says, "In whom also we have obtained an inheritance, being predestinated according to the purpose of him who worketh all things after the counsel of his own will." Those significant words appear again—"in whom." It is only as a believer is united with Christ that spiritual blessings are applied to him.

Speaking for believers, Paul said, "We have obtained an inheritance." An inheritance is something which a person comes into possession of because of his relationship with another. It is not something that is earned; it is a gift.

The believer's inheritance includes life itself. By receiving Christ as Saviour, the believer inherits eternal life. Jesus said, "He that heareth my word, and believeth on him that sent me, hath everlasting life, and shall not come into condemnation; but is passed from death unto life" (John 5:24).

The inheritance of the believer also includes everything he needs for his life. The believer is actually a citizen of heaven who is on a pilgrim journey on earth. However, God has made all spiritual blessings available to the believer. Paul told believers, "All things belong to you, and you belong to Christ; and Christ belongs to God" (I Cor. 3:22,23, NASB). God's riches made available to the believer are also emphasized in Romans 8:32: "He that spared not his own Son, but delivered him up for us all, how shall he not with him also freely give us all things?"

Our present blessings are only a small part of our spiritual inheritance, which is to be received in full in the future. The moment one receives Christ as Saviour he is placed as a mature son into the family of God and becomes an heir of an inheritance that is beyond human comprehension. We are to let Christ reign in our lives now, but our full spiritual inheritance includes being with Christ and reigning with Him throughout eternity.

Inheritance Through Suffering

Concerning reigning with Christ in the future, Romans 8:17 says, "If so be that we suffer with him, that we may be also glorified together." Being glorified with Him involves reigning with Him. Second Timothy 2:12 says, "If we suffer, we shall also reign with him: if we deny him, he also will deny us." This verse is not referring to salvation but to the way the believer lives for Christ.

Suffering for Christ involves more than physical suffering. Philippians 2 reveals how we can be identified with Christ in His suffering. Paul said, "Let this mind be in you, which was also in Christ Jesus" (v. 5). Paul then went on to describe the kind of attitude Jesus had: "Who, being in the form of God, thought it not robbery [a thing to be grasped] to be equal with God: but made himself of no reputation, and took upon him the form of a servant, and was made in the likeness of man" (vv. 6,7). The Lord Jesus Christ was willing to set aside His reputation in order to become our Redeemer. The believer is able to suffer with Christ when he adopts the same attitude. The Christian's desire should not be to establish a great reputation in the world but to live for Christ and win others to Him.

Jesus "humbled himself, and became obedient unto death, even the death of the cross" (v. 8). We suffer with Christ as we endure the taunts of the world while seeking to reveal to others that spiritual values are far more important than material values.

The result of Christ's suffering was that He was exalted by the Father: "Wherefore God also hath highly exalted him, and given him a name which is above every name" (v. 9). The believer who suffers with Christ is exalted by having the privilege of reigning with Christ.

The Lord Jesus referred to believers reigning with Him when He said, "To him that overcometh will I grant to sit with me in my throne, even as I also overcame, and am set down with my Father in his throne" (Rev. 3:21). Referring to what Christ has done for believers, Revelation 5:10 says, "Thou hast made them to be a kingdom and priests to our God; and they will reign upon the earth" (NASB). This is part of the inheritance believers have in Christ.

In this life, believers can expect persecution because they live in a world that is hostile to God. The Bible says, "All that will live godly in Christ Jesus shall suffer persecution" (II Tim. 3:12). This persecution may vary in form and degree, but those who diligently seek to please Jesus Christ in daily living will experience persecution from the unbelieving world.

The Lord Jesus wants the believer to share in His spiritual blessings. When He was on earth, the Lord Jesus prayed, "I in them, and thou in me, that they may be made perfect in one [perfectly united]; and that the world may know that thou hast sent me, and hast loved them, as thou hast loved me. Father, I will that they also, whom thou hast given me, be with me where I am; that they may behold my glory, which thou hast given me: for thou lovedst me before the foundation of the world" (John 17:23,24).

A Certain Inheritance

Peter made reference to the inheritance of believers when he told them that they had been begotten, or born again, "to an inheritance incorruptible, and undefiled, and that fadeth not away, reserved in heaven for you, who are kept by the power of God through faith unto salvation ready to be revealed in the last time" (I Pet. 1:4,5).

The Scriptures are emphatic about the certainty of the believer's inheritance. In this life people are sometimes cheated out of their inheritances, but this is never so concerning the spiritual inheritance that each believer will receive. Ephesians 1:11 emphasizes the certainty of the inheritance: "Being predestinated according to the purpose of him who worketh all things after the counsel of his own will." As we have seen, predestination means that God has undertaken to see something through to its end. There is no doubt about the believer's inheritance because God has set him aside for this purpose.

The certainty of the inheritance is further emphasized in verses 13 and 14. These verses reveal that God has given the Holy Spirit to the believer as the earnest of the believer's inheritance. The Holy Spirit is the down payment on the future inheritance. As seen from I Peter 1:4, this inheritance is "reserved in heaven" for believers. It is obvious from these verses that the believer never needs to be in doubt about his spiritual inheritance for he can be sure that God's eternal purpose will not be thwarted.

Ephesians 1:11 shows that all of this is "according to the purpose of him who worketh all things after the counsel of his own will." What God determines, He accomplishes—His sovereign will cannot be stalemated. Because God is sovereign, He has the power to perform what He has purposed. All the powers of spiritual darkness cannot defeat the divine purpose. It is no wonder that in his prayer Paul referred to "the exceeding greatness of his power to us-ward who believe" (v. 19). This power was great enough to raise Christ from the dead and to exalt Him above every name, and it is that same power that gives spiritual victory to every believer who will appropriate it.

Christ's Heritage

Not only do believers have an inheritance because they are joint heirs with Christ, but also Christ has an inheritance in the believer; that is, He inherits the believer. In His prayer recorded in John 17, Jesus said, "I pray for them . . . which thou hast given me" (v. 9).

Ephesians 1 reveals that believers have been chosen as Christ's inheritance—they have been made His heritage. This is seen in these passages: "That we should be to the praise of his glory" (v. 12), "until the redemption of the purchased possession" (v. 14), and "his inheritance in the saints" (v. 18).

Christ's inheritance in the saints is also seen in I Corinthians 6:19,20: "What? know ye not that your body is the temple of the Holy Ghost which is in you, which ye have of God, and ye are not your own? For ye are bought with a price: therefore glorify God in your body, and in your spirit, which are God's." Each believer belongs to God; he is God's heritage.

Throughout eternity, believers will declare the glory of God. This is seen in Ephesians 2:6,7, which says that God "hath raised us up together, and made us sit together in heavenly places in Christ Jesus: that in the ages to come he might show the exceeding riches of his grace in his kindness toward us through Christ Jesus." Throughout eternity, believers will be trophies of God's grace. God desires to display His praise and glory through His own. God has said, "The people whom I formed for Myself, will declare My praise" (Isa. 43:21, NASB).

Chapter 6

The Holy Spirit's Redemptive Work
(Eph. 1:13,14; 2:1)

Through the Spirit, the believer is quickened and sealed. It is to the work of the third Person of the Trinity that our attention is now turned.

Quickened

Paul told the Ephesians, "In whom [Christ] ye also trusted, after that ye heard the word of truth, the gospel of your salvation" (v. 13). In this verse Paul makes reference to the Ephesians' having believed the gospel. Other Scriptures reveal that when a person places his faith in Christ it is the ministry of the Holy Spirit to quicken him; that is, make him spiritually alive. Later in Paul's letter to the Ephesians he said, "And you hath he quickened, who were dead in trespasses and sins" (2:1).

The Spirit's ministry of making spiritually alive the person who receives Christ is also seen from Christ's words to Nicodemus: "Except a man be born of . . . the Spirit, he cannot enter into the kingdom of God" (John 3:5). At the very moment a person receives Christ he is born of the Spirit into the family of God.

Paul said the Ephesians had trusted in Christ after they had heard "the word of truth, the gospel of your salvation." It is essential that people hear the Word. Jesus said, "He that heareth my word, and believeth on him that sent me, hath everlasting life, and shall not come into condemnation; but is passed from death unto life" (John 5:24). Romans 10:17 says, "So then faith cometh by hearing, and hearing by the word of God." Hebrews 4:12 says that "the word of God is quick, and powerful, and sharper than any twoedged sword, piercing even to the dividing asunder of soul and spirit, and of the joints and marrow, and is a discerner of the thoughts and intents of the heart."

Because the Word must be proclaimed for people to be saved, it is no wonder Paul exhorted Timothy: "Preach the word; be instant in season, out of season; reprove, rebuke, exhort with all longsuffering and doctrine" (II Tim. 4:2).

The quickening ministry of the Holy Spirit is referred to in Colossians 2:13: "And you, being dead in your sins and the uncircumcision of your flesh, hath he quickened together with him, having forgiven you all trespasses." Romans 10:9,10 declares to all: "That if thou shalt confess with thy mouth the Lord Jesus, and shalt believe in thine heart that God hath raised him from the dead, thou shalt be saved. For with the heart man believeth unto righteousness; and with the mouth confession is made unto salvation."

Sealing

Paul told the Ephesians, "In whom also after that ye believed, ye were sealed with that holy Spirit of promise" (1:13). The words "after that" should not be understood to mean that the Ephesians were sealed by the Spirit sometime after they had received Christ. In the original language this verse literally reads: "In whom also having believed ye were sealed with the holy Spirit of promise." Paul was looking back at the time of the salvation of the Ephesians and was reminding them that having believed in Christ, they were sealed with the Holy Spirit. The sealing of the Spirit had taken place at the time of their salvation.

Ephesians 4:30 says, "Grieve not the holy Spirit of God, whereby ye are sealed unto the day of redemption." The sealing of the Spirit is not temporary; it is permanent—"unto the day of redemption." Some teach that if a person grieves the Holy Spirit the Spirit will leave him, but that is not what this verse teaches. The emphasis of the verse is that inasmuch as a believer is sealed with the Spirit until the day of redemption, he should not grieve the Spirit. In a physical sense, a child born into a family is a permanent member of that family; therefore, he should not grieve his parents by doing things that displease them. However, even if he does displease them, he is still a member of the family. So it is spiritually—the one who receives Christ is a member of the family of God forever and does not cease to be a member when he does something that grieves the Holy Spirit.

Notice that it is not just that the believer is sealed "by" the Holy Spirit but that he is sealed "with" the Holy Spirit (1:13). This means that the indwelling Holy Spirit Himself is the seal.

Before the Lord Jesus ascended, He told the disciples, "I will pray the Father, and he shall give you another Comforter, that he may abide with you for ever" (John 14:16).

A seal indicates three things: (1) a finished transaction, (2) ownership, and (3) security. Paul took a word that was used in the secular world and lifted it to a new level by associating spiritual truth with it.

A Finished Transaction

The spiritual transaction that has been finished is the salvation of the one who has received Christ. As such, this spiritual seal also indicates genuineness. Just as something is sealed to keep it from being tampered with, so the believer is sealed with the Holy Spirit, who is able to keep the believer safe. Inasmuch as the seal is the indwelling Holy Spirit, it is not visible outwardly although the results of the sealing are. Concerning genuineness, Christ said, "Verily, verily, I say unto you, he that entereth not by the door into the sheepfold, but climbeth up some other way, the same is a thief and a robber" (John 10:1). Jesus also said, "I am the door: by me if any man enter in, he shall be saved, and shall go in and out, and find pasture" (v. 9).

Concerning the Spirit, Jesus said, "Even the Spirit of truth; whom the world cannot receive, because it seeth him not, neither knoweth him: but ye know him; for he dwelleth with you, and shall be in you" (John 14:17). These words were spoken before the Spirit descended on the Day of Pentecost. Before that time He came upon individual believers to empower them for service, but it was not until the Day of Pentecost that the Holy Spirit permanently indwelled *every* believer. The indwelling of the Spirit is one of the key characteristics of the present Church Age. Spiritually, it evidences the finished transaction of salvation.

Ownership

The ownership indicated by a seal is seen in the words of Christ: "I am the good shepherd, and know my sheep, and am known of mine" (John 10:14). The Lord knows His own. Paul reminded Timothy of this truth: "Nevertheless the foundation of God standeth sure, having this seal, The Lord knoweth them that are his" (II Tim. 2:19). Just as cattle are sometimes given a brand as an outward seal of ownership, the believer is given the Holy Spirit as the inner seal of ownership. Thus, Romans 8:9 says, "But ye are not in the flesh, but in the Spirit, if so be that the Spirit of God dwell in you. Now if any man have not the Spirit of Christ, he is none of his." Because the Holy Spirit indwells every believer, Paul was able to tell the Corinthian Christians: "What? know ye not that your body is the temple of the Holy Ghost which is in you, which ye have of God, and ye are not your own? For ye are bought with a price: therefore glorify God in your body, and in your spirit, which are God's" (I Cor. 6:19,20).

Security

The security of a seal is seen in Ephesians 1:14. Having told the believers they were sealed with the Holy Spirit, Paul went on to say, "Which is the earnest of our inheritance until the redemption of the purchased possession, unto the praise of his glory." Notice that the Holy Spirit is the earnest of each believer's inheritance *until* God takes the believer to heaven. Because of all that God has accomplished in salvation, the believer is eternally secure. Some are afraid to teach the security of the believer because they are afraid there will be those who will think that if they are secure in Christ it is all right for them to live in sin. However, it should be remembered that the person who has received Christ has been given a desire to please Him. Although a believer will occasionally fall into sin, it will not be his desire to live in sin because he has a new nature that wants to please God.

According to Ephesians 1:11, an inheritance has been made sure for all believers: "In whom also we have obtained an inheritance, being predestinated according to the purpose of him who worketh all things after the counsel of his own will."

The indwelling Holy Spirit is the seal, and this seal is looked upon as "the earnest of our inheritance" (v. 14). An "earnest" is an assurance that the complete work will be accomplished. "Earnest money" is commonly referred to today. It serves as a down payment and indicates the purchaser's intent to follow through on the entire transaction. Although people sometimes fail in their arrangements, God never fails because He is able to accomplish what He sets out to do.

The Holy Spirit is God's earnest to the believer that he will someday have his full inheritance. Peter wrote: "Blessed be the God and Father of our Lord Jesus Christ, which according to his abundant mercy hath begotten us again unto a lively hope by the resurrection of Jesus Christ from the dead, to an inheritance incorruptible, and undefiled, and that fadeth not away, reserved in heaven for you, who are kept by the power of God through faith unto salvation ready to be revealed in the last time" (I Pet. 1:3-5).

Concerning what believers will receive and be in the future, John said, "Beloved, now are we the sons of God, and it doth not yet appear what we shall be: but we know that, when he shall appear, we shall be like him; for we shall see him as he is" (I John 3:2). Concerning the believer's future, Paul said, "And not only they [the things of creation], but ourselves also, which have the firstfruits of the Spirit, even we ourselves groan within ourselves, waiting for the adoption, to wit, the redemption of our body" (Rom. 8:23).

How wonderful it is that God has not only provided salvation but that He has also given the Holy Spirit as security to everyone who receives salvation! This should cause every believer to exclaim with Paul, "What shall we then say to these things? If God be for us, who can be against us? He that spared not his own Son, but delivered him up for us all, how shall he not with him also freely give us all things? Who shall lay anything to the charge of God's elect? It is God that justifieth. Who is he that condemneth? It is Christ that died, yea rather, that is risen again, who is even at the right hand of God, who also maketh intercession for us" (vv. 31-34).

Those who receive Christ as Saviour can be assured that they will someday be taken to be with Christ. The Lord Himself said, "I go to prepare a place for you. And if I go and prepare a place for you, I will come again, and receive you unto myself; that where I am, there ye may be also" (John 14:2,3). Paul described Christ's coming for Church Age believers in these words: "For the Lord himself shall descend from heaven with a shout, with the voice of the archangel, and with the trump of God: and the dead in Christ shall rise first: then we which are alive and remain shall be caught up together with them in the clouds, to meet the Lord in the air: and so shall we ever be with the Lord" (I Thess. 4:16,17). What a wonderful day that will be for those who know Christ as Saviour!

Those who know Christ may be sure that they will be caught up to be with Him. Jesus said concerning believers, "I give unto them eternal life; and they shall never perish, neither shall any man pluck them out of my hand. My Father, which gave them me, is greater than all; and no man is able to pluck them out of my Father's hand" (John 10:28,29). With verses such as these, no believer should have doubt about his security in Christ.

God's purpose in all this for the believer is seen in the words of Ephesians 1:14: "Unto the praise of his glory." It pleased God to make such provisions for the believer, and God can be counted on never to go back on His Word!

Chapter 7

Prayer for Spiritual Apprehension
(Eph. 1:15-23)

Having referred to what believers possess in Jesus Christ, Paul now prayed that they would understand the significance of their position and resources in Christ. This is not a parenthetic passage; rather, it is closely connected to what precedes it. It is a prayer that believers might realize what Christ has in them and what they have in Him.

Paul wrote: "Wherefore I also, after I heard of your faith in the Lord Jesus, and love unto all the saints, cease not to give thanks for you, making mention of you in my prayers" (Eph. 1:15,16). Paul rejoiced to know that these Ephesians had received Jesus Christ as Saviour, and he prayed faithfully for their spiritual progress.

Notice what Paul prayed for them: "That the God of our Lord Jesus Christ, the Father of glory, may give unto you the spirit of wisdom and revelation in the knowledge of him" (v. 17). Paul was not content with only stating spiritual truths; he realized that these truths would not profit anything unless believers grasped their significance. In his letter, therefore, he recorded his prayer that they might understand the significance of their position in Christ.

We always need to think deeply on the Word of God and pray that we might understand its significance. God no longer gives new revelation of Himself; He has not done so since the completion of the Bible. But He does give illumination so we can understand what has been revealed. Each time we read the Bible we need to pray that God will illuminate its truths to us so that we will understand their true significance. Every Christian has probably had the experience of reading the Bible and having the truth of a verse suddenly come to his

65

attention—a truth he had not noticed before, although he had read the passage many times. It was in this way that Romans 10:17 especially came to my attention early in my ministry. This verse says, "So then faith cometh by hearing, and hearing by the word of God." My grasping the principles stated in this verse changed my entire ministry. I immediately saw that if faith comes by the hearing of the Word, then my primary emphasis must be the preaching of the Word. As a result, God has burdened me over the years to give expository messages in which I seek to explain the riches of the Word. God has shown me that if I do this, those under my ministry will be able to exercise faith because they have heard the Word.

Paul was concerned that the Ephesian believers live according to their position in Christ. Paul wanted them to realize there was no need to live like spiritual paupers.

Occasionally, after a person has died, it is discovered that he had much wealth even though he lived as if he had none. Paul was concerned that believers live according to their spiritual resources in Christ. So burdened was he about this matter that he prayed that God would give them a "spirit of wisdom and revelation in the knowledge of him" (v. 17). The word translated "knowledge" means "full knowledge." Paul wanted believers to have full knowledge of their position in Christ, not to be content with partial knowledge.

Paul referred to the Father as "the God of our Lord Jesus Christ" (v. 17). Inasmuch as Jesus Christ Himself is God, Paul must have been emphasizing the humanity of Christ in this phrase. Of course, it is because of Christ's humanity that we now have spiritual resources in Him. It was necessary for Jesus Christ to come in the flesh to reveal the Father to mankind. John 1:18 says, "No man hath seen God at any time: the only begotten Son, which is in the bosom of the Father, he hath declared him."

When Jesus was on earth, He said, "If ye had known me, ye should have known my Father also" (John 14:7). To this statement, Philip answered, "Lord, show us the Father, and it is enough for us" (v. 8, NASB). Jesus responded, "Have I been so long with you, and yet you have not come to know Me, Philip? He who has seen Me has seen the Father; how do you say, 'Show us the Father'?" (v. 9, NASB). Jesus went on to explain that He was in the Father and the Father was in Him and that His purpose was to reveal the Father. This explains how Paul could refer to the Father as "the God of our Lord Jesus Christ" (Eph. 1:17).

God's Wisdom

Observe that Paul prayed for believers to be given a spirit of wisdom and understanding; he did not pray that the Holy Spirit would come to indwell believers. The reason for this is that the Holy Spirit already indwells every believer. But Paul did pray that God's truth would be illuminated so that believers could grasp its true significance. Paul wanted believers to have that knowledge which is from above—a knowledge which a natural, or unsaved, person does not have.

Paul referred to wisdom that originates with God when he said, "But of him are ye in Christ Jesus, who of God is made unto us wisdom" (I Cor. 1:30). Paul told the Corinthians, "But we speak the wisdom of God in a mystery, even the hidden wisdom, which God ordained before the world unto our glory" (2:7).

James wrote of a wisdom that is in contrast to God's wisdom. Referring to envying and strife, James said, "This wisdom descendeth not from above, but is earthly, sensual, devilish" (James 3:15). So that there might not be any mistaking of God's wisdom, James added, "But the wisdom that is from above is first pure, then peaceable, gentle, and easy to be intreated, full of mercy and good fruits, without partiality, and without hypocrisy" (v. 17).

Paul prayed for the Colossians similar to the way he prayed for the Ephesians. Paul told the Colossians, "For this cause we also, since the day we heard it, do not cease to pray for you, and to desire that ye might be filled with the knowledge of his will in all wisdom and spiritual understanding" (1:9). Paul recognized that only the Spirit of God could effectively communicate spiritual truths to believers.

It is important for us to recognize that it is not sufficient just to give information to others; we must pray that they will understand the significance of the information. This is not an excuse for shoddy preparation and presentation. The truth of God needs to be given out as clearly as possible, but we need to pray that the Spirit will illuminate it to those who hear.

More Than Salvation

Paul was concerned that the Ephesian believers progress beyond the point of salvation in their Christian experience. Salvation is spiritual birth but the believer is to go on to spiritual maturity. Paul expressed his personal desire for greater spiritual maturity when he wrote: "That I may know him, and the power of his resurrection, and the fellowship of his sufferings, being made conformable unto his death" (Phil. 3:10). Paul was thankful that he knew Jesus Christ as Saviour, but he wanted to progress into a fuller, deeper spiritual knowledge of Christ.

It cannot be overemphasized that meditation on the Word of God is one of the primary ways we grow in our understanding of God. As we study the Scriptures and wait expectantly on the Lord, He will illuminate the truths that have been read and will enable us to more completely grasp their significance. God gives spiritual insight to those who are willing to take the time to meditate on Him and His Word.

The psalmist had much to say about waiting on the Lord in meditation. Psalm 119 especially expresses the importance of the Word of God to the believer. The psalmist prayed, "Open thou mine eyes, that I may behold wondrous things out of thy law" (v. 18). The psalmist wanted his spiritual eyes to be opened so he could understand the significance of the truths he was reading. So important was the Word to the psalmist that he said, "Thy word is a lamp unto my feet, and a light unto my path" (v. 105). No wonder the psalmist could also say, "The entrance of thy words giveth light; it giveth understanding unto the simple" (v. 130).

Paul also prayed for the Ephesians, "The eyes of your understanding being enlightened" (1:18). There must be the divine operation of the Spirit of wisdom in the believer. When this is so, and when we respond to what the Spirit is teaching us, we will be growing more spiritually mature. God has not intended that we stop at the elementary level of salvation but that we go on to spiritual maturity. Thus, we are told, "Therefore leaving the principles of the doctrine of Christ, let us go on unto perfection [maturity]" (Heb. 6:1).

Paul prayed that the Ephesian Christians might know three things: (1) "what is the hope of his calling," (2) "what the riches of the glory of his inheritance in the saints" (v. 18), and (3) "what is the exceeding greatness of his power to us-ward who believe" (v. 19).

The Hope of His Calling

The hope of God's calling to which Paul referred extends beyond salvation. Salvation already belonged to the believers in Ephesus; thus, if "the hope of his calling" involved only salvation, there would have been no need for Paul to have prayed this prayer. Paul was concerned, however, that the believers know more than just the truths of salvation; he wanted them to grow spiritually.

It is a shame for a person to have been a Christian for years but not to have advanced beyond the knowledge of his salvation. The writer of Hebrews addressed such a group of believers when he wrote: "For when for the time ye ought to be teachers, ye have need that one teach you again which be the first principles of the oracles of God; and are become such as have need of milk, and not of strong meat. For every one that uses milk is unskilful in the word of righteousness: for he is a babe. But strong meat belongeth to them that are of full age, even those who by reason of use have their senses exercised to discern both good and evil. Therefore leaving the principles of the doctrine of Christ, let us go on unto perfection [maturity]" (5:12-14; 6:1).

Paul also wanted the Ephesian believers to go on to a greater understanding of all they had in Jesus Christ. In Ephesians 1:4 Paul said God had chosen believers in Him before the foundation of the world so they would "be holy and without blame before him in love." This is God's calling to each believer. In verse 18 Paul prayed that believers might know "what is the hope of his calling." Paul wanted them to understand that the power of the Godhead would be exercised until His plan and purpose were realized. Paul wanted the Ephesian Christians, and us, to know that God is going to continue His work with believers as He has determined to do.

Paul's consideration of God's work in and through believers caused him to write: "And we know that all things work together for good to them that love God, to them who are the called according to his purpose. For whom he did foreknow, he also did predestinate to be conformed to the image of his Son, that he might be the firstborn among many brethren" (Rom. 8:28,29). God begins working in us at the time of salvation and continues to work in us throughout our lifetime. He causes all things to work together for good, with the purpose of our becoming like His Son.

God's purpose in working in and through believers is also seen in Ephesians 4:13: "Till we all come in the unity of the faith, and of the knowledge of the Son of God, unto a perfect [mature] man, unto the measure of the stature of the fulness of Christ"; and in Ephesians 5:27: "That he might present it to himself a glorious church, not having spot, or wrinkle, or any such thing; but that it should be holy and without blemish." The high calling of God is again seen in I John 3:2: "Beloved, now are we the sons of God, and it doth not yet appear what we shall be: but we know that, when he shall appear, we shall be like him; for we shall see him as he is."

Paul referred to the high calling of God upon his own life when he said, "That I may know him, and the power of his resurrection" (Phil. 3:10). Paul did not consider himself to have attained what God desired for him; rather, he saw himself still in the process. He wrote: "Not that I have already attained it, or have already become perfect, but I press on in order that I may lay hold of that for which I also was laid hold of by Christ Jesus. Brethren, I do not regard myself as having laid hold of it yet; but one thing I do: forgetting what lies behind and reaching forward to what lies ahead, I press on toward the goal for the prize of the upward call of God in Christ Jesus" (vv. 12-14, NASB).

When we realize what God is trying to accomplish in our lives, it will give us an even greater desire to please Jesus Christ in all that we do. Our attitude will change because our values change the more we recognize what God wants to do in and through us. We need to heed Paul's words to the believers in Colosse: "If [since] ye then be risen with Christ, seek those things which are above, where Christ sitteth on the right hand of God. Set your affection on things above, not on things on the earth. For ye are dead, and your life is hid with Christ in God. When Christ, who is our life, shall appear, then shall ye also appear with him in glory" (Col. 3:1-4).

As Paul reflected on what he had in Christ in contrast to what he had before he knew Christ, he said, "But what things were gain to me, those I counted loss for Christ. Yea doubtless, and I count all things but loss for the excellency of the knowledge of Christ Jesus my Lord: for whom I have suffered the loss of all things, and do count them but dung [garbage], that I may win Christ" (Phil. 3:7,8). It was only as Paul had grasped the hope of God's calling that he had such a desire to know Christ better. This is why Paul prayed that the Ephesians might know "the hope of his calling."

God's Gloriously Rich Portion

Earlier, Paul told the Ephesians of the inheritance they had obtained because they had received Christ as Saviour (1:11). Now Paul told them that they were Christ's inheritance. Paul prayed that they might know "what [were] the riches of the glory of his inheritance in the saints" (v. 18). Williams translates this phrase: "How gloriously rich God's portion in his people is."

We belong to God because we have been purchased by Him. This is emphasized by Paul in I Corinthians 6:19,20: "What? know ye not that your body is the temple of the Holy Ghost which is in you, which ye have of God, and ye are not your own? For ye are bought with a price: therefore glorify God in your body, and in your spirit, which are God's." Every believer is God's purchased possession.

The extent to which believers make Christ complete is seen in Ephesians 1:23. Paul mentioned the Church, "which is his body, the fulness of him that filleth all in all." Paul referred to the Body of Christ, which is made up of all believers. Paul said that this Church is "the fulness of him"; that is, it makes Him complete as He desires to be. On the other hand, it is He that "filleth all in all"; that is, He fills and completes the Church. The Church could not be what it ought to be without Christ as the Head, and Christ could not be what He desires to be on earth without the Church.

An analogy of this relationship is seen in the relationship of husband and wife. God first created Adam but observed, "It is not good that the man should be alone; I will make him an help meet [fit] for him" (Gen. 2:18). The woman was then created. Woman complements man, even as man complements woman. So also, the Church complements Christ, and Christ complements the Church.

From Ephesians 1:18 it is apparent that we are more than a mere inheritance of Christ. Paul emphasized the kind of inheritance we are to Christ in the words "riches of the glory of his inheritance." Believers are an inheritance of glorious riches to Christ.

This reveals to us what God considers to be of greatest value in the universe. It is not the planets or stars; it is people. God created the universe by His might and power, but He purchased mankind by His precious blood. This universe will someday pass away and God will create a new heaven and a new earth. But man, who has been redeemed by Christ, shall abide forever! This reveals how important believers are to God. No wonder God is going to display the exceeding riches of His grace through us in ages to come (2:7). This is why Jesus desires to present the Church "to himself a glorious church, not having spot, or wrinkle, or any such thing; but that it should be holy and without blemish" (5:27).

When we consider the marvelous truths of what God thinks of us as believers, it causes us to be filled with praise because of our wonderful Saviour. Although there are times when, humanly speaking, there is only despair, we are able to lift our eyes to Christ and know that He is working in us to accomplish that which will bring glory to Him. So it is important that we do not become discouraged with circumstances; these are the very tools that God uses to make us more like Christ.

The Greatness of His Power

Paul prayed that believers might know "what is the exceeding greatness of his power to us-ward who believe, according to the working of his mighty power" (Eph. 1:19). The word translated "power" is the word from which the English word "dynamite" is derived, and here it refers to the omnipotence, or all-powerfulness, of God.

The Scriptures frequently refer to God's power as it relates to the believer. Ephesians 6:10 says, "Be strong in the Lord and in the power of his might." Philippians 1:6 says, "Being confident of this very thing, that he which hath begun a good work in you will perform it until the day of Jesus Christ." Colossians 1:29 records Paul's testimony: "I also labour, striving according to his working, which worketh in me mightily."

God's power is sufficient for our every need. None of us has to live a defeated life. But those who do not make use of God's available power live miserable, defeated lives. There's more than enough power to break the hold of all sinful habits; more than enough to give deliverance from temptation; more than enough to enable the believer to live above circumstances. Paul said that God's power is "to us-ward who believe" (v. 19). How this operates is seen in I Corinthians 10:13: "There hath no temptation taken you but such as is common to man: but God is faithful, who will not suffer you to be tempted above that ye are able; but will with the temptation also make a way to escape, that ye may be able to bear it."

God's power is made available to us by His indwelling presence. Paul referred to this when he told the Colossians that God's power "worketh in me mightily" (1:29). So the dynamo of Christian living is within the believer because God is within the believer. Hebrews 13:21 records the prayer, "Make you perfect [mature] in every good work to do his will, working in you that which is wellpleasing in his sight."

The person who has received Christ is a new creation. Referring to himself as a believer, Paul wrote: "I am [have been] crucified with Christ: nevertheless I live; yet not I, but Christ liveth in me: and the life which I now live in the flesh I live by the faith of the Son of God, who loved me, and gave himself for me" (Gal. 2:20).

Referring to being in Christ, Paul told the Ephesians, "And that ye put on the new man, which after God is created in righteousness and true holiness" (4:24). Those of us who know Christ share in the divine nature, so each of us is referred to as "a new man." However, there is a sense in which we become new men more fully as we become more and more like Christ. This is accomplished as we recognize the wealth and power we have available in Jesus Christ and then live accordingly. This is why Paul urged the Ephesians to walk in a worthy manner because of their calling (4:1). Paul also emphasized that believers have all the resources they need for spiritual warfare (6:10-18). These passages will be examined in detail later.

However, Paul indicated there is a condition that must be met before God's power is displayed through the believer. We must know that the greatness of God's power is to those "who believe" (1:19). God's power in us is limited only by the faith, or trust, which we have in Christ.

However, just as a person must cash a check for it to be of value to him, so must the believer avail himself of the riches he has in Christ. If one doubts that the writer of a check has money in the bank, or if the believer doubts his riches in Christ, he will never have what is intended for him to have. On the other hand, even if a person has no doubts about the sources behind a check, and the believer has no doubts about his riches in Christ, the resources become theirs only as they take the necessary action to claim them. The believer must not only know that he has riches in Christ but he must also avail himself of them by faith.

In the spiritual realm, victorious living is not to be a one-time experience. Some believers talk about an experience they had in the past, but the Lord intends that we live abundantly in the present. This we are able to do as we live according to the resources we have in Christ.

In Ephesians, Paul attempted to describe the immeasurable power of God by referring to what it had done—"raised him [Christ] from the dead" (1:20). This phrase includes Christ's resurrection, exaltation, lordship and headship.

The Resurrection of Christ

Just as in the Old Testament Scriptures the incidents of creation and Israel's deliverance through the Red Sea are frequently cited to remind believers of God's power, so in the New Testament the resurrection of Christ is frequently mentioned to remind believers of God's power.

After Christ gave His life on the cross for sin, His body was placed in a tomb and a guard was set to make sure no one stole the body. But in spite of this, God raised Jesus from the dead. Acts 2:24 says, "And God raised Him up again, putting an end to the agony of death, since it was impossible for Him to be held in its power" (NASB).

The power of God that raised Christ from the dead is the same power that raised us from spiritual death when we received Christ. As Paul told the Ephesians, "And you hath he quickened [made alive], who were dead in trespasses and sins" (2:1). Jesus Himself said, "He that heareth my word, and believeth on him that sent me, hath everlasting life, and shall not come into condemnation; but is passed from death unto life. Verily, verily, I say unto you, The hour is coming, and now is, when the dead shall hear the voice of the Son of God: and they that hear shall live. For as the Father hath life in himself; so hath he given to the Son to have life in himself" (John 5:24-26).

The life that the Son has is eternal life. The Bible says, "And this is the record, that God hath given to us eternal life, and this life is in his Son. He that hath the Son hath life; and he that hath not the Son of God hath not life" (I John 5:11,12). Every believer has this eternal life because he has the Son of God. Thus, God has already performed a miracle in us who have received Christ as Saviour. The living Christ indwells us and does a spiritual work in our lives. This is what Paul referred to when he said, "For we are his workmanship, created in Christ Jesus unto good works" (Eph. 2:10).

Paul frequently emphasized that Christ is the life of the believer. He wrote: "For ye are dead, and your life is hid with Christ in God. When Christ, who is our life, shall appear, then shall ye also appear with him in glory" (Col. 3:3,4). Notice particularly the words "Christ, who is our life." It is the realization of this truth that causes us to say with Paul, "I am [have been] crucified with Christ: nevertheless I live; yet not I, but Christ liveth in me: and the life which I now live in the flesh I live by the faith of the Son of God, who loved me, and gave himself for me" (Gal. 2:20). Does this describe your life?

We believers are also assured of a physical resurrection, at which time we will be made like Christ. Paul said, "For our conversation [citizenship] is in heaven; from whence also we look for the Saviour, the Lord Jesus Christ: who shall change our vile body, that it may be fashioned like unto his glorious body, according to the working whereby he is able even to subdue all things unto himself" (Phil. 3:20,21).

The resurrection of Church Age believers is referred to in I Thessalonians 4:16,17: "For the Lord himself shall descend from heaven with a shout, with the voice of the archangel, and with the trump of God: and the dead in Christ shall rise first: then we which are alive and remain shall be caught up together with them in the clouds, to meet the Lord in the air: and so shall we ever be with the Lord."

The Exaltation of Christ

Paul reminds us that God has displayed His power in the exaltation of Christ because after raising Christ from the dead, God "set him at his own right hand in the heavenly places" (v. 20). God not only raised Jesus Christ from the dead but exalted Him to His place in heaven. Acts 1:9 tells of Christ's ascension: "And when he had spoken these things, while they beheld, he was taken up; and a cloud received him out of their sight." When Stephen was being stoned by Christ-rejectors, he said, "Behold, I see the heavens opened, and the Son of man standing on the right hand of God" (7:56).

When the Father raised the Son from the dead, He gave the Son a glorified body that could exist both on earth and in heaven.

Christ's ascension to the Father assures us access to Him by prayer. Hebrews 4:14-16 says, "Seeing then that we have a great high priest, that is passed into the heavens, Jesus the Son of God, let us hold fast our profession. For we have not an high priest which cannot be touched with the feeling of our infirmities; but was in all points tempted like as we are, yet without sin. Let us therefore come boldly unto the throne of grace, that we may obtain mercy, and find grace to help in time of need."

Access to the Father has been made possible through the death, resurrection and ascension of the Son; therefore, we have the privilege of coming directly to God with our requests.

The Lordship of Christ

The power of God is evidenced by the lordship of Christ. Christ has been set "far above all principality, and power, and might, and dominion, and every name that is named, not only in this world, but also in that which is to come" (1:21). Another translation renders this verse: "Far above all rule and authority and power and dominion, and every name that is named—above every title that can be conferred—not only in this age and in this world, but also in the age and the world which are to come" (Amplified).

Jesus Christ became—and still is—victor over all human, angelic and satanic forces. The victory of Christ over Satan is referred to in Hebrews 2:14: "Forasmuch then as the children are partakers of flesh and blood, he also himself likewise took part of the same; that through death he might destroy him that had the power of death, that is, the devil." The word translated "destroy" in this verse means "to render powerless." By what Christ accomplished on the cross, He gained the victory over Satan and broke his power over mankind in that no one has to submit to Satan. Although Satan will be permitted to harass people until he is confined to the lake of fire, we may apply the power of God to reject him: "Resist the devil, and he will flee from you" (James 4:7). Every Christian needs to be aware that he is engaged in a spiritual battle against Satan: "We wrestle not against flesh and blood, but against principalities, against powers, against the rulers of the darkness of this world, against spiritual wickedness in high places" (Eph. 6:12).

Christ defeated all opposition by His death, burial and resurrection, and now He has been placed in a position of supreme authority over all created beings and over all the celestial hierarchy, whether they be good or bad.

Because Christ was obedient unto death, "God also hath highly exalted him, and given him a name which is above every name: that at the name of Jesus every knee should bow, of things in heaven, and things in earth, and things under the earth; and that every tongue should confess that Jesus Christ is Lord, to the glory of God the Father" (vv. 9-11).

The Headship of Christ

Ephesians 1:22 reveals that the exceeding greatness of God's power is shown by the headship of Christ. Paul said that the Father "hath put all things under his [Christ's] feet, and gave him to be the head over all things to the church." Notice that this act took place in the past and that nothing is excluded—He is head over "all things." Although positionally Christ became head over all things at His ascension, there is a sense in which things will be brought more completely under His headship in the future. Hebrews 2:8 alludes to this when it says, "Thou hast put all things in subjection under his feet. For in that he put all in subjection under him, he left nothing that is not put under him. But now we see not yet all things put under him."

Paul told the Corinthians, "Then comes the end, when He delivers up the kingdom to the God and Father, when He has abolished all rule and all authority and power. For He must reign until He has put all His enemies under His feet. The last enemy that will be abolished is death. For He has put all things in subjection under His feet. But when He says, 'All things are put in subjection,' it is evident that He is excepted who put all things in subjection to Him. And when all things are subjected to Him, then the Son Himself also will be subjected to the one who subjected all things to Him, that God may be all in all" (I Cor. 15:24-28, NASB).

Since Christ is the Head of the Church, of which every believer is a member, it is obvious that Christ is the Head of every believer. That is, every believer is subject to the supreme Head of the universal Church, Jesus Christ. Paul described the Church to which he was referring when he said, "Which is his body, the fulness of him that filleth all in all" (Eph. 1:23).

The mystical Body of Christ is made up of all who receive Christ as Saviour during the Church Age. Those of us who know Christ have Him as our source of life and power. He motivates our wills and performs through us all that He purposes to do.

Christ's being the Head of the Church is a parallel to the physical body. The head determines what the body will do and works through the body to accomplish its will. This kind of relationship is referred to in Philippians 2:13: "For it is God which worketh in you both to will and to do of his good pleasure." It has already been emphasized from the early portion of Ephesians 1 that God has chosen and set aside the believer for the purpose of working in and through him. As the Head of each believer, Christ not only desires to develop the inner life of a believer but also to direct and empower his activity.

During this age, Christ has purposely limited Himself to what He is able to accomplish through His Body—those who know Him as Saviour. Just as in the physical realm, the head and body cannot function without each other, so is this true in the spiritual realm. Although Christ has all power, He has chosen to work only through His Body; this is why He has made the resources of heaven available to us.

Ephesians 1:23 has been alluded to and explained previously. This verse refers to the Church, "which is his body, the fulness of him that filleth all in all." The Amplified Bible renders this verse: "Which is His body, the fullness of Him Who fills all in all—for in that body lives the full measure of Him Who makes everything complete, and Who fills everything everywhere [with Himself]." All that the Head is and has in the heavenlies is the possession of the Body. All that the Body is and has on earth is the possession of the Head.

The marriage relationship serves as an illustration of Christ and the Church. The husband and wife need each other to gain their greatest fulfillment. Thus, Paul said, "So ought men to love their wives as their own bodies. He that loveth his wife loveth himself. For no man ever yet hated his own flesh; but nourisheth and cherisheth it, even as the Lord the church: for we are members of his body, of his flesh, and of his bone" (5:28-30).

Just as there is a special sense in which the Church makes Christ complete during this age, the same will be true throughout eternity. In John's vision of the New Jerusalem, he explained that an angel said to him, " 'Come here, I shall show you the bride, the wife of the Lamb.' And He carried me away in the Spirit to a great and high mountain, and showed me the holy city, Jerusalem, coming down out of heaven from God" (Rev. 21:9,10, NASB). Revelation 19:7,8 also refers to Christ's relationship with the Church: "Let us be glad and rejoice, and give honour to him: for the marriage of the Lamb is come, and his wife hath made herself ready. And to her was granted that she should be arrayed in fine linen, clean and white: for the fine linen is the righteousness of saints."

In the Church "lives the full measure of Him Who makes everything complete, and Who fills everything everywhere [with Himself]." The fullness of the Godhead is mentioned in Colossians 2:9,10: "For in him dwelleth all the fulness of the Godhead bodily. And ye are complete in him, which is the head of all principality and power."

The divine power and qualities which are Christ's are imparted by Him to His Body. The Church is animated by His life and filled with His gifts and energies. The Church receives from Him what He possesses and is endowed by Him with all that is required for the realization of its heavenly vocation. Because so much has been made available to the Church, the Scriptures emphasize that the believer is to live according to what he possesses.

We are to put Christ first in everything. Colossians 1:18 says, "He is the head of the body, the church: who is the beginning, the firstborn from the dead; that in all things he might have the preeminence."

The special residence of the Head of the Church is in heaven, but the Body is on earth. We are to manifest His life to those on earth. It is only through us that the world is able to see the characteristics of Christ. The realization of this should cause us to seriously consider the sacred responsibility that is ours as a result of being in Christ. Each of us should ask himself, Do I shrink back in fear and collapse before human opposition and satanic influences? Do I conquer as one filled with the fullness of Him who is above all? Is it easy for me to become spiritually discouraged and depressed? Am I a victor because of my unshakeable confidence in the Lord Jesus Christ?

We do not need to be "under the circumstances," because Jesus Christ is the God of circumstances. How wonderful it is that God has made His power available to those who believe!

Chapter 8

Man Made New
(Eph. 2:1-10)

Paul was writing to believers when he wrote his letter to the Ephesians, and because he wrote by inspiration, his words are applicable to all believers of this age. In verses 1-10 of chapter 2, four truths are especially emphasized: (1) what we were (vv. 1-3); (2) what we are (vv. 4-6); (3) what we shall be (v. 7); (4) how we are made new (vv. 8-10).

What We Were

Ephesians 2:1 says, "And you hath he quickened, who were dead in trespasses and sins." The word "dead" refers to a state of spiritual death, not physical death.

Spiritually Dead

The Bible never speaks of death as annihilation or cessation of existence but of separation. Whereas physical death is the separation of the soul from the body, spiritual death is the separation of the soul from God.

In Ephesians 4:18 spiritual death is seen as a broken relationship. This verse refers to those "having the understanding darkened, being alienated from the life of God through the ignorance that is in them, because of the blindness of their heart." It is sin that separates a person from God. Sin entered the human race through Adam and Eve when they chose to disobey God and eat of the forbidden fruit. Spiritual death came upon them immediately, for they were separated from God because of their sin. Although physical death was not immediate, the seeds of physical death began to work in their lives so that they eventually died physically. Romans 5:12 attributes sin to Adam: "Wherefore, as by one man sin entered into the world, and death by sin; and so death passed upon all men, for that all have sinned." From this verse we see that both physical death and spiritual death are the results of sin.

Every person is spiritually dead until he receives Jesus Christ as his personal Saviour. If he passes from this life without receiving Christ, he experiences the second death, which is eternal separation from God. Revelation 20:14,15 says, "And death and hell [hades] were cast into the lake of fire. This is the second death. And whosoever was not found written in the book of life was cast into the lake of fire."

It is important to realize that the person without Christ is considered by the Scriptures to be much more than just morally degraded or diseased—he is considered to be dead. Paul reminded believers that before they had been made alive spiritually by God, they were dead "in trespasses and sins" (Eph. 2:1).

Unbelievers have a sin nature that produces "trespasses and sins." One cannot change his nature by changing his actions any more than the nature of a fruit tree can be changed by removing the fruit. Thus, self-reform avails nothing in bringing a person into right relationship with Jesus Christ; he must receive Christ as Saviour in order to receive a new nature.

One who is dead cannot do anything to change his state; it must be changed from a source outside of himself. God has made it possible for the spiritually dead person to receive Christ as Saviour, at which time forgiveness of sin is applied to the person and he is given eternal life. This is why Jesus said, "Except a man be born again, he cannot see the kingdom of God" (John 3:3). Jesus added, "Marvel not that I said unto thee, Ye must be born again" (v. 7). When a person receives Christ, he experiences the second birth. He is no longer spiritually dead because he has received eternal life. As has been emphasized previously, eternal life is in the Son of God, so whoever has received Him has eternal life (I John 5:11,12).

Paul described what the Ephesians were like—and what all believers were like—before they received Christ: "Wherein in time past ye walked according to the course of this world, according to the prince of the power of the air, the spirit that now worketh in the children of disobedience" (2:2).

Bound by Fleshly Lusts

Concerning the children of disobedience, Paul went on to say, "Among whom also we all had our conversation in times past in the lusts of our flesh, fulfilling the desires of the flesh and of the mind; and were by nature the children of wrath, even as others" (v. 3). This verse reveals that before receiving Christ, people are in bondage to the desires of the old nature.

The "flesh" refers to the natural life each person has in Adam. It is a depraved nature inherited from Adam by birth. Romans 8:5 refers to this nature: "For they that are after the flesh do mind the things of the flesh." Verse 8 adds, "So then they that are in the flesh cannot please God." That is, the unsaved person is not able to please God. The second birth is necessary; he must receive Jesus Christ as Saviour in order to please God. So verse 9 says, "But ye are not in the flesh, but in the Spirit, if so be that the Spirit of God dwell in you. Now if any man have not the Spirit of Christ, he is none of his."

The person who receives Christ receives a new nature, but he still retains the old, or adamic, nature. This causes a struggle within each believer because he must decide whether to yield to the desires of the old nature or to the desires of the new nature. Galatians 5:16 says, "Walk in the Spirit, and ye shall not fulfil the lust of the flesh." Verse 17 adds, "For the flesh lusteth against the Spirit, and the Spirit against the flesh: and these are contrary the one to the other: so that ye cannot do the things that ye would." As the believer yields to the Holy Spirit, he will not fulfill the desires of the old nature.

Dominated by the World System

Before people receive Christ they are dominated by the world system. This is indicated in verse 2: "Wherein in time past ye walked according to the course of this world." The word translated "world" is *kosmos*, which is used here to refer to the world system. For the unbeliever, all influence comes from his environment because he has no communication with heaven.

In Subjection to Satan

Ephesians 2:2 also shows that those without Christ are under Satan's dominion: "Wherein in time past ye walked . . . according to the prince of the power of the air, the spirit that now worketh in the children of disobedience." In II Corinthians 4:3,4 Satan is referred to as "the god of this world": "But if our gospel be hid, it is hid to them that are lost: in whom the god of this world hath blinded the minds of them which believe not, lest the light of the glorious gospel of Christ, who is the image of God, should shine unto them."

Although unbelievers make jokes about Satan and speak lightly of him, he is a real person with great intelligence, although he is not omniscient. Satan is active in two spheres—in the air and on the earth. The title "the prince of the power of the air" shows his activity in this sphere. The fact that he works in the children of disobedience reveals he is active on the earth. Satan is the chief enemy of God; he opposes God and desires to have the worship that belongs only to God. Satan's tactics are to try to keep people under his dominion and when they leave his dominion by receiving Christ, to endeavor to get them to dishonor God. Sin began with Satan and it is his desire to keep people under the condemnation of sin. However, Satan himself will someday be cast into the lake of fire (Rev. 20:10).

Under God's Wrath

Before a person receives Christ as Saviour he is condemned under God's wrath. This is evident from verse 3 where Paul reminded the Ephesians that before they were made spiritually alive they "were by nature the children of wrath, even as others."

It is easy for people to accept that God is a God of love, but it is extremely difficult for many to accept that He is also a God of wrath. However, John 3:18 says, "He that believeth on him is not condemned: but he that believeth not is condemned already, because he hath not believed in the name of the only begotten Son of God." Verse 36 further emphasizes this truth: "He that believeth on the Son hath everlasting life: and he that believeth not the Son shall not see life; but the wrath of God abideth on him."

So everyone is condemned under God's wrath until he receives Jesus Christ as Saviour. The only hope for the person under the wrath of God is to receive the love of God as it has been manifested in the death of Jesus Christ for our sin.

What We Are

Having reminded the Ephesian Christians of what they were before they received Christ, Paul now reminded them of what they are because of their position in Christ. These same truths apply to those of us who now know Jesus Christ as personal Saviour.

There is an emphatic break between verses 3 and 4. Verses 1-3 revealed the dark picture of those without Christ, and verse 4 begins: "But God." How wonderful it is when God intervenes for man! Look at verse 4 in its entirety: "But God, who is rich in mercy, for his great love wherewith he loved us." This verse reveals God's love for men. Our sin is repulsive to His holiness, yet our souls are precious to Him. It has never been man's tendency to seek God, but God has sought man. This is seen throughout the Scriptures.

When Adam and Eve sinned against God, they did not seek Him. They hid from God but He "called unto Adam, and said unto him, Where art thou?" (Gen. 3:9). Although man was out of fellowship and needed to be reconciled to God, the first move toward this reconciliation did not come from man but from God.

Because of His great love, God desired to dwell with man. Therefore, He said, "Let them make me a sanctuary; that I may dwell among them" (Ex. 25:8). Later, God lived among men in the Person of His Son, the Lord Jesus Christ. The Bible says, "But when the fulness of the time was come, God sent forth his Son, made of a woman, made under the law, to redeem them that were under the law, that we might receive the adoption of sons" (Gal. 4:4,5).

God's love and reaching out toward man is also seen in Christ's return. The Lord Jesus Christ told His disciples, "Let not your heart be troubled: ye believe in God, believe also in me. In my Father's house are many mansions: if it were not so, I would have told you. I go to prepare a place for you. And if I go and prepare a place for you, I will come again, and receive you unto myself; that where I am, there ye may be also" (John 14:1-3).

The fact that God first acted to reconcile man to Himself does not mean that He changes His attitude toward the unregenerate person. God is still a consuming fire, and He never shows mercy at the expense of justice. His justice was satisfied when Jesus Christ was crucified. Isaiah prophesied this when he wrote by revelation: "All we like sheep have gone astray; we have turned every one to his own way; and the Lord hath laid on him the iniquity of us all. He shall see the travail of his soul, and shall be satisfied" (Isa. 53:6,11).

The righteous demands of God concerning sin were satisfied through the death of Jesus Christ. This is why the Bible says, "For God so loved the world, that he gave his only begotten Son, that whosoever believeth in him should not perish, but have everlasting life" (John 3:16). Concerning Christ, I John 2:2 says that "he is the propitiation [satisfaction] for our sins: and not for our's only, but also for the sins of the whole world."

God's mercy, mentioned in Ephesians 2:4, is based on His justice having been satisfied. The Bible says, "But now the righteousness of God without the law is manifested, being witnessed by the law and the prophets; even the righteousness of God which is by faith of Jesus Christ unto all and upon all them that believe: for there is no difference: for all have sinned, and come short of the glory of God; being justified freely by his grace through the redemption that is in Christ Jesus: whom God hath set forth to be a propitiation through faith in his blood, to declare his righteousness for the remission of sins that are past, through the forbearance of God; to declare, I say, at this time his righteousness: that he might be just, and the justifier of him which believeth in Jesus" (Rom. 3:21-26).

God could not bypass His justice to deliver man from condemnation, and it was not necessary for Him to do so. His justice was satisfied by the death of Jesus Christ for the sin of the world. Now, God could be just and could also justify any who believed in Jesus Christ as their Saviour. Concerning Christ, Ephesians 1:7 reminds us, "In whom we have redemption through his blood, the forgiveness of sins, according to the riches of his grace."

Pondering these tremendous thoughts about God caused Dr. Louis T. Talbot to write: "Therefore, when Christ was crucified, God was glorified, justice was satisfied, the law was magnified, and sin was nullified, and the sinner justified" (*Lectures on Ephesians*, p. 60).

Ephesians 2:5,6 states what is true of every believer today: "Even when we were dead in sins, [God] hath quickened us together with Christ (by grace ye are saved;) and hath raised us up together, and made us sit together in heavenly places in Christ Jesus." Salvation, which was planned in the heart of God in eternity past, is seen in three aspects in these verses. First, we were spiritually dead, so God quickened us—made us spiritually alive. Second, we were subject to Satan, but God raised us up together with Jesus Christ. Third, we were bound by the flesh, or old nature, but God seated us in a new environment—in the heavenlies.

Dead, But Made Alive

How can a dead person be made alive? By a miracle of God. Before one receives Christ as Saviour he is "dead in trespasses and sins" (v. 1), but upon receiving Christ he is "quickened" (v. 5). Those spiritually dead are made spiritually alive by receiving Christ.

The power of God to accomplish this was emphasized in Ephesians 1: "According to the working of his mighty power, which he wrought in Christ, when he raised him from the dead" (vv. 19,20). We are reconciled to God by Christ's death: "For if, when we were enemies, we were reconciled to God by the death of his Son, much more, being reconciled, we shall be saved by his life" (Rom. 5:10). This is the first operation of God's power "to us-ward who believe" (Eph. 1:19).

God does not patch up, or rework, the old life; He gives a new life by means of the new birth. Thus, Christ told

Nicodemus, "That which is born of the flesh is flesh; and that which is born of the Spirit is spirit. Marvel not that I said unto thee, Ye must be born again" (John 3:6,7). The process of the new birth is a mystery to which Christ drew this parallel: "The wind bloweth where it listeth [pleases], and thou hearest the sound thereof, but canst not tell whence it cometh, and whither it goeth: so is every one that is born of the Spirit" (v. 8). Even though it is impossible for us to understand the process of the new birth, we can see its effects. However, the means of the new birth is clearly revealed in verses 14,15: "As Moses lifted up the serpent in the wilderness, even so must the Son of man be lifted up: that whosoever believeth in him should not perish, but have eternal life."

Being made spiritually alive involves more than pardon. A criminal already executed may be pardoned, but he remains dead. Also, a bullet may be removed from a dead person, but he remains dead even though the cause of death has been removed. So also, more than forgiveness of sin is accomplished when a person receives Christ as Saviour; the person is given life—the Lord Jesus Christ Himself. John 5:25,26 says, "Verily, verily, I say unto you, The hour is coming, and now is, when the dead shall hear the voice of the Son of God: and they that hear shall live. For as the Father hath life in himself; so hath he given to the Son to have life in himself." Thus, I John 5:12 says, "He that hath the Son hath life; and he that hath not the Son of God hath not life."

Subject, But Raised Up

Before receiving Christ we were subjected to Satan, but now God "hath raised us up together . . . in Christ Jesus" (Eph. 2:6). Whereas quickening refers to the impartation of new life, the raising up indicates the act by which God has lifted us into a new realm. He has taken us out of the realm of Satan and placed us in a heavenly realm. Colossians 1:13 tells us that God "hath delivered us from the power of darkness, and hath translated us into the kingdom of his dear Son."

At His resurrection, Christ demonstrated His victory over Satan: "When He had disarmed the rulers and authorities, He made a public display of them, having triumphed over them through Him" (2:15, NASB). Christ overcame Satan by His death and resurrection, and He gives enablement for believers to overcome him. James 4:7 instructs believers, "Submit yourselves therefore to God. Resist the devil, and he will flee from you."

So we see that we are not only given new life in Christ, but we are also freed from bondage. By receiving Christ, the sinner is made a saint, is lifted from the pit, and is placed upon a rock. Thus the psalmist wrote: "I waited patiently for the Lord; and he inclined unto me, and heard my cry. He brought me up also out of an horrible pit, out of the miry clay, and set my feet upon a rock, and established my goings. And he hath put a new song in my mouth, even praise unto our God: many shall see it, and fear, and shall trust in the Lord" (40:1-3). Because believers are raised up together in Christ Jesus, Paul exhorted the Ephesians, "Walk worthy of the vocation wherewith ye are called" (4:1). Our position in Christ is always the basis for our life.

In the Flesh, But in Christ

Not only has God "raised us up together," but He has also "made us sit together in heavenly places in Christ Jesus" (2:6). Ephesians 1:20 tells of Christ's being set in heavenly places: "Which he [the Father] wrought in Christ, when he raised him from the dead, and set him at his own right hand in the heavenly places." It is the spiritual privilege of every believer to be seated in heavenly places in Christ, and it is the spiritual responsibility of every believer to live accordingly. "[Since] ye then be risen with Christ, seek those things which are above, where Christ sitteth on the right hand of God. Set your affection on things above, not on things on the earth. For ye are dead, and your life is hid with Christ in God. When Christ, who is our life, shall appear, then shall ye also appear with him in glory" (Col. 3:1-4).

Because we are seated in the heavenlies in Christ, we should have spiritual rest and relaxation. However, many who know Christ as Saviour are characterized by worrying. The Bible says, "Fret not thyself because of evildoers, neither be thou envious against the workers of iniquity" (Ps. 37:1). The believer is commanded, "Rest in the Lord, and wait patiently for him: fret not thyself because of him who prospereth in his way, because of the man who bringeth wicked devices to pass. Cease from anger, and forsake wrath: fret not thyself in any wise to do evil" (vv. 7,8). We need not worry, "for our conversation [citizenship] is in heaven; from whence also we look for the Saviour, the Lord Jesus Christ" (Phil. 3:20).

Paul was writing these great truths from a dungeon in Rome, but he was deeply conscious of his position in Christ. This was the secret of his victorious living. He realized what his spiritual resources were in Christ.

Christ has been set "far above all principality, and power, and might, and dominion, and every name that is named, not only in this world, but also in that which is to come" (1:21). He has been raised far above everything and everyone else. He is not contaminated by the things of this world. As we live according to our heavenly position in Christ, we will not be contaminated by the world either. This involves having a proper attitude of the heart and mind and living by faith. As we appropriate what we have in Christ, we will share in the power and conquests of that exalted position.

Because we are in Christ, we are as far above the power of Satan as Christ is above the power of Satan. Therefore, if we resist Satan, he will flee from us (James 4:7).

The statements in Romans 8:37-39 are true of every believer: "Nay, in all these things we are more than conquerors through him that loved us. For I am persuaded, that neither death, nor life, nor angels, nor principalities, nor powers, nor things present, nor things to come, nor height, nor depth, nor any other creature, shall be able to separate us from the love of God, which is in Christ Jesus our Lord." Because Christ has triumphed, those in Him also triumph. Thus we can say, "Thanks be unto God, which always causeth us to triumph in Christ" (II Cor. 2:14).

Notice the difference in prepositions in Ephesians 2:5,6. Believers are quickened *with* Christ, but they are seated in heavenly places *in* Christ. Everyone who has received Christ as Saviour has already been made alive with Him. However, we have not yet been seated *with* Him, as He said, "To him that overcometh will I grant to sit with me in my throne" (Rev. 3:21). Even though we are not seated with Him yet, we are seated in heavenly places in Him. Christ is our representative in heaven while we live here on earth. Yet, He also indwells us because He is omnipresent.

Christ's special ministry in heaven at the present time is that of intercession. Hebrews 7:25 says, "He ever liveth to make intercession for them." Thus, in His glorified body He is in heaven making intercession for us, guarding our salvation.

Christ guards believers on earth and evidences this by sealing them with the Holy Spirit, "who is given as a pledge of our inheritance, with a view to the redemption of God's own possession, to the praise of His glory" (Eph. 1:14, NASB). On earth, Jesus Christ seals our lives by the Holy Spirit, and in heaven He guards our lives by interceding for us. First John 2:1 says, "We have an advocate with the Father, Jesus Christ the righteous."

Christ intercedes for us in heaven but indwells us on earth and energizes us to do that which pleases Him. Christ lives within the believer, and Paul referred to this as a mystery (not previously revealed): "Christ in you, the hope of glory" (Col. 1:27). Because Paul realized this truth, he wrote: "Whereunto I also labour, striving according to his working, which worketh in me mightily" (v. 29). Paul knew that Christ in him was his true source of spiritual strength. It is no wonder that he wrote: "I am [have been] crucified with Christ: nevertheless I live; yet not I, but Christ liveth in me: and the life which I now live in the flesh I live by the faith of the Son of God, who loved me, and gave himself for me" (Gal. 2:20). The believer has Christ living within him. What a privilege!

What We Shall Be

God's purpose for the believer is seen in Ephesians 2:7: "That in the ages to come he might show the exceeding riches of his grace in his kindness toward us through Christ Jesus." Notice when this shall be—"in the ages to come." This phrase literally means "the ages that are coming, one upon another." It indicates not just a particular age but age upon age. God's eternal purpose in the ages to come is to exhibit, through and to believers, His eternal kindness. Of course, this implies there will be spectators, and no doubt those are the angels. The saints are the objects of God's kindness and will be displayed throughout eternity.

Ephesians 1:4 tells us that we have been chosen "in him before the foundation of the world"; that is, before the world existed. Verse 10 reveals the purpose of God's choosing: "That in the dispensation of the fulness of times he might gather together in one all things in Christ, both which are in heaven, and which are on earth; even in him." Even after all dispensations have run their course, there will still be a ministry for Church Age believers—to show "the exceeding riches of his grace in his kindness toward us through Christ Jesus" (2:7). We who have accepted His wonderful grace by receiving Christ as Saviour will display throughout eternity what God has done for us. God will use us to display His grace and power and will lead us into a deeper and deeper understanding of His marvelous work in our behalf. There will be no end to this, for even after a million years we will still be amazed at the unfolding of God's wonders and marvelous power.

How We Are Made New

What Paul said of the Ephesian Christians is true of every believer: "For by grace are ye saved through faith; and that not of yourselves: it is the gift of God: not of works, lest any man should boast. For we are his workmanship, created in Christ Jesus unto good works, which God hath before ordained that we should walk in them" (vv. 8-10).

The believer is God's workmanship, as is also indicated in II Corinthians 5:17,18: "Therefore if any man be in Christ, he is a new creature: old things are passed away; behold, all things are become new. And all things are of God."

Every believer has been delivered from condemnation— "For by grace are ye saved" (Eph. 2:8). From the construction in the original language, we see that Paul was referring to a salvation that had been completed in the past. The Ephesian believers to whom he was writing were not then being saved from condemnation; they had already been saved from condemnation. A person is delivered from condemnation the moment he places his trust in Christ alone for his salvation. The progressive aspect of salvation is not deliverance from condemnation but walking according to one's position in Christ.

Notice from Ephesians 2:8 the agent of our salvation—"faith." Because faith is the means of salvation, salvation is placed within the reach of everyone. People have various degrees of faith, but it is not the degree of faith that saves—it is the object of one's faith—Jesus Christ.

Even the faith to be saved is a gift from God: "For by grace are ye saved through faith; and that not of yourselves: it is the gift of God" (v. 8). God not only provides the Substitute for our sin, but He also provides the faith that enables us to believe Him for salvation. Such faith comes by means of God's Word: "Faith cometh by hearing, and hearing by the word of God" (Rom. 10:17).

Paul emphasized that salvation is not earned by our doing good deeds: "Not of works, lest any man should boast" (Eph. 2:9). If salvation were by works, some would not be able to attain it because they would not be physically able to do the necessary things. But salvation is available to all because it is acquired by faith. If anyone were able to earn salvation by works, he would have the right to boast of his accomplishment. However, salvation is a gift to be received; it cannot be earned.

Even though works have no part in a person's acquiring salvation, they have a large part in his life *after* he has received Christ by faith. Thus, verse 10 says, "For we are his workmanship, created in Christ Jesus unto good works, which God hath before ordained that we should walk in them." Notice that a person is created in Christ Jesus *unto* good works, not *by* good works. A person is saved apart from works but he is to perform good works after salvation. Titus 3:5,8 also shows that salvation is gained not by works but that a believer is to produce good works: "Not by works of righteousness which we have done, but according to his mercy he saved us, by the washing of regeneration, and renewing of the Holy Ghost. . . . These things I will that thou affirm constantly, that they which have believed in God might be careful to maintain good works. These things are good and profitable unto men." Thus we see that the Scriptures abound in references stating that we are not saved by good works, but we are to produce good works after we are saved.

From the first chapter of Ephesians we have seen that God chose us "before the foundation of the world, that we should be holy and without blame before him in love: having predestinated us unto the adoption of children" (vv. 4,5). God has set us apart as full-grown sons; therefore, let us produce good works which will bring glory to Him.

Chapter 9

Jew and Gentile Made One

(Eph. 2:11-22)

Ephesians 2:11-22 reveals that the Jew and Gentile are made one by the blood of Jesus Christ. Within this passage are three classifications of mankind: Jew, Gentile and the new man.

A similar division of mankind is seen in I Corinthians 10:32: "Give none offence, neither to the Jews, not to the Gentiles, nor to the church of God." The person who is part of the Body of Christ is part of the "church of God" and is a new man.

"Jews" are the descendants of Abraham whom God chose so He might produce a special people for special purposes. These people were first called "Hebrews," later "Israelites," and still later "Jews." By the time all three names had come into existence they had begun to be used interchangeably.

Those not descendants of Abraham are known as "Gentiles." When the Scriptures refer to the "nations," it is referring to Gentiles in contrast to the nation of Israel.

From Adam to Abraham—about 2000 years—there were only Gentiles because God had not yet chosen Abraham for the purpose of producing through him a special people. However, with God's call of Abraham and the resulting descendants, there were two groups, Jews (Hebrews) and Gentiles. Since the Day of Pentecost, when the Holy Spirit descended as recorded in Acts 2, a person who has experienced spiritual birth is considered a "new man," even though he is still considered either a Jew or a Gentile according to his physical birth. Thus we see that when a person receives Christ as Saviour, he is lifted to a position that transcends all physical aspects.

As individuals, both the Jew and the Gentile were equally under the condemnation of sin, with its resulting penalty of death. They were equally far from God and needed to be reconciled to Him. Because of the extreme differences between Jews and Gentiles, there was little harmony between the two throughout Old Testament times. However, in Ephesians 2:11-22, Paul showed that these two peoples with radically different backgrounds are elevated to a new position in Christ. Both the Jew and the Gentile who know Christ as Saviour are "new men." In this spiritual realm there is no distinction as Jew or Gentile because both are one in Christ.

The words "new man" in Ephesians 2:11-22 refer to the Church in a collective sense rather than the believer as an individual. Gentiles are referred to in this passage as "uncircumcision," and Jews are referred to as "circumcision." Paul told the Ephesians, "Wherefore remember, that ye being in time past Gentiles in the flesh, who are called Uncircumcision by that which is called the Circumcision in the flesh made by hands" (v. 11). Notice that Paul said "ye" rather than "we." Paul was a Jew; therefore, he could not include himself in what he was saying about the Gentiles. He went on to tell them, "That at that time ye were without Christ, being aliens from the commonwealth of Israel, and strangers from the covenants of promise, having no hope, and without God in the world" (v. 12).

In considering the contrast between the Jews and the Gentiles, it is important to remember that the Jew had special privileges, although he misinterpreted these as merit before God. In the Book of Romans, when Paul showed that the Jew was also under the condemnation of sin, he asked the questions, "What advantage then hath the Jew? or what profit is there of circumcision?" (3:1). Paul then answered his own questions: "Much every way: chiefly, because that unto them were committed the oracles of God" (v. 2). Later in the same letter he mentioned other privileges: "Who are Israelites; to whom pertaineth the adoption, and the glory, and the covenants, and the giving of the law, and the service of God, and the promises; whose are the fathers, and of whom as concerning the flesh Christ came" (9:4,5).

Genesis 12 records God's call to Abraham to make of him a great nation. This was part of God's plan to fulfill the promise of Genesis 3:15: "I will put enmity between thee and the woman, and between thy seed and her seed; it shall bruise thy head, and thou shalt bruise his heel." God had promised to send the woman a descendant who would bruise the head of Satan. This person was Jesus Christ, who was God Himself but who entered the human race through the Jewish nation.

Although God called the nation for this and other specific purposes, He reminded the people often that He had not chosen them because they deserved to be chosen. Moses reminded the people, "For thou art an holy people unto the Lord thy God: the Lord thy God hath chosen thee to be a special people unto himself, above all people that are upon the face of the earth. The Lord did not set his love upon you, nor choose you, because ye were more in number than any people; for ye were the fewest of all people: but because the Lord loved you, and because he would keep the oath which he had sworn unto your fathers, hath the Lord brought you out [of Egypt] with a mighty hand, and redeemed you out of the house of bondmen, from the hand of Pharaoh king of Egypt" (Deut. 7:6-8). God brought the Jewish nation into existence through Abraham for specific purposes. Because of this, the Jews were a privileged people. Three major purposes of God are clearly evident from the Scriptures: (1) to be the channel for the Messiah, (2) to be custodians of the oracles of God, the Bible, and (3) to be recipients of the covenants of promise concerning future earthly blessings.

God chose to bring blessing to all the people of the earth through His people, Israel. Being such a privileged people brought great responsibility, for the Jews were to be a witness of God to all mankind.

The Gentiles, called "uncircumcision" by the Jews, were regarded by the Jews as outcasts and as having no hope in God. However, even though the Jew had been chosen for specific purposes by God, the Jew was condemned under sin, as was the Gentile, and both had to come to God by faith. The Jew's privileges did not merit him a spiritual position with God. Both Jews and Gentiles "have sinned, and come short of the glory of God" (Rom. 3:23). What is said in

Ephesians 2 is true of all mankind—everyone is dead in trespasses and sins until he receives Christ as Saviour.

The New Man

The new man mentioned in Ephesians 2 is the Church, the Body of Christ, not the individual believer. Verse 14 says that Christ "hath made both one"; verse 15 says, "to make in himself of twain one new man."

Ephesians 2:12-22 can be divided by three phrases: "at that time ye were" (v. 12); "but now in Christ Jesus" (v. 13); and "now therefore ye are" (v. 19).

The first division reveals what the Gentiles were. In its entirety, verse 12 says, "That at that time ye were without Christ, being aliens from the commonwealth of Israel, and strangers from the covenants of promise, having no hope, and without God in the world." Especially notice five phrases from this verse. "Without Christ"—the promise of the Messiah was given to Israel, not to the Gentiles. However, even though Christ came to be the Messiah of Israel, He came to be the Saviour of the entire world. "Aliens from the commonwealth of Israel"—the Gentiles had no part in the inheritance of the Chosen People. "Strangers from the covenants of promise"—the Gentiles did not have the promise of future blessing as a result of natural birth. "Having no hope"—the Gentiles had no divine revelation concerning the future. "Without God in the world"—the Gentiles had no knowledge of the true God. God revealed Himself to the world through the Jewish nation, not through the Gentiles. The Gentiles were opposed to the true God and were under the dominion of Satan.

The emphasis of Ephesians 2:13-18 is seen in the words "but now in Christ Jesus" (v. 13). In its entirety verse 13 says, "But now in Christ Jesus ye who sometimes were far off are made nigh by the blood of Christ." This verse reveals how God has intervened in behalf of the Gentiles.

This is also seen earlier in the same chapter. Verses 1-3 remind the Gentiles of what they were without Christ, and then God's intervention is seen in the words "but God" (v. 4). Then follows the account of how God provided salvation by grace through faith. As Romans 5:6 tells us,

"For when we were yet without strength, in due time Christ died for the ungodly." The hopeless situation has been completely changed because of what Christ accomplished at Calvary.

Romans 5:8-11 reveals what we have because of Christ: "But God commendeth his love toward us, in that, while we were yet sinners, Christ died for us. Much more then, being now justified by his blood, we shall be saved from wrath through him. For if, when we were enemies, we were reconciled to God by the death of his Son, much more, being reconciled, we shall be saved by his life. And not only so, but we also joy in God through our Lord Jesus Christ, by whom we have now received the atonement."

Notice especially that those who have been reconciled by Christ's death shall be saved by His life. We have Christ's life within us. Second Corinthians 5:17,18 says, "Therefore if any man be in Christ, he is a new creature: old things are passed away; behold, all things are become new. And all things are of God, who hath reconciled us to himself by Jesus Christ."

Before salvation we were without Christ, without hope, and without God; after salvation these are ours because we "are made nigh by the blood of Christ" (Eph. 2:13).

Ephesians 2:19 shows what believers are in Christ: "Now therefore ye are no more strangers and foreigners, but fellowcitizens with the saints, and of the household of God." Although both Jews and Gentiles were separated from God and each other, now—through Christ—they are members of the same Body and "household of God." Verse 19 will be dealt with more fully when we consider believers as a building.

Conciliation of Jew and Gentile

Verses 14-18 reveal that the believing Jew and Gentile have a permanent union in Christ. Christ has a threefold relationship to this peace that unites Jew and Gentile: (1) He is our peace (v. 14), (2) He made peace (v. 15), and (3) He preached peace (v. 17).

Verse 14 tells us, "For he is our peace, who hath made both one, and hath broken down the middle wall of partition between us." Here we see that Christ is not merely a peacemaker; He Himself is our peace. Before He left the earth He told His disciples, "Peace I leave with you, my peace I give unto you: not as the world giveth, give I unto you. Let not your heart be troubled, neither let it be afraid" (John 14:27). The one who desires to receive Christ's peace must receive Him as Saviour because He is our peace. What a contradiction it is that man attempts to bring about peace today but leaves Christ entirely out of his considerations. It is impossible to have peace on earth without the Prince of Peace Himself. Jesus said, "These things I have spoken unto you, that in me ye might have peace. In the world ye shall have tribulation: but be of good cheer; I have overcome the world" (John 16:33).

That Christ is our peace is also seen in the prophecy of Isaiah 9:6,7: "For unto us a child is born, unto us a son is given: and the government shall be upon his shoulder: and his name shall be called Wonderful, Counsellor, The mighty God, The everlasting Father, The Prince of Peace. Of the increase of his government and peace there shall be no end, upon the throne of David, and upon his kingdom, to order it, and to establish it with judgment and with justice from henceforth even for ever. The zeal of the Lord of hosts will perform this."

Ephesians 2:15 reveals that Christ has made peace: "Having abolished in his flesh the enmity, even the law of commandments contained in ordinances; for to make in himself of twain one new man, so making peace." Notice what was involved in Christ's work of making peace. First, the "middle wall of partition" between Jew and Gentile had to be broken down (v. 14). Second, He had to abolish "in His flesh the enmity" (v. 15). Third, He had to "make in Himself of twain one new man" (v. 15). Fourth, He had to reconcile both "unto God in one body" (v. 16).

The temple in Jerusalem had a wall that separated the Gentiles from the Jews. For any Gentile to go beyond that wall meant death. Of course, many Jews were just as evil as the Gentiles in the sight of God, but nevertheless the wall existed to separate the two peoples. The Jews had been called for specific purposes and were to remain a separate people although they were to be witnesses of God to the Gentiles.

Many Jews were Jews outwardly but not inwardly. Paul told the Jews, "For he is not a Jew, which is one outwardly; neither is that circumcision, which is outward in the flesh: but he is a Jew, which is one inwardly; and circumcision is that of the heart, in the spirit, and not in the letter; whose praise is not of men, but of God" (Rom. 2:28,29).

Middle Wall of Partition

The temple wall that separated the Jews and Gentiles was small in comparison to the greater wall of social and religious separation. Many Jews became bigoted because of the privileges God had extended to them. They had a superiority complex that produced many other problems between the two peoples.

The spirit of many of the Jews was similar to what is frequently seen today in denominations and local churches. Such a feeling of superiority is also responsible for many of the severe racial problems that exist today. This passage in Ephesians is highly significant in seeing how such problems can be resolved.

Christ broke down the middle wall of partition "having abolished in his flesh the enmity, even the law of commandments contained in ordinances; for to make in himself of twain one new man, so making peace" (Eph. 2:15). Israel was separated from other nations, and to it was committed the Mosaic Law system. Many Israelites considered those not having the Law as inferior, which brought disrepute to God. Writing by inspiration, Paul said, "Behold, thou are called a Jew, and restest in the law, and makest thy boast of God, and knowest his will, and approvest the things that are more excellent, being instructed out of the law; and art confident that thou thyself art a guide of the blind, a light of them which are in darkness, an instructor of the foolish, a teacher of babes, which hast the form of knowledge and of the truth in the law" (Rom. 2:17-20). Paul pressed his point by saying, "Thou that makest thy boast of the law, through breaking the law dishonourest thou God? For the name of God is blasphemed among the Gentiles through you" (vv. 23,24).

The Gentiles sinned without having the Law, and the Jews sinned while having the Law. As a result, both were under the penalty of death and the condemnation of God. The Bible says, "For there is no respect of persons with God. For as many as have sinned without law shall also perish without law: and as many as have sinned in the law shall be judged by the law" (vv. 11,12). So both Jews and Gentiles were under the penalty of sin. For them to be delivered from this penalty someone had to pay it in their behalf. This is what Christ did when He shed His blood on the cross—He "abolished in his flesh the enmity" (Eph. 2:15).

It is clear from the Scriptures that the Law does not justify anyone. "That no man is justified by the law in the sight of God, it is evident: for, The just shall live by faith. And the law is not of faith: but, The man that doeth them shall live in them. Christ hath redeemed us from the curse of the law, being made a curse for us: for it is written, Cursed is every one that hangeth on a tree" (Gal. 3:11-13).

The cross is the only meeting place of Jew and Gentile—here they are on equal grounds. This is true of all individuals regardless of their differences. If this truth would be realized and acted on, it would solve most of the religious and social problems so prevalent today. When we see ourselves as we really are—sinners without hope—and receive Jesus Christ as Saviour, we will realize we have no basis to feel superior to anyone else. We need the grace of God for salvation the same as any other person.

From Ephesians 2:15 we learn that Jesus Christ made "in himself of twain one new man, so making peace." Christ removed the barriers to peace between Jews and Gentiles and then established a basis for real unity with continuing peace. Of these two peoples—Jews and Gentiles—God made "one new man."

It must be remembered that God still has an earthly program for Israel which He will resume in the future when the nation receives Christ as Messiah. However, during the present age when a Jew or a Gentile receives Christ as Saviour he becomes a new man, a member of the Body of Christ. Notice especially that the Jew is not converted into a Gentile nor the Gentile into a Jew but into a "new man." Redemption through the blood of Christ eliminates barriers between peoples. If there are such barriers after redemption it is because Christians are walking according to the flesh rather than the Spirit. The Bible calls such a believer a "carnal person" (I Cor. 3:1-4). In Christ, both Jews and Gentiles are raised to a new heavenly position far transcending anything ever heard of or seen before by either. The "one new man" transcends all barriers. Through salvation, the Jew and the Gentile become of one race of people in which all old differences are obliterated.

A New Outlook

Every person in Christ has a new citizenship: "For our conversation [citizenship] is in heaven; from whence also we look for the Saviour, the Lord Jesus Christ" (Phil. 3:20). Think of it! In Christ, we are citizens of heaven although we are living on earth.

Of Abraham and his descendants who had faith in God, the Bible says, "These all died in faith, not having received the promises, but having seen them afar off, and were persuaded of them, and embraced them, and confessed that they were strangers and pilgrims on the earth. But now they desire a better country, that is, an heavenly: wherefore God is not ashamed to be called their God: for he hath prepared for them a city" (Heb. 11:13,16).

Because we have been raised to a new position by receiving Christ as Saviour, the Scriptures exhort us: "If [since] ye then be risen with Christ, seek those things which are above, where Christ sitteth on the right hand of God. Set your affection on things above, not on things on the earth. For ye are dead, and your life is hid with Christ in God. When Christ, who is our life, shall appear, then shall ye also appear with him in glory" (Col. 3:1-4).

First John 3:2,3 tells us, "Beloved, now are we the sons of God, and it doth not yet appear what we shall be: but we know that, when he shall appear, we shall be like him; for we shall see him as he is. And every man that hath this hope in him purifieth himself, even as he is pure."

God has reconciled both Jews and Gentiles to Himself. Therefore, when the Jew and the Gentile receive Christ as Saviour, they can be at peace with each other because they are at peace with God. Once God has become their Father, they can gladly call each other "brother." And it is only when individuals are in right relationship with God that they can be in complete harmony with each other. This means that our deepest racial problems can never be completely solved until those involved come to know Christ as their Saviour and yield their lives to His control. Only the Christian has the basis for truly solving the problems that people face.

Jesus Christ reconciled both Jew and Gentile to God "in one body by the cross" (Eph. 2:16). The moment they were united to God through faith in Christ, they were united to one another. They became members of the same body—the Body of Christ.

In I Corinthians 12:12,13 we are told more about the Body made up of Jews and Gentiles. These verses say, "For as the body is one, and hath many members, and all the members of that one body, being many, are one body: so also is Christ. For by one Spirit are we all baptized into one body, whether we be Jews or Gentiles, whether we be bond or free; and have been all made to drink into one spirit."

So all the redeemed of this age are spiritually united on earth as the Body of Christ, and the risen, ascended Christ is in heaven as the Head of the Body. As the Head, He gives life and direction to the members of the Body. Each believer is to no longer consider what he was in the natural realm but is to consider what he is in Christ. Regardless of one's nationality, color or denominational preference, he becomes one in Christ with every other believer when he receives Christ. Colossians 3:11 says of the Body of Christ, "Where there is neither Greek nor Jew, circumcision nor uncircumcision, Barbarian, Scythian, bond nor free: but Christ is all, and in all." This is a position that surpasses all racial, social, religious and class barriers.

The oneness is not an external but an internal one. It is an inner oneness that results from life in Jesus Christ. Therefore, the peace between Jew and Gentile is not man-made but God-made. Attempts at peacemaking that originate with man usually fail because they are attempts to reconcile man with man before man is reconciled to God.

Although there can be temporary peace in such situations, there is no basis for a lasting peace.

Internationally, the world will not have peace until the Prince of Peace returns to establish the kingdom of God. Now, the Prince of Peace is not taken into consideration in peace negotiations between nations, but someday He will return and bring about world peace. At the end of seven years of tribulation, Christ will return to earth to bring an end to wars and to establish His kingdom. Those who have received Christ as Saviour will "reign with him a thousand years" (Rev. 20:6). What a glorious future we have to look forward to!

Those redeemed from every nation during the Tribulation—prior to Christ's reign of peace—rejoice together in their salvation. Revelation 5:9 says, "And they sung a new song, saying, Thou art worthy to take the book, and to open the seals thereof: for thou wast slain, and hast redeemed us to God by thy blood out of every kindred, and tongue, and people, and nation." Revelation 7 tells us that "a great multitude, which no man could number, of all nations, and kindreds, and people, and tongues, stood before the throne, and before the Lamb, clothed with white robes, and palms in their hands. . . . These are they which came out of great tribulation, and have washed their robes, and made them white in the blood of the Lamb" (vv. 9,14).

At present, God is not in the process of making a new world but a new man. God is not now attempting to improve world conditions by improving world systems; rather, God replaces the old, earthly nationalism by a new order of people whose citizenship is in heaven. Thus, the greatest and most lasting way we can affect our society is to take the gospel to others so they can come into right relationship with Jesus Christ by receiving Him as Saviour. Their influence for good and righteousness will then be felt by others around them.

Ephesians 2:17 says that Christ preached peace: "[Christ] came and preached peace to you which were afar off, and to them that were nigh."

After His resurrection, Christ appeared to the disciples to proclaim peace to them and to send them to proclaim peace to others: "Then the same day at evening, being the first day of the week, when the doors were shut where the disciples were assembled for fear of the Jews, came Jesus and stood in the midst, and saith unto them, Peace be unto you. And when he had so said, he shewed unto them his hands and his side. Then were the disciples glad, when they saw the Lord. Then said Jesus to them again, Peace be unto you: as my Father hath sent me, even so send I you" (John 20:19-21).

The peace that Jesus proclaimed and the peace that was later proclaimed by the apostles and disciples is now to be proclaimed by us. Second Corinthians 5:18,19 tells us, "Now all these things are from God, who reconciled us to Himself through Christ, and gave us the ministry of reconciliation, namely, that God was in Christ reconciling the world to Himself, not counting their trespasses against them, and He has committed to us the word of reconciliation" (NASB). As we proclaim the gospel to others, they have the opportunity to receive it and to be reconciled to God.

A Building

The words "now therefore" (v. 19) mark a division in Ephesians 2:11-22. In verses 11-18 Paul describes the believers in Christ as a "body," but he changed the metaphor with verse 19 and described the Church as a "building." In his other writings, Paul sometimes referred to the Church as the Bride of Christ.

In using "body" as a metaphor, the Bible emphasizes that Christians have Christ's life. As a body, the Church is not an organization; it is an organism. The Holy Spirit unites all the members of the Body of which Jesus Christ is the Head. This metaphor also emphasizes that believers are to be in submission to the will of the Head. Just as the physical body responds to the decision of the mind, so the members of the Body of Christ are to respond to carry out His will.

By referring to the Church as the Bride of Christ, the Scriptures emphasize the love relationship of the bridegroom (Jesus Christ) and the bride (those who receive Him as Saviour). The analogy of bridegroom and bride shows how enjoyable this relationship is to be between Christ and believers. Furthermore, it emphasizes that we have all we need because Christ loves us and is able to provide whatever we need. The unsearchable riches of Christ are ours because we are the Bride and He is the Bridegroom.

However, in Ephesians 2:19-22 Paul likened Christians to a building. He told believers, "Now therefore ye are no more strangers and foreigners, but fellowcitizens with the saints, and of the household of God; and are built upon the foundation of the apostles and prophets, Jesus Christ himself being the chief corner stone" (vv. 19,20).

Implications of a Building

Any structure requires a process of building for it to become what the architect desires. As people receive Jesus Christ as Saviour, they become parts of this building, so in a sense it is in the process of being built so it will be exactly what the Master Architect desires.

The main purpose of a building is to be inhabited. In referring to the Church as a "building," Paul was emphasizing that believers are inhabited, or indwelt, by God.

The fact that believers are God's building coincides with Paul's previous statement that "we are his workmanship, created in Christ Jesus unto good works, which God hath before ordained that we should walk in them" (v. 10). God began His building process on the Day of Pentecost, when the Church came into existence, and it will continue until Christ returns to catch away believers from the earth (I Thess. 4:16,17).

Inasmuch as both Jews and Gentiles have equal access to the Father through the Son, all believers are fellow citizens of heaven and part of the household of God. Just as children have responsibilities in the home, so the children of God have responsibilities in His household: "What? know ye not that your body is the temple of the Holy Ghost which is in you, which ye have of God, and ye are not your own? For ye are bought with a price: therefore glorify God in your body, and in your spirit, which are God's" (I Cor. 6:19,20). I Peter 2:5 says, "You also, as living stones, are being built up as a spiritual house for a holy priesthood, to offer up spiritual sacrifices acceptable to God through Jesus Christ" (NASB). We are not to be idle—we have responsibilities that must be fulfilled if we are to please the Lord. We are His living quarters on earth and as such we are also His headquarters for carrying out His will on earth.

When Jesus was on earth, He said He had no place to lay His head, but today the Church is His home on earth. Paganism had, and has, its temples. Judaism had its temple in Jerusalem from which the knowledge of God was to encircle the earth. Christianity has its temple but it is not a physical one—it is made up of all who know Jesus Christ as Saviour. The body of every believer is a "temple" of the Holy Spirit because every believer is inhabited by the Holy Spirit (I Cor. 6:19).

Foundation

As God's building, we are built on the foundation which is Jesus Christ. Paul said, "According to the grace of God which is given unto me, as a wise masterbuilder, I have laid the foundation, and another buildeth thereon. But let every man take heed how he buildeth thereupon. For other foundation can no man lay than that is laid, which is Jesus Christ" (I Cor. 3:10,11). All building must be done upon this foundation.

Ephesians 2:20 says that we "are built upon the foundation of the apostles and prophets, Jesus Christ himself being the chief corner stone." As "the chief corner stone," Christ served as the starting point for the building—all else is determined by and built upon Him. The apostles and prophets immediately followed and we were added later.

Notice it says "apostles and prophets," not "prophets and apostles." The prophets referred to are not Old Testament prophets but those in the New Testament; therefore, they are mentioned after the apostles. A prophet is one who not only speaks concerning the future (foretelling) but speaks for God at the present (forthtelling). The forthtelling of prophets is seen in I Corinthians 14: "Pursue love, yet desire earnestly spiritual gifts, but especially that you may prophesy. For one who speaks in a tongue does not speak to men, but to God; for no one understands, but in his spirit he speaks mysteries. But one who prophesies speaks to men for edification and exhortation and consolation" (vv. 1-3, NASB). Although the gift of prophecy included forthtelling, in those days it especially had to do with new truth being given from God. Although men today can be prophets in the general sense of speaking forth for God, they are not prophets in the New Testament sense of the word inasmuch as they do not give forth new truth.

Jesus Christ is building His Church. When He was on earth He said, "I will build my church; and the gates of hell shall not prevail against it" (Matt. 16:18). We are living stones within God's building, and we also have a part as co-builders as we take the gospel to others so they can receive Christ as Saviour. Christ came and preached peace; now we who know Him as Saviour are to preach the gospel to others so they may have this peace. Jesus told the Father, "As thou hast sent me into the world, even so have I also sent them into the world" (John 17:18). Just before Jesus ascended to the Father, He gave believers the Great Commission: "All power is given unto me in heaven and in earth. Go ye therefore, and teach all nations, baptizing them in the name of the Father, and of the Son, and of the Holy Ghost: teaching them to observe all things whatsoever I have commanded you: and, lo, I am with you alway, even unto the end of the world. Amen" (Matt. 28:18-20).

Those who receive Christ as Saviour become living stones, precisely fitted into the building of God. Just as there are many shapes and sizes of stones, so individual believers vary from one another, but God has a special place for each in the building. Those in Paul's day knew that it took much work to shape stones so they would fit precisely in a building. So Paul was emphasizing not only that believers are stones in God's building but also that it takes the shaping work of God to make them fit properly into the building. The harder the stone, the longer it takes the builder to make it what he wants it to be. As living stones we sometimes find the process painful, but the end result is good. That's why Romans 8:28 says, "And we know that all things work together for good to them that love God, to them who are the called according to his purpose."

According to the Scriptures, God's building is not yet completed. Ephesians 2:21 pictures the Church as a building that is being developed: "In whom all the building fitly framed together groweth unto an holy temple in the Lord."

Paul concluded his comments about the building of God with the words: "In whom ye also are builded together for an habitation of God through the Spirit" (v. 22). Because God is omnipresent, He is able to be where His family is—on earth—while also being in heaven. Those who know Christ as Saviour are the habitation, or dwelling place, of God on earth. This is why the Scriptures say that the believer's body is a temple of the Holy Spirit (I Cor. 6:19).

How does it affect us to realize that God lives in us as believers? Think of what great respect the Jews had for the physical temple of God. This gives us some idea of the awe with which we should view ourselves as a living temple of God. How wonderful it is to realize that Jesus Christ not only died for us but that when we received Him as Saviour, He came to live in us and empowers us to do that which brings glory to Him!

Chapter 10

God's Eternal Mystery Revealed
(Eph. 3:1-12)

In Ephesians 3:1-5 Paul introduced the fact that the mystery of God concerning the Church had been revealed. A "mystery" in the Scriptures refers to something that had been hidden in the past but was then revealed.

The words "for this cause" (v. 1) connect chapters 1 and 2 with what follows. In the first two chapters Paul told some of the greatest truths ever known concerning the believer and his relationship to God through Jesus Christ. But now Paul was about to write the Ephesian believers concerning the plan and purpose God had in mind for the Church from ages past.

Ephesians 3 begins by revealing Paul's excellent attitude in spite of the hardship he was suffering: "For this cause I Paul, the prisoner of Jesus Christ for you Gentiles" (v. 1). Humanly speaking, Paul was a prisoner of Nero, the Roman emperor, and was probably chained continuously to guards, but he saw himself only as "the prisoner of Jesus Christ." What a tremendous attitude in the midst of such horrible circumstances! He could have despaired because he was not able to go from place to place to preach the gospel, but instead he saw himself as a prisoner of the Lord and wrote letters during his confinement that have influenced the world. The Book of Ephesians, written during this time, ranks as one of his greatest letters and is one of the most significant New Testament books.

The kind of attitude Paul had, whether in prison or out, is also seen from what he wrote to the Corinthians who had been critical of him: "For, I think, God has exhibited us apostles last of all, as men condemned to death; because we have become a spectacle to the world, both to angels and to men. We are fools for Christ's sake, but you are prudent in Christ; we are weak, but you are strong; you are distinguished, but we are without honor. To this present hour we are both hungry and thirsty, and are poorly clothed, and are roughly treated, and are homeless; and we toil, working with our own hands; when we are reviled, we bless; when we are persecuted, we endure; when we are slandered, we try to conciliate; we have become as the scum of the world, the dregs of all things, even until now" (I Cor. 4:9-13, NASB).

As Paul wrote to the Ephesians, he was in prison because the Jews could not understand how God could bring the Gentiles into a loving relationship with Himself. Such a thought was not according to their tradition and what they understood the Old Testament to teach. They thought the Gentiles were beyond reconciliation—they called them "dogs." Nothing stirred the Jews more to anger than the message that Paul preached. Paul proclaimed that God was not dwelling in temples made with hands, that He was not dealing with Israel as a nation but had turned to the Gentiles with salvation, that all people who were saved were being framed into the same body, and that saved Jews and Gentiles alike were indwelt by the Holy Spirit and were members of the same Body.

Once, when the Jews saw Paul in the temple they cried out, "This is the man, that teacheth all men every where against the people, and the law, and this place" (Acts 21:28). When Paul was finally able to give a defense to the crowd, he told them how God had said to him, "Depart: for I will send thee far hence unto the Gentiles" (22:21). At this statement, the crowd cried out, "Away with such a fellow from the earth: for it is not fit that he should live" (v. 22). Why all this uproar that finally led to Paul's imprisonment? Because he was teaching the grace of God in a way it had never before been presented.

Opposition to Grace

Those who emphasize the grace of God today sometimes find opposition also. This opposition comes from those who fail to comprehend the extent of the riches of God's grace. When it is taught that works not only have nothing to do with attaining salvation but also that they have nothing to do with retaining salvation, opposition sometimes arises. There are those who teach that one must work in order to keep his salvation. To teach the grace of God—that past, present and future sins are paid for when a person receives Christ—is looked upon by these teachers as giving approval to sin. They imply that people will live in sin unless a works standard is held over them. However, such teachers fail to understand that a person who receives Christ becomes a new creature and does not desire to live a sinful life, even though he may occasionally commit sin.

Because of the opposition Paul met as he taught the grace of God, he told Timothy, "Yea, and all that will live godly in Christ Jesus shall suffer persecution" (II Tim. 3:12). When a Christian lives according to his position "in Christ" rather than according to a system of works, he frequently suffers persecution by others.

Paul also warned believers, "Beware lest any man spoil you through philosophy and vain deceit, after the tradition of men, after the rudiments [elementary principles] of the world, and not after Christ" (Col. 2:8). In verses 20-23 Paul said, "Wherefore if ye be dead with Christ from the rudiments of the world, why, as though living in the world, are ye subject to ordinances, (Touch not; taste not; handle not; which all are to perish with the using;) after the commandments and doctrines of men? Which things have indeed a shew of wisdom in will worship, and humility, and neglecting of the body; not in any honour to the satisfying of the flesh."

Paul's emphasis on grace was frequently misunderstood. He wrote the Romans: "Moreover the law entered, that the offence might abound. But where sin abounded, grace did much more abound" (5:20). Paul expected the Romans to ask, "If grace abounds more than sin then is it good to live in sin to focus attention on God's grace?" Therefore, he wrote: "What shall we say then? shall we continue in sin, that grace may abound? God forbid. How shall we that are dead to sin, live any longer therein?" (6:1,2).

The truth that needs to be emphasized in this dispensation is that believers have died to sin and have Christ indwelling them, motivating them, and constraining them by His love. The evidence that a person has a genuine relationship with Christ is that he does not desire to live in sin.

This is one of the most significant things to be remembered as we consider how the grace of God is worked out in daily living. Therefore, the Christian does not want to do those things that displease Christ. As D. L. Moody put it, a person's "wanter" is changed when he comes to know Christ. The law was like a whip over a person, which said in effect, "Do this, or die." The law meant only condemnation; it gave no power to a person to do right. However, Christ indwells every believer and enables him to do right as he depends on Christ.

Those who oppose the teaching of God's grace are ignorant of the great and wonderful truth that the believer is "in Christ." Not only this, but Christ is in the believer and works in him to accomplish His will. Thus Paul wrote: "To whom [the saints] God would make known what is the riches of the glory of this mystery among the Gentiles; which is Christ in you, the hope of glory: whom we preach, warning every man, and teaching every man in all wisdom; that we may present every man perfect [mature] in Christ Jesus: whereunto I also labour, striving according to his working, which worketh in me mightily" (Col. 1:27-29).

So we have seen that it was because of Paul's firm stand for the grace of God that he was a prisoner as he wrote to the Ephesians. But Paul did not consider himself a prisoner of man but a "prisoner of Jesus Christ" (3:1).

Dispensation of Grace

To the Ephesians, Paul described himself as "the prisoner of Jesus Christ for you Gentiles, if ye have heard of the dispensation of the grace of God which is given me to you-ward" (vv. 1,2). A dispensation is like an administration. Just as in the United States there are different administrations under different Presidents, so throughout the ages God has placed the world under administrations that have originated with Him. Because an administration has a beginning and an end, a time element is implied in the word "dispensation." Thus, it is a period of time during which God deals with man in a particular manner.

Five dispensations preceded the present one. These are commonly referred to by the names "Innocence," "Conscience," "Human Government," "Promise" and "Law." The Dispensation of Innocence extended from the creation of Adam and Eve until their expulsion from the Garden of Eden. The Dispensation of Conscience followed and came to an end with the judgment of the universal flood. The Dispensation of Human Government followed but was brought to an end with the judgment at the tower of Babel. The Dispensation of Promise was associated with God's call of Abraham and the promises that were given to and through him. This dispensation ended with the Israelites' being in Egypt, out of the will of God. The Dispensation of the Law began when God gave the Law to Moses after the Israelites had been delivered from Egypt. This dispensation extended until Jesus Christ died on the cross, thus bringing an end to the Mosaic system as a rule of life. The Dispensation of Grace, the present one, extends from the Day of Pentecost until the Rapture of the Church.

It is exceedingly important to understand that salvation has been by the same means in every dispensation—by grace through faith. However, the dispensation during which the believer lived determined what his rule of life was for that age. But even though the rule of life has changed during the various ages, the way of salvation has never changed.

The present dispensation is also sometimes called the "Dispensation of the Church" or the "Dispensation of the Holy Spirit." The reason for this is that this is the age of the Church, the Body of Christ, and every believer is indwelt by the Holy Spirit.

A Mystery

To Paul was committed the responsibility of revealing how God was working with mankind during the Church Age. Previously it had not been revealed; thus, it was referred to as a "mystery." Special revelation had been given to Paul concerning God's method of dealing with Jews and Gentiles.

Paul showed how he was qualified to speak concerning the mystery when he said, "How that by revelation he made known unto me the mystery; (as I wrote afore in a few words, whereby, when ye read, ye may understand my knowledge in the mystery of Christ)" (vv. 3,4). Paul said he had written something before to the Ephesians concerning the mystery. He may have been referring to the previous chapter (vv. 14-22) or to a letter he had written to the Ephesians earlier that is not part of the Scriptures.

As has been indicated, a "mystery" in the Scriptures refers to something that was previously unknown but has now been made known. C. I. Scofield summed up the meaning when he said, "A 'mystery' in Scripture is a previously hidden truth, now divinely revealed, but in which a supernatural element still remains despite the revelation" (*Scofield Reference Bible*, p. 1014). There are many mysteries referred to in the Bible, among which are mysteries of the kingdom of heaven, Israel's blindness during the present age, the translation of believers at the end of this age, the New Testament Church as one body composed of both Jews and Gentiles, and the inliving Christ.

One of the key mysteries of the present age is known as the "mystery among the Gentiles," which is "Christ in you, the hope of glory" (Col. 1:27). The rule of life for the believer during the present age is not the Mosaic Law system but obedience to the convicting and empowering work of the indwelling Christ.

The mystery of Ephesians 3 has to do also with the present-age believer, especially concerning his relationship with others in the Body of Christ. Ephesians 2 revealed how God had made Jews and Gentiles into "one new man, so making peace" (v. 15). Chapter 3 continues to develop this subject. Regarding the mystery of Christ, Paul said, "Which in other ages was not made known unto the sons of men, as it is now revealed unto his holy apostles and prophets by the Spirit" (v. 5).

The mystery now revealed to the apostles and New Testament prophets was not understood during Old Testament times. The Old Testament prophets spoke concerning the suffering of Christ and the glory of His kingdom on earth, but it was not revealed to them what would take place between these times.

Because they did not know what would take place during the present age, the disciples asked Christ when He was about to return to heaven, "Wilt thou at this time restore again the kingdom to Israel?" (Acts 1:6). Jesus' response was "It is not for you to know the times or the seasons, which the Father hath put in his own power" (v. 7). However, Jesus told them the next significant event: "But ye shall receive power, after that the Holy Ghost is come upon you: and ye shall be witnesses unto me both in Jerusalem, and in all Judaea, and in Samaria, and unto the uttermost part of the earth" (v. 8).

But the mystery of the Church, Paul said, was now revealed to the apostles and prophets (Eph. 3:5). The "prophets" to which Paul referred were New Testament prophets. He referred to them earlier when he said that the household of God was "built upon the foundation of the apostles and prophets" (2:20). The mystery of the Church was not revealed in Old Testament times, which explains why there is no direct reference to the Church in the Old Testament. Although certain events might serve as illustrations of the Church, they did not serve as specific teaching about the Church; nor would anyone have known from them at that time that the Church would later come into existence.

There are those who teach that the mystery of the Church was revealed only to Paul. However, it is evident from Ephesians 3:5 that it had been revealed to God's "holy apostles and prophets by the Spirit." Paul was especially chosen to proclaim the truths concerning the Church, but he was not the only one to whom it was revealed. For instance, God caused Peter to understand that he, a Jew, was no longer to consider the Gentile as unclean. God gave Peter a vision in which he saw something like a great sheet coming down from heaven with all kinds of animals on it (Acts 10:9-12). Peter then heard a voice saying, "Rise, Peter; kill, and eat" (v. 13). But Peter responded, "By no means, Lord, for I have never eaten anything unholy and unclean" (v. 14, NASB). Peter heard the voice again and this time it said, "What God has cleansed, no longer consider unholy" (v. 15, NASB). By this experience, God prepared Peter to witness to Cornelius, a Gentile.

It is important to realize that the mystery to which Paul referred in Ephesians 3 was not that Christ was to suffer for sin and later establish His kingdom on earth. These truths had already been proclaimed in Old Testament times. Nor was it the mystery that the gospel was to be preached to the Gentiles. This truth was implied in the Abrahamic covenant: "In thee shall all families of the earth be blessed" (Gen. 12:3).

The mystery to which Paul referred in Ephesians 3 is evident from verse 6: "That the Gentiles should be fellowheirs, and of the same body, and partakers of his promise in Christ by the gospel." The Jews realized that the message of salvation should be taken to the Gentiles, but it was new to them to realize that the Gentiles—considered by them to be unclean—would be on an equal basis with them in the Body of Christ.

As J. Sidlow Baxter has so well stated it, the mystery is "that during the present age an elect people, the Church, should be gathered out, irrespective of nationality—an elect people who should be brought collectively into such an intimate union of life and love and eternal glory with Him as can only be expressed by saying that the Church is His 'body,' and His 'bride,' and His 'temple' (three metaphors which, respectively, express union in *life*, and in *love*, and in *glory*)!" (*Explore the Book*, Vol. 6, p. 176).

Unsearchable Riches

Paul rejoiced in his special privilege of proclaiming to both Jew and Gentile that they were one in Christ. Concerning the gospel, Paul said, "Whereof I was made a minister, according to the gift of the grace of God given unto me by the effectual working of his power. Unto me, who am less than the least of all saints, is this grace given, that I should preach among the Gentiles the unsearchable riches of Christ" (vv. 7,8). Paul's descriptions of himself reveal his humble attitude before God. Here he described himself as "less than the least of all saints." In I Corinthians 15:9 he said of himself, "For I am the least of the apostles, that am not meet [fit] to be called an apostle, because I persecuted the church of God." In I Timothy 1:15, one of his last letters, Paul said, "This is a faithful saying, and worthy of all acceptation, that Christ Jesus came into the world to save sinners; of whom I am chief."

Because Paul realized what he himself really was, he never ceased to marvel at the grace of God in making provision for his sin. This is why he considered preaching the gospel as preaching "the unsearchable riches of Christ" (Eph. 3:8). The unsearchable riches of Christ include more than salvation. It is regrettable that some people never go beyond this stage in their knowledge of Christ. In the spiritual realm, we will live abundantly only as we recognize the resources we have in Christ and live accordingly. The contrast between salvation truths and Christian living truths is seen in II Corinthians. Paul wrote: "For ye know the grace of our Lord Jesus Christ, that, though he was rich, yet for your sakes he became poor, that ye through his poverty might be rich" (8:9). This is primarily salvation truth. But Paul also told believers, "God is able to make all grace abound toward you; that ye, always having all sufficiency in all things, may abound to every good work" (9:8). This is primarily Christian living truth. God's grace is sufficient to meet all our needs and to enable us to have an abundance of good works that bring glory to Him. God has expressed His grace not only in our salvation but in providing what we do not deserve as we live for Him. However, when we do not appropriate what He has provided by His grace, we are thrown back on our own resources and live frustrated Christian lives.

From the nation of Israel we learn what happens when we rely on ourselves. God had delivered the Israelites from Egypt, had enabled them to pass through the Red Sea, had destroyed their enemies, had given them the Law, and had cared for them in the desert. Yet, when the Israelites came to Kadesh-barnea, just south of the land of Canaan, they refused to trust the Lord to conquer the land of Canaan through them, and they turned back into the desert. Their trust was in themselves, not God. They nullified the grace of God because they refused to trust God to enable them to take the land He had promised to them.

Because of what we have in Christ, we ought to live on the high plane made possible by His unlimited grace.

We need a new appreciation of the kind of relationship we have with Christ. Sometimes people say it would have been a tremendous privilege to have lived on earth when Jesus was here and to have had the opportunity to know Him then. This is true, but it does not compare with the privilege we believers have now. He actually lives within us to work His will in and through us. Paul said, "Yea, though we have known Christ after the flesh, yet now henceforth know we him no more [after the flesh]. Therefore if any man be in Christ, he is a new creature: old things are passed away; behold, all things are become new" (II Cor. 5:16,17).

Those who walked with the Lord while He was on earth were not to consider themselves as privileged over those who did not have this opportunity. It is the spiritual relationship that is of most importance, and when we receive Jesus Christ we become new creations. Think of it! Each of us who knows Christ as Saviour is a special creation of God and is indwelt by the Son of God Himself! No wonder Paul rejoiced over the privilege of proclaiming the unsearchable riches of Christ.

Paul stated his burden when he said, "And to make all men see what is the fellowship of the mystery, which from the beginning of the world hath been hid in God, who created all things by Jesus Christ: to the intent that now unto the principalities and powers in heavenly places might be known by the church the manifold wisdom of God" (Eph. 3:9,10).

All of this, Paul said, was "according to the eternal purpose which he purposed in Christ Jesus our Lord: in whom we have boldness and access with confidence by the faith of him" (vv. 11,12). From Ephesians 1:4, we have seen that God's purpose is "that we should be holy and without blame before him in love." This was the purpose for which God chose us before the foundation of the world. And because people must hear the message and be saved before they can enter into this purpose, Paul saw himself as a part of the plan of God in that he was proclaiming the unsearchable riches of Christ.

Access to Grace

What a privilege it is to be able to tell others that they can have not only salvation but also resources in Christ for everything they need. This is the message Paul gave in Romans 5. He said, "Therefore being justified by faith, we have peace with God through our Lord Jesus Christ" (v. 1).

But Paul didn't stop at this point. He went on to tell us of our access into God's grace for daily living: "By whom also we have access by faith into this grace wherein we stand, and rejoice in hope of the glory of God" (v. 2).

Salvation, then, gives us access to God so that we might constantly depend on Him for all we need. "Having therefore, brethren, boldness to enter into the holiest by the blood of Jesus, by a new and living way, which he hath consecrated for us, through the veil, that is to say, his flesh; and having an high priest over the house of God; let us draw near with a true heart in full assurance of faith, having our hearts sprinkled from an evil conscience, and our bodies washed with pure water. Let us hold fast the profession of our faith without wavering; (for he is faithful that promised;)" (Heb. 10:19-23).

Christ tells us in John 15:16: "Ye have not chosen me, but I have chosen you, and ordained you, that ye should go and bring forth fruit, and that your fruit should remain: that whatsoever ye shall ask of the Father in my name, he may give it you." But we will never fully appreciate our position in Christ and our privilege of bearing fruit unless we faithfully study the Bible so that we might know of our unsearchable riches in Christ.

We are not doomed to defeat in the Christian life; God has made victory possible through Christ. Therefore, we can say with Paul, "Thanks be to God, which giveth us the victory through our Lord Jesus Christ" (I Cor. 15:57).

Chapter 11

Prayer for Realization and Application
(Eph. 3:13-21)

Because Paul considered it such a high privilege to proclaim God's eternal mystery concerning the Church, he said, "Wherefore I desire that ye faint not [do not lose heart] at my tribulations for you, which is your glory" (v. 13).

Having said this, Paul recorded what he was praying for believers. This is one of Paul's greatest prayers, and it reveals what we should pray for ourselves as well as for other believers.

In the preceding passages Paul had been describing the believer's great wealth in Christ. Now Paul prayed that every member of the Body of Christ might realize and appropriate these benefits.

There are several interesting comparisons that can be made between Paul's first prayer, in Ephesians 1, and his second prayer, in Ephesians 3. The first prayer was for revelation; the second prayer was for realization. The first was for spiritual comprehension of the riches of His grace; the second was for spiritual appropriation of these riches. In the first prayer Paul was concerned that believers might understand what they had; in the second, that believers might be what God desires.

Ruth Paxson has ably set forth the contrasts and complements of Paul's two prayers in Ephesians:

First Prayer (1:15-23)	Second Prayer (3:14-21)
Revelation	Realization
Enlightenment	Enablement
Light	Life
Know what you are	Be what you know

Know the power of God	Experience the fulness of God
Power working for us	Power working in us
Ye in Christ	Christ in you
Christ fulness Church	Church fulness Christ

—*The Wealth, Walk and Warfare of the Christian*, p. 72.

So we see that in Paul's first prayer he was concerned that we understand our relationship with God and what we have as a result. In his second prayer, Paul was concerned that we fulfill God's purpose and be what He wants us to be. These purposes are introduced by the word "that." But it is important to remember that we must know the "what" before we can fulfill the "that."

Paul's second prayer reaches its climax in the words "that ye might be filled with all the fulness of God" (v. 19). As we have seen from Ephesians, not every one who has eternal life also lives abundantly. This is why Paul prayed that believers "might be filled with all the fulness of God" (3:19). We fully possess Christ as Saviour the moment we believe, but we are to live, by faith, according to the riches we have in Him. And the wonderful thing is that He always has more in store for us! In fact, Ephesians 2:7 reveals that we'll still be learning about His riches throughout eternity: "That in the ages to come he might show the exceeding riches of his grace in his kindness toward us through Christ Jesus."

In Paul's second prayer there are four petitions, each one providing the basis for the succeeding one:

1. "That he would grant you, according to the riches of his glory, to be strengthened with might by his Spirit in the inner man" (v. 16).

2. "That Christ may dwell in your hearts by faith" (v. 17).

3. "That ye, being rooted and grounded in love, may be able to comprehend with all saints what is the breadth, and length, and depth, and height; and to know the love of Christ, which passeth knowledge" (vv. 17,19).

4. "That ye might be filled with all the fulness of God" (v. 19).

These are great petitions; so great, in fact, that one might wonder if they can possibly be fulfilled. However, there are statements in the passage that provide the basis for believing they can be fulfilled. In Paul's first petition are these significant words: "According to the riches of his glory" (v. 16). The words "according to" show proportion or relationship. God's riches are infinite. Thus, when He grants benefits to us in proportion to His riches, it is obvious that we have much more than we will ever need. It is as if a millionaire gave you a signed check and said, "Make it out for any amount you need." No wonder Paul said that God has "blessed us with all spiritual blessings in heavenly places in Christ" (1:3).

There is another statement in Ephesians 3 that gives assurance of the fulfillment of the petitions. Paul said that God "is able to do exceeding abundantly above all that we ask or think, according to the power that worketh in us" (v. 20).

Especially notice the words "according to the power that worketh in us." By the indwelling Holy Spirit's enablement, we can benefit from what God has provided. All that Christ did on earth He did by the power of the Holy Spirit. Before Christ left the earth, He promised that the same Holy Spirit would come to live in believers and do the work in and through them that He had done in Him. Christ told believers, "Verily, verily, I say unto you, He that believeth on me, the works that I do shall he do also; and greater works than these shall he do; because I go unto my Father" (John 14:12). Christ also said, "When he, the Spirit of truth, is come, he will guide you into all truth: for he shall not speak of himself; but whatsoever he shall hear, that shall he speak: and he will shew you things to come. He shall glorify me: for he shall receive of mine, and shall shew it unto you" (16:13,14).

The Holy Spirit descended on the Day of Pentecost and since that time has indwelt every believer. The Holy Spirit convicts, empowers, guides, teaches and produces the fruit of the Spirit in us.

From Paul's prayer in Ephesians 3 we see that we must be strengthened in the inner man, indwelt by Christ by faith, and rooted and grounded in love before we can expect to know the fullness of God. We now turn our attention to each petition in detail.

Strengthened by the Spirit

Paul prayed, "That he would grant you, according to the riches of his glory, to be strengthened with might by his Spirit in the inner man" (v. 16). One translator renders the phrase "to be strengthened with might" as "to be made strong with power." Another says, "to be mightily strengthened." This verse coincides in meaning with Ephesians 6:10: "Finally, my brethren, be strong in the Lord, and in the power of his might."

Of necessity, this is a power outside of ourselves. Our own strength—the strength of our flesh—is woefully inadequate. We will not have victory in our Christian lives until we trust in God's strength rather than our own.

Notice that the strengthening mentioned in Paul's first petition is "by his Spirit." As the Holy Spirit indwells, He imparts power for daily living the new life in Christ Jesus. This power is not a once-and-for-all act of the Spirit; it is a continual process. Before He ascended, Jesus told believers, "Ye shall receive power, after that the Holy Ghost is come upon you: and ye shall be witnesses" (Acts 1:8).

Paul prayed that believers might be strengthened by the Spirit "in the inner man." God always begins His work within a person and then expresses that work outwardly. Emphasis is placed on the external in such an expression as "the body, soul and spirit" because the body is mentioned first. However, the emphasis of the Scriptures and the process by which God works changes the order to "the spirit, soul and body."

The spirit enables man to communicate with God. The soul enables man to think, decide and feel. The body enables man to be aware of his world and is the part of him through which the spirit and the soul find expression. The "inner man" refers to the spirit and soul, which need to be strengthened by the Holy Spirit in order that the proper things may be expressed through the body.

In this physical world one does not act apart from his body. This is why the Bible says, "Present your bodies a living sacrifice, holy, acceptable unto God, which is your reasonable service" (Rom. 12:1). When we present our bodies to God, nothing is excluded because we are unable to express ourselves apart from our bodies. In contrast to those in Old Testament times who brought dead sacrifices, every believer is to present his body as a "living sacrifice."

Indwelling by Faith

Paul's second petition for the Ephesians—and for all believers—was "that Christ may dwell in your hearts by faith" (3:17). Although at first glance this statement might seem to be a reference to Christ's coming to live within a person at the time of salvation, more is intended in this context. It is true that Christ indwells every believer, but sometimes the word "dwell" is used in the sense of "settle down" or "be at home."

Paul referred to his relationship to the indwelling Christ when he wrote: "I am [have been] crucified with Christ: nevertheless I live; yet not I, but Christ liveth in me" (Gal. 2:20). Thus, as Paul prayed for the Ephesians, he prayed that Christ might dwell in their hearts in the sense of being enthroned in their lives—that He might be truly at home, not just a guest. He will be completely at home in our lives to the extent that He is truly Lord of our lives. When we received Him as Saviour He came to permanently indwell us, but our need now is to put Him first in everything so that He will be at home in us. When we come to this point, our desire will be the same as Paul's when he said, "That I may know him, and the power of his resurrection, and the fellowship of his sufferings, being made conformable unto his death" (Phil. 3:10).

Notice that the place of Christ's dwelling is "in your hearts" (v. 17). Christ dwells in the inner man and desires to control the person he indwells. Of course, Christ indwells every person who receives Him as Saviour, but this does not necessarily mean He is in control of the person's life.

In order for Christ to control our lives, we must give up the self-life—we must desire to please Him rather than ourselves. This means we will have to say No to our own desires when they conflict with His. We will have victory in our lives only as we submit ourselves to the Lord and by faith live in dependence on Him. We must not underestimate the importance of denying ourselves when our desires conflict with His. Jesus said, "If any man will come after me, let him deny himself, and take up his cross daily, and follow me. For whosoever will save his life shall lose it: but whosoever will lose his life for my sake, the same shall save it" (Luke 9:23,24).

Notice from Paul's prayer that the kind of relationship with Christ he is speaking of is "by faith" (Eph. 3:17). We are to appropriate what He has provided for us. We do this by faith. We rely on Him to live His life in and through us.

'Rooted and Grounded in Love'

Paul's third petition is recorded in verses 17, 18: "That ye, being rooted and grounded in love, may be able to comprehend with all saints what is the breadth, and length, and depth, and height; and to know the love of Christ, which passeth knowledge." This rooting and grounding had already taken place in the lives of the Ephesians. We know this because in the original language the words appear in a tense that refers to a completed act with a continuing effect. Because these Ephesians had received Christ, they were rooted and grounded in love, and this provided the basis to further understand the love of God.

Being properly rooted and grounded was a primary concern of Paul's. In another letter he wrote: "As ye have therefore received Christ Jesus the Lord, so walk ye in him: rooted and built up in him, and stablished in the faith, as ye have been taught, abounding therein with thanksgiving" (Col. 2:6,7).

Being rooted and grounded in love is the same as being rooted and grounded in Christ, for the kind of love Paul referred to originates with God. This love is expressed as we seek to know Him better. We must always be aware of the tendency to focus our attention on the gifts rather than on the Giver, Christ Himself. When we are more concerned about the gift than the Giver, we are similar to those who have left their first love. Revelation 2:4,5 records Christ's words to the Church of Ephesus: "Nevertheless I have somewhat against thee, because thou hast left thy first love. Remember therefore from whence thou art fallen, and repent, and do the first works; or else I will come unto thee quickly, and will remove thy candlestick out of his place, except thou repent."

The word "rooted" is taken from the figure of a tree that draws its life from the earth. As believers, we draw our life from the Lord Jesus Christ. The word "grounded" is taken from the figure of a building that requires a solid foundation for it to be a sturdy structure. All that the believer has is based on the finished work of Christ. The Bible says, "For other foundation can no man lay than that is laid, which is Jesus Christ" (I Cor. 3:11). Every believer will be judged as to whether he builds on this foundation "gold, silver, precious stones" or "wood, hay, stubble" (v. 12).

Paul prayed that believers "may be able to comprehend" (Eph. 3:18). The word translated "comprehend" means "to lay hold of, to seize, to appropriate." Paul wanted believers to grasp what God had done for them and apply it specifically to their lives. This emphasizes it is not enough just to know what God has done for us; we must make it our own through appropriation.

Paul wanted believers to understand and appropriate "with all saints" (v. 18). Not one of us will completely grasp all the truth of God's love, but as we share with each other what we have learned and continue to study the Word of God, we will become mature believers. Paul urged believers to spiritually contribute to each other "till we all come in the unity of the faith, and of the knowledge of the Son of God, unto a perfect [mature] man, unto the measure of the stature of the fulness of Christ" (4:13).

From this we see the importance of Christian fellowship. In fact, the Scriptures give a divine rebuke to spiritual isolationism. Those of us who are members of His Body are to have fellowship with each other even though we may belong to different local churches. Any believer who has reservations about this should carefully read I Corinthians 12:14-27.

Paul wanted believers to experience God's love in the four dimensions spoken of in Ephesians 3:18: "the breadth, and length, and depth, and height." The four dimensions indicate Paul wanted believers to know everything there is to know about God's love. However, it is also possible to see each dimension as suggesting a special aspect of God's love.

"Breadth" suggests the extent of God's love. It is all inclusive—it encompasses everyone. However, only those who receive Jesus Christ as Saviour can fully experience God's love because only they become "new men" in Jesus Christ (2:15).

"Length" suggests the duration of God's love—it extends from eternity past to eternity future. Ephesians 1:4 refers to eternity past when it says that God "hath chosen us in him before the foundation of the world." Ephesians 2:7 refers to eternity future: "That in the ages to come he might show the exceeding riches of his grace in his kindness toward us through Christ Jesus." God's love is without beginning, interruption, or end. God's love does not depend on human response. Nothing we did set God's love in operation, nothing we do can interrupt His love, and nothing we do can bring an end to God's love. No wonder Paul exclaimed, "Who shall separate us from the love of Christ?" (Rom. 8:35). After mentioning several possibilities in this passage, Paul concluded that nothing "shall be able to separate us from the love of God, which is in Christ Jesus our Lord" (v. 39).

"Depth" suggests the condescension of God's love. Perhaps Paul was thinking of man's spiritual death, from which he was delivered by receiving Christ as Saviour. Paul's words in Ephesians 2:1-3 reveal how far we believers had fallen before we received Jesus Christ as Saviour. We "walked according to the course of this world, according to the prince of the power of the air, the spirit that now worketh in the children of disobedience" (v. 2). How wonderful it is to realize that God's love reached to such a depth. The depth to which Jesus went is seen from Philippians 2:8: "And being found in fashion as a man, he humbled himself, and became obedient unto death, even the death of the cross."

"Height" suggests the position to which the believer is raised. Paul said that God "hath raised us up together, and made us sit together in heavenly places in Christ Jesus" (v. 6). We have been raised from the depth of our sin to the height of His glory! The height to which God raised Christ after His death on the cross is seen in Philippians 2:9: "Wherefore God also hath highly exalted him, and given him a name which is above every name."

Not only are we raised to new heights by our position in Christ but also we will someday be raised from this earth to meet Him. Jesus said, "In my Father's house are many mansions: if it were not so, I would have told you. I go to prepare a place for you. And if I go and prepare a place for you, I will come again, and receive you unto myself; that where I am, there ye may be also" (John 14:2,3). First Thessalonians 4:16,17 refers to our being taken to be with Christ: "For the Lord himself shall descend from heaven with a shout, with the voice of the archangel, and with the trump of God: and the dead in Christ shall rise first: then we which are alive and remain shall be caught up together with them in the clouds, to meet the Lord in the air: and so shall we ever be with the Lord."

Having prayed that the believers might know the dimensions of God's love, Paul added, "And to know the love of Christ, which passeth knowledge" (Eph. 3:19). The word translated "know" refers to an experiential knowledge. Because we are finite, it is impossible for us to ever comprehend the love of God, but we can experience what we cannot fully comprehend. Even if we could comprehend God's love, mere intellectual knowledge is not enough—it must be appropriated in order to be beneficial to us. It is possible for a person to know God loves him and that Christ gave His life on the cross for him and yet not be a believer because he has not exercised his will to receive Christ as his Saviour. When he does so, Christ will come into his life and will express a love in and through him that is so great he will not be able to comprehend it. The more we experience Christ's love, the more we will understand what an inexhaustible source it is. The expression of this love is what is so desperately needed today.

The Fullness of God

Paul's fourth petition builds on his first three. It is only when the first three are fulfilled in a person's life that the fourth can be fulfilled. Paul prayed, "That ye might be filled with all the fulness of God" (v. 19). Paul was concerned that we realize the wealth we have in Christ Jesus.

The word "fill" in its various forms is one of Paul's key words in his letter to the Ephesians. It is used in 1:23: "Which is his body, the fulness of him that filleth all in all"; 4:10: "that he might fill all things"; v. 13: "unto the measure of the stature of the fulness of Christ"; 5:18: "be filled with the Spirit."

The Holy Spirit strengthens us in the inner man so Christ may be at home in every aspect of our lives. He is to be Lord of all.

Consider the marvelous truth that every believer has the fullness of God within him! But how can this be? Can the ocean be contained in a glass? Can God be contained in a believer?

Colossians 1:19 says, "For it pleased the Father that in him [Christ] should all fulness dwell." Colossians 2:9 tells us that in Christ "dwelleth all the fulness of the Godhead bodily." Verse 10 adds, "And ye are complete in him, which is the head of all principality and power." The first part of this verse literally reads: "And ye are in him, having been filled." Because Christ is the fullness of God, we are filled with God's fullness when we are filled with Christ.

In Paul's prayer "That ye might be filled with all the fulness of God" (Eph. 3:19), the word "with" is actually "unto" or "to." Thus, it is used in the sense of "to the measure of." The fullness of God is that which becomes the believer's through the indwelling Christ. So we see why Paul also prayed "that Christ may dwell in your hearts by faith" (v. 17). Having received Christ, we possess Him, but He desires to fully possess us. He possesses us only as we submit our lives to Him. The fullness of God is limited only by our refusal to believe Him and yield to His control. As we submit to Christ and thereby allow Him to direct our lives and empower us for service, we will mature in the Christian life as He intends.

Paul's Doxology

Do you think that what Paul had been praying for is unattainable? Then closely observe his closing doxology: "Now unto him that is able to do exceeding abundantly above all that we ask or think, according to the power that worketh in us, unto him be glory in the church by Christ Jesus throughout all ages, world without end. Amen" (Eph. 3:20,21).

Verse 20 emphasizes the power for realizing God's plan and purpose in us and for us. By our own strength we are not able to live as God desires, but He enables us to do His will. What He purposes, He undertakes to produce in us.

The Amplified Bible translates Ephesians 3:20, "Now to Him Who, by (in consequence of) the [action of His] power that is at work within us, is able to [carry out His purpose and] do superabundantly, far over and above all that we [dare] ask or think—infinitely beyond our highest prayers, desires, thoughts, hopes or dreams."

The power must be from God, not from within ourselves. The emphasis so common today, even in Christian circles, is that we become what we ought to be by doing what we ought to do. This is like saying one should pretend he's living abundantly and eventually he will be. Such thinking can lead only to frustration and defeat. We must know and appropriate what we have in Christ to live abundantly. Only when we realize what we are will we glorify God in what we do.

The scriptural principle is that God works within us to accomplish His will. Philippians 2:13 says, "For it is God which worketh in you both to will and to do of his good pleasure." It is only after a person becomes a believer that God works in him to accomplish His will. The power to accomplish that which pleases God does not lie in our own strength. We must look to Jesus who purposes, promises and is able to perform such works in and through us. Hebrews 12:2 reveals what should be the characteristic of our lives: "Looking unto Jesus the author and finisher of our faith."

Paul said that God "is able to do" (Eph. 3:20). No petition, however great, can exceed God's ability to grant it. What God has commenced, as we saw in chapters 1 and 2, He will surely consummate.

Notice the progression and climax of Paul's words: God is "able to do"—"able to do exceeding abundantly"—"able to do exceeding abundantly above all"—"able to do exceeding abundantly above all that we ask"—"able to do exceeding abundantly above all that we ask or think." From these words we see that it is impossible to exhaust what God is able to do for us.

All of this is ours because we are in Christ. Having loved us enough to die for us, He certainly can be counted on to provide all we need for daily living. But even after we stop asking because of our unbelief, He continues providing because these provisions are "according to the power that worketh in us" (v. 20). From the words "according to" we see that God is working in proportion to, or in conformity with, the power working in us. Imagine what this proportion is since it is God Himself working in us! It is the special ministry of the Holy Spirit to work in the believer to mold him into the image of Christ. The Spirit abides in us to make Christ real to us and to make Him the Lord of our lives. This is why Paul prayed that we might "be strengthened with might by his Spirit in the inner man" (v. 16).

As we have seen from Ephesians 1:13,14, the indwelling Spirit is God's pledge of His limitless power in us to perform and perfect what He desires. That is, in effect God says to believers, "I have already given you the Holy Spirit, and My pledge is that all of My limitless power is available to you."

In his petition Paul referred to the power that works "in us" (Eph. 3:20). Christ works in us to make us what He wants us to be. The words "in us" also emphasize what we have because of our position in Christ.

But the question arises, Since God has pledged His power to us, why don't we see more evidence of it in our lives? Remember, we are not robots; we are created in God's image, as free moral agents. Therefore, we must *choose* to let God have His way in our lives; He does not force Himself on us.

The need to respond is seen in Romans 6. Verses 6,7 give us the facts: "Knowing this, that our old man is crucified with him, that the body of sin might be destroyed, that henceforth we should not serve sin. For he that is dead is freed from sin." Verses 11,12 call on the believer to act on the basis of the facts: "Likewise reckon ye also yourselves to be dead indeed unto sin, but alive unto God through Jesus Christ our Lord. Let not sin therefore reign in your mortal body, that ye should obey it in the lusts thereof." Verse 13 calls for a further exercising of the will: "Neither yield [present] ye your members as instruments of unrighteousness unto sin: but yield [present] yourselves unto God, as those that are alive from the dead, and your members as instruments of righteousness unto God."

Romans 12:1 calls for the same all-out commitment: "Present your bodies a living sacrifice, holy, acceptable unto God, which is your reasonable service." Each day we should say in effect, "Lord, here I am; I make myself available to You to work in me and through me as it pleases You." When we fail because we stop depending on the Lord and begin depending on ourselves, we need to confess our sin and claim His promise to forgive it (I John 1:9).

In the light of all that Paul said in his prayer, it is pathetic when a believer lives on a lower level than what God wants him to live. How pathetic it is when God is kept from working in our lives because of our unbelief. When Jesus was on earth, Matthew recorded that in one locality "he did not many mighty works there because of their unbelief" (Matt. 13:58). May this not be true of us. Remember also the solemn words of Hebrews: "But with whom was he grieved forty years? was it not with them that had sinned, whose carcases fell in the wilderness? And to whom sware he that they should not enter into his rest, but to them that believed not? So we see that they could not enter in because of unbelief. Let us therefore fear, lest, a promise being left us of entering into his rest, any of you should seem to come short of it" (3:17-19;4:1).

Thus we see that the believer determines what God is able to do for him. In all that God desires to do during this age, He is limited only by our unbelief. We limit His working in and through us by the degree that we fail to yield to the indwelling Holy Spirit.

The last words of Paul's prayer in Ephesians 3 are: "Unto him be glory in the church by Christ Jesus throughout all ages, world without end. Amen" (v. 21). Notice to whom the glory is due—"unto him." Here Paul referred to the Father and the desire for glory to be given to Him through the Body of Christ. This is accomplished as we allow the Holy Spirit to have His way in our lives. Glory rightfully belongs to the Heavenly Father, and the source of it during this age is believers, who make up the Church. God's tremendous work is being done in us, and we are to give Him praise and honor not only in words but also in actions. We are to allow Him to accomplish His purpose in and through us.

The Father is to be glorified in the Church "by Christ Jesus," or literally, "in Christ Jesus." From the prayer of Jesus recorded in John 17, we see how He glorified the Father: "I have glorified thee on the earth: I have finished the work which thou gavest me to do. I have manifested thy name unto the men which thou gavest me out of the world: thine they were, and thou gavest them me; and they have kept thy word. For I have given unto them the words which thou gavest me; and they have received them, and have known surely that I came out from thee, and they have believed that thou didst send me" (vv. 4,6,8).

The Father now desires to be glorified anew by Christ Jesus, but through us who have received Him as Saviour. Christ is now able to glorify the Father by working through believers, who are His Body, the Church. As the Head of the Body, He purposes what we should do and then motivates us to perform that which brings glory to the Father. How important it is, therefore, that we not limit Him by our unbelief. He died, rose, ascended, was seated and exalted, and was made Lord of all for the purpose of bringing glory to the Father through the saints. And this glory is "throughout all ages, world without end" (Eph. 3:21).

As Paul concluded his prayer with "Amen," so let us say, "Amen," to all that God has done for us. How wonderful it is that He has provided not only all we need for salvation but also all we need—and more—for daily living. This should cause us to exclaim with Paul: "O the depth of the riches and wisdom and knowledge of God! How unfathomable (inscrutable, unsearchable) are His judgments—His decisions! And how untraceable (mysterious, undiscoverable) are His ways—His methods, His paths! For who has known the mind of the Lord and who has understood His thoughts, or who has [ever] been His counselor? Or who has first given God anything that he might be paid back or that he could claim a recompense? For from Him and through Him and to Him are all things.—For all things originate with Him and come from Him; all things live through Him, and all things center in and tend to consummate and to end in Him. To Him be glory forever! Amen—so be it" (Rom. 11:33-36, Amplified).

Chapter 12

The Conduct of the Church United

(Eph. 4:1-16)

Ephesians 1—3 deals with the doctrinal teaching of the believer's position in Christ. Ephesians 4—6 deals with how to live according to this position in Christ—how Christ works in and through the believer. Having examined the first three chapters of Ephesians, we now turn our attention to the last three chapters. Ephesians 4—6 deals with practice—the believer's earthly conduct.

We turn our attention now to Paul's appeal for believers to walk worthy of their calling and to his exhortation for them to keep the unity of the Spirit (4:1-3). Paul wrote: "I therefore, the prisoner of the Lord, beseech you that ye walk worthy of the vocation wherewith ye are called" (v. 1). The word "therefore" connects the latter half of Ephesians with the former half. In Ephesians 1—3 we see our standing in the heavenlies; we are told how God sees us in Christ. These chapters reveal our wealth in Christ, which is based on the finished work of Christ. Beginning in chapter 4, however, the emphasis is on the believer's walk, or how he should live because of his position in Christ. These chapters tell how men should see Christ in us as we live on earth. Believers are the light of the world so we should heed Christ's command, "Let your light so shine before men, that they may see your good works, and glorify your Father which is in heaven" (Matt. 5:16). We let, not make, our lights shine as we appropriate our wealth in Christ, described in Ephesians 1—3, in our daily living.

Just as with earthly wealth, our wealth in Christ is not to be hoarded but is to be used wisely. Proverbs 11:24 says, "There is that scattereth, and yet increaseth; and there is that

137

withholdeth more than is meet, but it tendeth to poverty."
Here we see the spiritual principle that the one who shares his
spiritual wealth with others actually increases it. Verse 25
says, "The liberal soul shall be made fat: and he that
watereth shall be watered also himself." Unless we use the
wealth that we have in Christ we will become spiritually
emaciated. However, the more we appropriate what we have
in Christ, the more we will grow in our knowledge of Him
and thus increase our spiritual wealth.

With Ephesians 4:1, Paul transfers the focus of attention
from "being" to "doing." The first three chapters emphasize
"being" because they tell what we are in Christ; the last three
chapters emphasize "doing" because they tell how we ought
to live. What we are concerns doctrine; how we should live
concerns practice. The Scriptures give careful attention to
both. The "therefore" of Ephesians 4:1 joins the doctrine of
position with practice. But it must always be remembered
that the doing results from the being.

It is common for the Bible to reveal doctrine before it
emphasizes living. Two examples are Romans and Galatians.
The first 11 chapters of Romans basically deal with doctrine,
whereas chapters 12—16 deal with practical daily living.
Galatians 1—4 is primarily doctrine, whereas chapters 5 and 6
emphasize practice. The word "therefore" is found in the
first verse in both Romans and Galatians where the subject
changes from doctrine to the applying of doctrine to daily
living. Thus we see that proper living is based on proper
doctrine.

Two extremes are common today. One is that believers
have a thorough knowledge of the Word of God but fail to
apply the doctrine to daily living. The other
extreme—perhaps an overreaction to the first—is that
believers are concerned about experience to the extent they
almost entirely ignore doctrine. It is important that doctrine
and experience be given their rightful places. A proper
understanding of doctrine results in experience. However,
experience that is not based on doctrine is never trustworthy.

When Paul appealed to believers in Ephesians for
particular action, he carefully laid the doctrinal groundwork
first so that his appeal was based on the believer's

relationship to Christ. This is a relationship that has been provided through God's eternal purpose and grace.

Ephesians 2:10 gives us the doctrine: "For we are his workmanship, created in Christ Jesus unto good works, which God hath before ordained that we should walk in them." Ephesians 4—6 describes in detail what these works are and what the walk is to be like. The good works and walk of the believer are to conform to his relationship to Christ; that is, his standing in Him. From the first three chapters of Ephesians we see that believers have His nature, life and presence; therefore, we are to produce good works that will conform to our position. This is accomplished by being available to Christ for Him to live His life in and through us.

No believer needs to attempt to produce good works in his own strength. The Scriptures are clear that the works of the flesh do not please God. One does not become spiritual by doing certain things; he is spiritual because of his relationship with Jesus Christ. It is possible for a person to maintain a set of standards that give an outward spiritual appearance yet be unspiritual and maybe even unsaved. This was my condition when I was young. I conformed to the standards of a godly home and church, but it was not until I was 20 that I realized that conformity to the standards did not make me a Christian. It was only by receiving Christ as my Saviour that I personally obtained forgiveness of sins and everlasting life.

Having received Christ, we are "partakers of the divine nature" (II Pet. 1:4). The result is that our desires are changed so that basically we want to please Him and tell others of Him. Our heavenly standing is in Christ; His earthly testimony is in and through us. In order that others might see Christ, we must express Him through our lives. Christ indwells us and desires to live His life through us. Second Corinthians 6:16 tells believers, "Ye are the temple of the living God; as God hath said, I will dwell in them, and walk in them; and I will be their God, and they shall be my people." Christ dwells in us to walk in us; that is, live out His life through us. First John 4:12 says, "No man hath seen God at any time. If we love one another, God dwelleth in us, and his love is perfected in us." Because no one can see the Person of God, it is essential that believers express His nature through their lives. Loving one another is the outworking of God's love, which is in the believer.

Colossians 2:6 tells us how to walk: "As ye have therefore received Christ Jesus the Lord, so walk ye in him." We received Christ by faith; therefore we are to live by faith. We are to appropriate God's eternal power for daily living.

The need to appropriate God's power is seen from Ephesians 3:20: "Now unto him that is able to do exceeding abundantly above all that we ask or think, according to the power that worketh in us."

If we are to have a walk that pleases God we must rely entirely on Him. Romans 7 shows what it will be like if we rely on our own strength to live the Christian life. In this chapter, Paul told of his frustration because of his attempt to live abundantly by self-effort. He knew how he should live but he was unable to effectively do it on his own. Paul said, "For I know that in me (that is, in my flesh,) dwelleth no good thing: for to will is present with me; but how to perform that which is good I find not. For the good that I would I do not: but the evil which I would not, that I do" (vv. 18,19).

Paul also said, "For I delight in the law of God after the inward man: but I see another law in my members, warring against the law of my mind, and bringing me into captivity to the law of sin which is in my members. O wretched man that I am! who shall deliver me from the body of this death?" (vv. 22-24). Paul answered his own question in the following verse: "I thank God through Jesus Christ our Lord. So then with the mind I myself serve the law of God; but with the flesh the law of sin" (v. 25). Then begins the glorious eighth chapter of Romans, which describes how God has undertaken to make the Christian walk possible. Verse 2 sounds the triumphant note: "For the law of the Spirit of life in Christ Jesus hath made me free from the law of sin and death."

We need to constantly remind ourselves that it is impossible to effectively live the Christian life in our own strength. Each believer needs to say to himself in effect, "Since I am a child of God through Christ, I share the life of Christ; and since I share the life of Christ, I have resident within me power enough to make me all that God meant me to be from all eternity." The power of God is embodied in

Christ, who indwells us. Colossians 2:9,10 says, "For in him dwelleth all the fulness of the Godhead bodily. And ye are complete in him." Whatever we need, we have in Christ. Our need is to recognize and appropriate the power available to us.

The "power" is a Person—the Person of the Holy Spirit working in the believer to make him like Christ. This is why the Bible has much to say about being filled (controlled) with the Holy Spirit. We must be filled by Him before we can have a walk that is worthy.

We are to walk worthy as His Body. This means we represent Him by expressing His mind and by living His life. We are not to attempt to merely imitate His life; we are to let Him live His life in and through us. Our attempts will be miserable attempts, but when we recognize the truth of Galatians 2:20—"Christ liveth in me"—our lives will be showcases for Him.

We are also to walk worthy as the temple of God. Although we do not normally associate "walking" with a temple, believers are a temple of God and He desires to "walk in them," or to live His life in and through them (II Cor. 6:16). The temple indicates God's presence in our midst, and we are the presence of God in the midst of the world.

Thus, in our worthy walk we express His life as seen in the Body, and His presence as seen in the building.

The question is, What does the world see in you and me? Do they clearly see the Lord Jesus Christ reflected in our lives? The Holy Spirit has much to do with our worthy walk. In Ephesians 1—3 we are told what the Holy Spirit has done for the believer, whereas in 4—6 we are told what the believer is to do in his relationship to the Holy Spirit. For instance, 1:13 tells us we have been sealed with the Holy Spirit of promise and verse 14 says that He is "the earnest of our inheritance." This is what He is to us. Ephesians 4:30 shows us our responsibility: "Grieve not the holy Spirit of God, whereby ye are sealed unto the day of redemption." This, then, is a walk after the Spirit.

Other New Testament books also have much to say about walking after the Spirit. Romans 8:4 says, "That the righteousness of the law might be fulfilled in us, who walk not after the flesh, but after the Spirit." Galatians 5:16 says,

"This I say then, Walk in the Spirit, and ye shall not fulfil the lust of the flesh."

To walk "after the Spirit" or "in the Spirit" involves a daily submission to Him, allowing Him to teach us through the Word and to control our lives.

Walking worthy of our vocation—divine calling—is appropriating what we have in Christ. The walk after the flesh is the self-life; the walk after the Spirit is the Spirit-controlled life—it is completely His undertaking. The one who walks after the Spirit depends completely on the Spirit for all he needs.

Living Step-by-Step

The word "walk" also implies living one step at a time. Much can be learned about the Christian's walk from considering what it is like for a child to learn to walk. It is difficult for him at first as he pulls himself up beside some object and attempts to balance himself on his unsteady legs. In order for him to let go of the object and attempt to take the first step, he usually needs to be encouraged by someone he trusts who extends outstretched arms. That's exactly what the Lord does for us. Having shown us from Ephesians 1—3 what we are in Him, He now extends His outstretched arms and encourages us to walk, or follow, after Him.

Paul zealously sought to follow the Lord. He said, "Wherefore, my beloved, as ye have always obeyed, not as in my presence only, but now much more in my absence, work out your own salvation with fear and trembling. For it is God which worketh in you both to will and to do of his good pleasure. Do all things without murmurings and disputings" (Phil. 2:12-14). Paul's testimony was that he was following the Lord. He was forgetting past falls he had taken and mistakes he had made and was seeking God's approval on his life at the present.

The Lord Jesus said concerning following, "If any man will come after me, let him deny himself, and take up his cross daily, and follow me. For whosoever will save his life shall lose it: but whosoever will lose his life for my sake, the same shall save it" (Luke 9:23,24).

Romans 6 reveals what is necessary to have a walk that is pleasing to God. First, we must know the facts: "Knowing this, that our old man [was] crucified with him" (v. 6). Second, we must count these things as so because they are so: "Likewise reckon ye also yourselves to be dead indeed unto sin, but alive unto God through Jesus Christ our Lord" (v. 11). Third, we must say No to evil: "Let not sin therefore reign in your mortal body, that ye should obey it in the lusts thereof" (v. 12). Fourth, we must say Yes to Christ, committing all to Him: "Neither yield ye your members as instruments of unrighteousness unto sin: but yield yourselves unto God, as those that are alive from the dead, and your members as instruments of righteousness unto God" (v. 13).

It is interesting to note the difference between the ways Paul referred to himself in the first half of Ephesians and the last half. In beginning the first half, or doctrinal portion, Paul referred to himself as "an apostle of Jesus Christ" (1:1). Paul emphasized his apostleship because he had a special message to give believers, and that message was given in the first three chapters. In the last half of Ephesians, which emphasizes the practice of Christians, Paul referred to himself as "the prisoner of the Lord" (4:1). This last section of Ephesians is an intense appeal by Paul for believers to walk worthy of their calling, and Paul underscored his appeal by calling himself a prisoner of the Lord.

How interesting that Paul should have this viewpoint. He was a prisoner of Rome and was in a damp dungeon because of preaching the gospel, but he really considered himself to be a prisoner of the Lord. Paul recognized that the Lord could use him where he was and this is precisely what the Lord did. During this imprisonment, Paul wrote letters to Philemon, the Colossians, the Ephesians and the Philippians. These letters are now contained in the Scriptures and have had great impact on the world down through the ages.

It is good to ask ourselves, "Whose prisoner am I? Do I consider myself a prisoner of circumstances or of the Lord Jesus Christ?"

Paul wanted believers to know of his apostleship so they would know his authority, and he wanted them to know he was a prisoner of the Lord so they would know he spoke from experience on matters of daily living. Paul realized that an appeal to godly living is not effective unless those making the appeal have subjected themselves to God. Paul spoke with authority, but it was authority in subjection.

Paul exhorted believers to walk "with all lowliness and meekness, with longsuffering, forbearing one another in love" (4:2). Two of these characteristics—meekness and long-suffering—are mentioned elsewhere as the fruit of the Spirit: "But the fruit of the Spirit is love, joy, peace, longsuffering, gentleness, goodness, faith, meekness, temperance" (Gal. 5:22,23). Although the words "lowliness" and "forbearing one another in love" were not used in listing the fruit of the Spirit, it is evident that these qualities are included.

Lowliness

Lowliness refers to an attitude of the mind—humility. Such an attitude is possible only when the believer is under the control of the indwelling Spirit. It is not natural for fallen man to have an attitude of humility. In fact, the opposite characteristic is evidenced in every person from birth to the grave. The natural characteristics are self-assertiveness and the tendency to pride and boastfulness. But when the indwelling Christ is allowed control of the believer's life, it is evidenced in an attitude of humility.

In writing to the Philippians, Paul's primary example of humility was the Lord Jesus Christ Himself, who gave up His position with the Father to come to earth to die for our sin (2:5-8). When we allow Him to express His life through us, this attitude of humility will be evident to others. When humility is not evidenced in our lives, it is because self is in control instead of Christ.

Paul's humble attitude is seen in Ephesians 3:8, where he referred to himself as "less than the least of all saints." It is also seen from his statement in I Corinthians 15:10: "By the grace of God I am what I am." Paul exhorted each believer "not to think of himself more highly than he ought to think" (Rom. 12:3). One translator renders this verse, "Do not be uplifted with unjustifiable notions of your own importance."

Paul was one of the greatest apostles because he realized he was one of the greatest sinners. The concept of the grace of God completely overwhelmed Paul and motivated him to keep on sharing the gospel in spite of extremely difficult circumstances.

Lowliness of mind was evident in Job's case when God was finally able to communicate with his heart. Job exclaimed: "I have heard of thee by the hearing of the ear: but now mine eye seeth thee. Wherefore I abhor myself, and repent in dust and ashes" (Job 42:5,6). When we are in submission to the indwelling Christ, we, too, will recognize that our confidence is not to be in ourselves, but God (Rom. 7:18).

Meekness

Paul also urged believers to walk in "meekness" (Eph. 4:2). This word expresses the opposite of revenge, resentment or retaliation; the one who is meek is slow to take offense. Moses was described as "very meek, above all the men which were upon the face of the earth" (Num. 12:3).

In New Testament times the Greek word for "meekness" was used in referring to a wild animal that had been tamed, such as a horse. In this sense, the word implies a controlled strength. This is what Moses had, and this is what we need to have.

When Christ is at home in our lives—when He really has dominion over every aspect of our lives—we will be meek. This does not mean we will be without strong convictions; it means that our attitudes will be in control as we carry out our convictions.

Of course, the meekest of all persons was the Lord Jesus who said, "Come unto me, all ye that labour and are heavy laden, and I will give you rest. Take my yoke upon you, and learn of me; for I am meek and lowly in heart: and ye shall find rest unto your souls" (Matt. 11:28,29). Peter referred to Christ's humble attitude in these words: "Who, when he was reviled, reviled not again; when he suffered, he threatened not; but committed himself to him that judgeth righteously" (I Pet. 2:23).

It is only when Christians have a humble attitude toward each other that they will be able to keep the unity of the Spirit. When we do God's will we can expect opposition, but

this is no excuse for a bad attitude. When we are controlled
by the Spirit we will have Christ's attitude. The Bible says,
"All that will live godly in Christ Jesus shall suffer
persecution" (II Tim. 3:12), but even in persecution there
will be meekness in the Christ-controlled believer.

Long-suffering

Paul also said that the walk of believers should be marked
by "longsuffering" (Eph. 4:2). This means that we should be
without irritation or annoyance, that we should patiently
endure even when suffering wrongfully. The Bible says, "For
this is thankworthy, if a man for conscience toward God
endure grief, suffering wrongfully. For what glory is it, if,
when ye be buffeted for your faults, ye shall take it
patiently? but if, when ye do well, and suffer for it, ye take it
patiently, this is acceptable with God" (I Pet. 2:19,20).

What do you do when people misrepresent you and
falsely accuse you? Do you fight fire with fire? Love is
long-suffering, for the Bible says love "suffereth long, and is
kind" (I Cor. 13:4). This attitude contributes to the keeping
of the unity of the Spirit.

Long-suffering means that we do not surrender to
circumstances or succumb under trial; it also implies that we
should not yield to despondency.

Forebearing One Another

The fourth characteristic Paul mentioned for the
believer's walk is "forbearing one another in love" (Eph.
4:2). This has to do with lovingly putting up with all that is
disagreeable in other people. Our attitude toward them
should be love and patience even though they do things with
which we cannot agree. Impatience tends to result in
destructive criticism. When we love each other we will live
together peaceably even though we do not share the same
viewpoints.

The believer's walk is to be characterized by lowliness,
meekness, long-suffering and forbearance while "endeavouring to keep the unity of the Spirit in the bond of
peace" (4:3). This can be considered the first major step in

the believer's walk—"endeavouring to keep the unity of the Spirit." Another translation renders verse 3, "Be eager and strive earnestly to guard and keep the harmony and oneness of [produced by] the Spirit in the binding power of peace" (Amplified). As believers, we are not asked to create, legislate or organize this unity but to keep it. We will do this as our walk is characterized by lowliness, meekness, long-suffering and forbearance (v. 2).

The word translated "keep" means "to watch over, to guard, to preserve." The unity of believers came into being on the Day of Pentecost with the coming of the Holy Spirit to indwell every person who is a member of the Body of Christ. A person becomes a member of the Body of Christ by receiving Christ as Saviour. First Corinthians 12:13 says, "For by one Spirit are we all baptized into one body, whether we be Jews or Gentiles, whether we be bond or free; and have been all made to drink into one Spirit."

There is unity in the members because they are indwelt by the same Spirit. However, when those in the Body of Christ get out of fellowship with the Head of the Body they disrupt the unity of the members. Just as a member of the physical body disrupts the harmony of the other members when it malfunctions, so a believer out of fellowship disrupts the spiritual harmony that is intended among believers.

The unity spoken of in Ephesians 4:3 is not an organizational unity of denominations or a federation of churches. The unity referred to is a spiritual unity of everyone within the Body of Christ; that is, all who have received Him as personal Saviour. This means that our unity must always be based on the truth of the Scriptures, which tell who Christ is and what we are in Him. Any unity that compromises the teaching of the Scriptures regarding Jesus Christ is not a unity that has God's approval. However, the ecumenism of our day seems far more concerned about unity for unity's sake, than it does about adhering to the truth of the Scriptures. In fact, the teaching of the Scriptures is sometimes de-emphasized so much that for the sake of unity some groups do not even have doctrinal statements. Such groups tend to emphasize God's love and the need of working in harmony with those with whom we disagree. It is naive, however, to emphasize love at the expense of truth—to emphasize God's love but not His holy standards and justice. Organizational unity is not necessarily wrong if only believers are involved. However, it is wrong—no matter how good the cause may be—for believers to compromise their message in order to work with unbelievers.

When Paul said we are to be "endeavouring to keep the unity of the Spirit," the word he used for "endeavouring" was a word that originally meant "to make haste" and then came to mean "to be zealous or eager, to give diligence." Each believer is to give his utmost attention to see that harmony is preserved within the Body of Christ. It is a spiritual unity, or oneness, that exists among all who know Christ as Saviour, but it can be maintained only as we walk in fellowship with Him.

Chapter 13

The Basis for Unity

(Eph. 4:4-6)

Having made the appeal for believers to walk in a worthy manner, endeavoring to keep the unity of the Spirit, Paul then revealed that this unity is based on seven unities that already exist. These are given in verses 4-6. Notice that these unities are spiritual, not physical or organizational.

'One Body'

First, "there is one body" (v. 4). This refers to the Body of Christ, of which every believer is a member. This Body was formed on the Day of Pentecost and exists entirely apart from man's efforts. Believers are not commanded to organize a body, for Paul said, "There *is* one body."

When He was on earth, Jesus prayed for a oneness in the organism that was to be His Body, the Church. He prayed, "And now I am no more in the world, but these are in the world, and I come to thee. Holy Father, keep through thine own name those whom thou hast given me, that they may be one, as we are. That they all may be one; as thou, Father, art in me, and I in thee, that they also may be one in us: that the world may believe that thou hast sent me. And the glory which thou gavest me I have given them; that they may be one, even as we are one: I in them, and thou in me, that they may be made perfect in one; and that the world may know that thou hast sent me, and hast loved them, as thou hast loved me" (John 17:11, 21-23).

The believers to which Christ referred in these verses are members of the Church, of which He prophesied, "I will build my church; and the gates of hell shall not prevail

149

against it" (Matt. 16:18). This Body of Christ is composed of individuals who have been washed in the blood of Jesus Christ, having been regenerated by the Holy Spirit. These people are from every background, color and nationality. But regardless of how they differ, all believers in Christ are part of the one Body, and they are one in Him. Ephesians 5:30 says, "For we are members of his body, of his flesh, and of his bones." Earlier, Paul told the Ephesians that the Church is "his body, the fulness of him that filleth all in all" (1:23).

It is important to realize that since every believer is united to Christ by the Holy Spirit, all believers are one with each other. As members of the Body, they are to be in submission to the Head, Jesus Christ. Members of the Body are to have special concern for each other. Paul told believers, "But now hath God set the members every one of them in the body, as it hath pleased him. That there should be no schism in the body; but that the members should have the same care one for another. And whether one member suffer, all the members suffer with it; or one member be honoured, all the members rejoice with it. Now ye are the body of Christ, and members in particular" (I Cor. 12:18, 25-27). There should not be divisions in the Body because there is only one Head, the Lord Jesus Christ. "He is the head of the body, the church: who is the beginning, the firstborn from the dead; that in all things he might have the preeminence" (Col. 1:18).

Disruption of harmony among believers is evidence of their living to please themselves instead of Jesus Christ. Walking according to the flesh is known as carnality. Paul had to tell the Corinthian believers, "For ye are yet carnal: for whereas there is among you envying, and strife, and divisions, are ye not carnal, and walk as men?" (I Cor. 3:3).

'One Spirit'

Second in Paul's list of seven unities is "one Spirit" (Eph. 4:4). There is only one Holy Spirit, and it is He who places every person into the Body of Christ at the time of regeneration: "For by one Spirit are we all baptized into one body" (I Cor. 12:13).

The disruption and divisions in the church at Corinth resulted from some believers thinking that their gifts were better than other believers' gifts. However, Paul strongly reminded them that all gifts have been given by the same Holy Spirit. Paul said, "Now there are diversities of gifts, but the same Spirit. And there are differences of administrations, but the same Lord. And there are diversities of operations, but it is the same God which worketh all in all. But the manifestation of the Spirit is given to every man to profit withal. For to one is given by the Spirit the word of wisdom; to another the word of knowledge by the same Spirit; to another faith by the same Spirit; to another the gifts of healing by the same Spirit; to another the working of miracles; to another prophecy; to another discerning of spirits; to another divers kinds of tongues; to another the interpretation of tongues: but all these worketh that one and the selfsame Spirit, dividing to every man severally as he will" (I Cor. 12:4-11).

It is important to remember that the Holy Spirit has the responsibility of producing all life and all actions of the "one body."

When He was on earth, Jesus Himself told of the ministry of the Holy Spirit. He told His disciples, "Nevertheless I tell you the truth; It is expedient for you that I go away: for if I go not away, the Comforter will not come unto you; but if I depart, I will send him unto you. And when he is come, he will reprove the world of sin, and of righteousness, and of judgment. Howbeit when he, the Spirit of truth, is come, he will guide you into all truth: for he shall not speak of himself; but whatsoever he shall hear, that shall he speak: and he will shew you things to come. He shall glorify me: for he shall receive of mine, and shall shew it unto you" (John 16:7,8,13,14). From these verses we see that it is the special responsibility of the Holy Spirit to minister to believers and to glorify Christ.

Before Christ ascended to heaven, He told His followers, "But ye shall receive power, after that the Holy Ghost is come upon you: and ye shall be witnesses unto me" (Acts 1:8). When the Holy Spirit came on the Day of Pentecost, He unified believers into one Body and is now in the process of taking the things of Christ and making them real to believers.

One of the key things for us to remember concerning the "one Spirit" is that to Him has been delegated the responsibility of being in charge of the Body so that believers carry out the will and work of Christ on earth. He is to be sovereign in our lives, and when we submit to Him, there will be the harmony among us that Christ desires. This harmony is disrupted only as we walk according to the desires of the flesh, rather than according to the desires of the Spirit. Galatians 5:16 tells us, "Walk in the Spirit, and ye shall not fulfil the lust of the flesh." Romans 8:13 says, "If ye through the Spirit do mortify the deeds of the body, ye shall live." Through the power of the indwelling Holy Spirit, we are to put to death those actions that disrupt the unity of the Body of Christ. Not heeding the Spirit's convicting work in our lives will lead to conflict, but there will be harmony when we confess our sins and walk in fellowship with Him.

It must be understood, however, that disobedience does not actually destroy the oneness of the Body of Christ produced by the Spirit. The enjoyment and the functional aspect of that unity can be destroyed, but the unity itself cannot be destroyed.

Christ is working in believers so their practice might become more like their position. His purpose in working in the Church is stated in Ephesians 5:26,27: "That he might sanctify and cleanse it with the washing of water by the word, that he might present it to himself a glorious church, not having spot, or wrinkle, or any such thing; but that it should be holy and without blemish." Even though some have no regard for this unity in Christ, it still remains because it is the work of Christ. As the Bible says, "If we believe not, yet he abideth faithful" (II Tim. 2:13). What He has undertaken, He will see through to its end. A spiritual unity exists among all believers, whether they recognize and enjoy it or not.

'One Hope'

The third unity mentioned by Paul in Ephesians 4:4 has to do with the call of believers: "Even as ye are called in one hope of your calling." The believer has one main hope, which will be fulfilled when Christ returns for His Church. This hope is to be with the Lord Himself and to be completely like Him—transformed into His image. "As we have borne the image of the earthy, we shall also bear the image of the heavenly" (I Cor. 15:49). The Apostle John told believers, "Beloved, now are we the sons of God, and it doth not yet appear what we shall be: but we know that, when he shall appear, we shall be like him; for we shall see him as he is. And every man that hath this hope in him purifieth himself, even as he is pure" (I John 3:2,3).

If you are a child of God, then this is the hope of the future for you—to be like Jesus Christ. Notice how this hope affects the believer—it causes him to purify himself. That is, knowing that he will someday meet Christ and be like Him causes the believer to want to live a pure life now.

Nothing so unifies believers as the blessed hope of His return for the Church, which could take place at any time. Paul spoke of the way we should live with Christ's return in view: "For the grace of God that bringeth salvation hath appeared to all men, teaching us that, denying ungodliness and worldly lusts, we should live soberly, righteously, and godly, in this present world; looking for that blessed hope, and the glorious appearing of the great God and our Saviour Jesus Christ" (Titus 2:11-13).

James wrote of the same truths in these words: "Be patient therefore, brethren, unto the coming of the Lord. Behold, the husbandman waiteth for the precious fruit of the earth, and hath long patience for it, until he receive the early and latter rain. Be ye also patient; stablish your hearts: for the coming of the Lord draweth nigh. Grudge not one against another, brethren, lest ye be condemned: behold, the judge standeth before the door" (5:7-9).

The hope of the believer's calling is also mentioned in the early chapters of Ephesians. In particular, Ephesians 1:18 says, "The eyes of your understanding being enlightened; that ye may know what is the hope of his calling."

'One Lord'

The fourth unity mentioned by Paul is "one Lord" (4:5). The title "Lord" means "Master." In the good sense of the word, Christ is our "Boss." Earlier in Ephesians He is presented as our Saviour; now He is presented to us as our Lord. This ties in with the emphasis on the unity in the Church. When we are submitting to His lordship, this unity will be clearly evidenced in our lives. It is essential for unity that there be one Head. Jesus Christ is that Head, for He is "the head of the body, the church" (Col. 1:18).

The emphasis on the lordship of Christ runs throughout the New Testament. Philippians 2:11 reveals that God has highly exalted Christ "that every tongue should confess that Jesus Christ is Lord, to the glory of God the Father." He is Lord—He is in a class by Himself. Revelation 17:14 says He is "Lord of lords, and King of kings." This same Jesus is our Lord—there is no other Lord beside Him. He is the Head of the Church—this excludes anyone else as head of the Church.

As we live for Him, let us learn from Peter's experience. Peter had a vision in which he saw heaven opened and a sheet lowered, upon which were all kinds of animals, both clean and unclean. A voice commanded, "Rise, Peter; kill, and eat" (Acts 10:13). Peter's reply was "Not so, Lord; for I have never eaten any thing that is common or unclean" (v. 14). Notice the contrast of the words "not so" and "Lord." If Jesus Christ is truly Lord, then we should never say no to His commands. If we say no to His commands, then He is really not Lord in that area of our lives. He is the Lord; therefore, let us gladly submit to His will.

'One Faith'

The fifth unity to which Paul referred is "one faith" (Eph. 4:5). The word "faith" is used in two primary ways in the Scriptures. It refers to the body of truth concerning the Person and work of Jesus Christ, and it also refers to the means by which the benefits of Christ's redemptive work are applied to our lives.

Jude used the word "faith" to refer to the body of truth concerning Jesus Christ when he wrote: "Beloved, when I gave all diligence to write unto you of the common salvation, it was needful for me to write unto you, and exhort you that ye should earnestly contend for the faith which was once delivered unto the saints" (Jude 1:3).

In this sense, the word "faith" is similar to the word "gospel." Concerning the gospel, Paul wrote: "Moreover, brethren, I declare unto you the gospel which I preached unto you, which also ye have received, and wherein ye stand; by which also ye are saved, if ye keep in memory what I preached unto you, unless ye have believed in vain. For I delivered unto you first of all that which I also received, how that Christ died for our sins according to the scriptures; and that he was buried, and that he rose again the third day according to the scriptures" (I Cor. 15:1-4).

The body of truth concerning Christ's Person and work has been revealed to us by God in the Bible, His written Word. Therefore, it is imperative that we recognize the authority of the Scriptures. The divine standard of truth is not a creed or a denominational statement—it is the Scriptures. The Bible is God's Word from Genesis to Revelation and was without error when it was originally written. Beware of a religion or cult that places another book on an equal basis with the inspired Word of God. Only the Bible has been inspired by God; therefore, only the Bible is the final authority concerning "the faith which was once delivered unto the saints" (Jude 1:3).

The word "faith" is also frequently used throughout the Scriptures to describe the means by which a person is able to have redemption through Jesus Christ. Ephesians 2:8,9 says, "For by grace are ye saved through faith; and that not of yourselves: it is the gift of God: not of works, lest any man should boast." Faith is the means of salvation, not works.

Romans 4:5 emphasizes the same truth: "But to him that worketh not, but believeth on him that justifieth the ungodly, his faith is counted for righteousness." No work that man can do, regardless of how valuable he considers it, can bring him into right relationship with Jesus Christ. Having received Christ by faith, Romans 5:1 tells of the peace that results: "Therefore being justified by faith, we have peace with God through our Lord Jesus Christ."

Having come into right relationship with Jesus Christ, we are to live the Christian life by faith. "The just shall live by faith" (Rom. 1:17). We live by the same principle by which we received Christ as Saviour. This is further emphasized in Colossians 2:6: "As ye have therefore received Christ Jesus the Lord, so walk ye in him." We received him by faith, and we are to live by faith.

Faith is almost synonymous with believing, and Romans 10 has much to say about faith and believing. "For Christ is the end of the law for righteousness to every one that believeth" (v. 4). "The word is nigh thee, even in thy mouth, and in thy heart: that is, the word of faith, which we preach; that if thou shalt confess with thy mouth the Lord Jesus, and shalt believe in thine heart that God hath raised him from the dead, thou shalt be saved. For with the heart man believeth unto righteousness; and with the mouth confession is made unto salvation" (vv. 8-10). "So then faith cometh by hearing, and hearing by the word of God" (v. 17).

Thus, the "one faith" of Ephesians 4:5 is faith in the Person and work of Jesus Christ as revealed in the Scriptures.

'One Baptism'

The sixth unity to which Paul referred was that of "one baptism" (v. 5). In seeking to establish whether this is water baptism or Spirit baptism, it must be remembered that it is a baptism that unifies the Body of Jesus Christ. As such, only Spirit baptism fulfills all that is required.

The baptism of, or by, the Spirit is mentioned in I Corinthians 12:13: "For by one Spirit are we all baptized into one body, whether we be Jews or Gentiles, whether we be bond or free; and have been all made to drink into one Spirit." A person is baptized into the Body of Christ by the Holy Spirit the moment the person receives Christ as Saviour.

Spirit baptism is also referred to in Romans 6:3,4: "Know ye not, that so many of us as were baptized into Jesus Christ were baptized into his death? Therefore we are buried with him by baptism into death: that like as Christ was raised up from the dead by the glory of the Father, even so we also should walk in newness of life." Galatians 3:27 also speaks of Spirit baptism: "For as many of you as have been baptized into Christ have put on Christ." The baptism of the Spirit into the Body of Christ at the time of salvation joins the believer to the one Body for his life and to the one Lord as his Master.

The baptism of the Holy Spirit is an inner process accomplished by the Holy Spirit alone. It is not something man does; it is what God does. On the other hand, water baptism is man's outward testimony of this inner work.

There are at least three reasons why water baptism could not have been the "one baptism" referred to in Ephesians 4. First, the context speaks of being made one with Christ and other believers. Inasmuch as water baptism does not accomplish either of these, it does not fit the context. Water baptism is an outward expression of the Spirit-produced inner unity with Christ and other believers.

Second, the unity spoken of in Ephesians 4 is a divinely produced unity—it is a "unity of the Spirit" (v. 3). Because water baptism is not a divine, or supernatural, act but a human one, it cannot be the "one baptism" referred to.

Third, the "one baptism" is that which places us into the Body of Christ, where we share in the unity of the Spirit. Inasmuch as only Spirit baptism places us into the Body of Christ, the "one baptism" must be Spirit baptism, not water baptism.

'One God and Father'

The seventh unity mentioned by Paul is "one God and Father of all, who is above all, and through all, and in you all" (v. 6). Previously, Paul mentioned the "one Spirit" (v. 4) and the "one Lord" (v. 5). Now he mentions the "Father" (v. 6). Thus, in these statements we see references to the three Persons of the Trinity—Father, Son and Spirit.

When Paul mentioned that God is the "Father of all," he did not use the phrase as it is being used by theological liberals today. They speak of the universal Fatherhood of God and the Brotherhood of Man in referring to a spiritual relationship with God. However, the Scriptures clearly teach that not all are spiritually in right relationship to God. Those who are not do not have God as their spiritual Father but Satan. Jesus told unbelievers, "Ye are of your father the devil, and the lusts of your father ye will do" (John 8:44).

God is the Father of all in the sense that He has brought all into existence. Acts 17:26 says that God has "made from one [common origin, one source, one blood] all nations of men to settle on the face of the earth, having definitely determined [their] allotted periods of time and the fixed boundaries of their habitation—their settlements, lands and abodes" (Amplified).

Even though men reject God and even claim to be atheists, they are still responsible to God and will someday be judged by Him. The Bible says, "As it is appointed unto men once to die, but after this the judgment" (Heb. 9:27). Revelation 20:12-15 reveals that all unbelievers will someday be raised to stand before God to be judged and to be cast into the lake of fire. Acts 17:31 says that God has "appointed a day, in the which he will judge the world in righteousness."

There is "one God and Father" (Eph. 4:6); therefore, He is absolutely sovereign and is able to do what He desires to do (1:5,11).

God is "above all" (4:6); therefore, all must eventually acknowledge His Son, Jesus Christ. The Father has exalted the Son so "that at the name of Jesus every knee should bow, of things in heaven, and things in earth, and things under the earth; and that every tongue should confess that Jesus Christ is Lord, to the glory of God the Father" (Phil. 2:10,11).

No believer can dictate what the Body of Christ should be like because God is sovereign over the "one body." He is "above all" and has delegated the responsibility for spiritual unity to the Holy Spirit.

Paul also described God as one who is "through all" (Eph. 4:6). God is "through all" the Church in that His presence pervades every believer.

Paul also told believers that God is "in you all" (v. 6). From these words we see that the Father, as well as the Son and the Spirit, indwells the believer. Jesus alluded to the indwelling of the Father when He said, "I in them, and thou in me, that they may be made perfect in one" (John 17:23). However, even though all three Persons of the Godhead indwell the believer, it is the special ministry of the Holy Spirit to work in the believer to make him like Christ.

The word "you" in Ephesians 4:6 emphasizes that Paul is referring to believers. The fact that God is "in" believers establishes a relationship among all believers of the present age. Paul previously stated in his letter to the Ephesians that both Jew and Gentile are one in the Body of Christ, and this is because they have been united by God.

Conclusions

Because of the seven unities, which Paul emphasized, there are certain things that we need to keep clearly in mind.

First, we must remember that the Church is an organism, not an organization. There is "one body" of which Christ is the "one head." There is nothing wrong with organization itself, but it must be remembered that unity of believers is not the result of organizational unity but spiritual unity. A local church should be well organized, but those who are part of the local church may not necessarily be a part of the universal Church, the Body of Christ. Faith in Christ alone makes one a part of the Body of Christ. Of course, one who has received Christ should become involved in a local church where he can fellowship with other believers and have a greater outreach to a lost world.

Second, caution should be exercised that there not be a departure from the headship of Christ to the headship of men. Christ uses men in accomplishing His will in the Church, but Christ is the "one head" of the Church.

It is important, therefore, that we be followers of Christ, not followers of men. Whenever believers become followers of men they are like the church at Corinth, which divided into various groups, each following a different person. Paul had stern words for the Corinthian church and asked, "Is Christ divided? was Paul crucified for you? or were ye baptized in the name of Paul?" (I Cor. 1:13).

There will always be those who will seek to draw attention to themselves to the extent that they divide believers. In Paul's last meeting with the Ephesians he told them, "For I know this, that after my departing shall grievous wolves enter in among you, not sparing the flock. Also of your own selves shall men arise, speaking perverse things, to draw away disciples after them" (Acts 20:29,30). Paul warned the Colossians, "Beware lest any man spoil you through philosophy and vain deceit, after the tradition of

men, after the rudiments of the world, and not after Christ"
(Col. 2:8).

Third, believers need to be aware of the tendency for one
particular teaching to predominate. In fact, a doctrine may
be taught by some almost to the exclusion of all others. This
may be a doctrine that is overemphasized, or it may be an
experience-centered approach that deemphasizes the
authority of God's Word. It is common for believers to try to
fit other believers into the same mold. There were those in
Corinth who thought their gifts were better than others' and
they treated others as second-class Christians if they didn't
have particular gifts.

Divisions can also arise because of different viewpoints on
what the Bible teaches. For instance, there are many things
about prophecy that have not been revealed to us, and in
those areas we must not be dogmatic. However, those things
the Bible clearly teaches we must not compromise for the
sake of man-made unity.

Fourth, we must be on the alert for those who are guilty
of disrupting the unity of the Spirit. Invariably, these people
justify themselves by claiming to be contenders for the faith.
Certainly, every believer should contend for the faith but he
should not display an unChristlike attitude. We must stand
for the truth, but in the process we should evidence the fruit
of the Spirit. We are to endeavor to keep the unity of the
Spirit while "forbearing one another in love" (Eph. 4:2). In
verse 15 Paul exhorted the believers to be "speaking the truth
in love." It is imperative that our lives be characterized by
Christ's love as we stand for the truth. Someone has said,
"The unity that is rooted in truth, ripens in love."

Chapter 14

Victory Accomplished;
Gifted Men Appointed

(Eph. 4:7-11)

Beginning with Ephesians 4:7, there is an abrupt change of thought. Attention is turned from the unity of all believers to what has been done for each believer. Paul said, "But unto every one of us is given grace according to the measure of the gift of Christ" (v. 7). Not one member of the Body has been left out in the distribution of gifts. Some may have gifts that are more outstanding because of their public nature, but every believer has a gift that should be exercised to the glory of Christ.

A key chapter on the subject of gifts is I Corinthians 12. This chapter emphasizes that the various gifts have been given to believers by the same Holy Spirit; thereby, showing the unity of the Body. There are "diversities of gifts," there are "differences of administrations," and there are "diversities of operations" (vv. 4-6). "But to each one is given the manifestation of the Spirit for the common good" (v. 7, NASB). Verse 11 further emphasizes, "But one and the same Spirit works all these things, distributing to each one individually just as He wills" (NASB).

A fuller understanding of Ephesians 4:7 is gained from another translation: "All these [achievements and abilities] are inspired and brought to pass by one and the same (Holy) Spirit, Who apportions to each person individually [exactly] as He chooses" (Amplified). Every believer has some contribution to make toward the Body of Christ as a whole. Not one can say that he is not significant, because all the gifts must be faithfully exercised if the Body is to function as Christ intends.

If a member does not function properly, the rest of the Body will be less efficient because it will have to compensate for the loss, even as the physical body must compensate when one of its members does not function properly. Paul said, "And the eye cannot say unto the hand, I have no need of thee: nor again the head to the feet, I have no need of you. Nay, much more those members of the body, which seem to be more feeble, are necessary: and those members of the body, which we think to be less honourable, upon these we bestow more abundant honour; and our uncomely parts have more abundant comeliness. For our comely parts have no need: but God hath tempered the body together, having given more abundant honour to that part which lacked: that there should be no schism in the body; but that the members should have the same care one for another" (I Cor. 12:21-25).

Enabling Grace

Notice from Ephesians 4:7 that grace is given "according to the measure of the gift of Christ." If the gift for ministry requires much enablement, God gives it accordingly—there is sufficient grace to meet any need. A noted Greek scholar says concerning this verse, "The gift is measured; and while each individual receives, he receives according to the will of the sovereign Distributor. And whether the measure be great or small, whether its contents be of more brilliant endowment or of humbler or unnoticed talent, all is equally Christ's gift, and of Christ's adjustment; all is equally indispensable to the union and edification of that body in which there is 'no schism,' and forms an argument why each one gifted with such grace should keep the unity of the Spirit" (John Eadie, *Commentary on the Epistle to the Ephesians*, p. 280).

Notice that the grace referred to has to do with the exercise of special gifts for service—it is the Spirit's enablement for ministry. Paul told believers, "God is able to make all grace abound toward you; that ye, always having all sufficiency in all things, may abound to every good work" (II Cor. 9:8).

Paul then gave background in telling of the gifts for service that Christ has given: "Wherefore he saith, When he ascended up on high, he led captivity captive, and gave gifts unto men. (Now that he ascended, what is it but that he also descended first into the lower parts of the earth? He that descended is the same also that ascended up far above all heavens, that he might fill all things.) And he gave some, apostles; and some, prophets; and some, evangelists; and some, pastors and teachers" (Eph. 4:8-11).

Christ's Ascension

Notice the phrase in verse 8, "When he ascended up on high." These words refer to Christ's going to heaven after His resurrection. Previously, He had been with the Father, but He had come to earth to take upon Himself a human body, live an obedient life and die for the sin of the world. He then descended to hades but rose from there and was on the earth for 40 days before ascending into heaven. The Scriptures say that after He had risen from the dead and had given instructions to His disciples, "When he had spoken these things, while they beheld, he was taken up; and a cloud received him out of their sight" (Acts 1:9). This ascension took place before the Day of Pentecost, when the Church was born.

Speaking of Christ's descent into hades, Peter said, "His soul was not left in hell [hades], neither his flesh did see corruption" (2:31).

Ephesians 4:8 says, "When he ascended up on high, he led captivity captive, and gave gifts unto men." Psalm 68:18 is a prophecy concerning the same truths: "Thou hast ascended on high, thou hast led captivity captive: thou hast received gifts for men."

Christ's Triumph

The words "He led captivity captive" (Eph. 4:8) have commonly been understood as teaching that Christ led believers from hades to heaven at the time of His resurrection. It is commonly thought that before the cross hades consisted of two compartments—one for the righteous dead and one for the unrighteous dead. The account of Luke 16:19-31 supports this. Inasmuch as Christ entered hades at the time of His death, it is thought that He led the righteous dead from the one compartment and took them to heaven to be with Himself. The words "He led captivity captive" have been commonly used to imply that the righteous who were held captive in hades were now taken captive by Christ and led to heaven.

Although this view has merit, upon further research I do not believe that this is what is being taught in Ephesians 4:8. The key reason for not thinking so is that the context does not support it. A particular verse or phrase must be interpreted in the light of its context. The context of Ephesians 4:8 has to do primarily with victory and gifts. As has been indicated, Psalm 68:18 is a parallel passage. The Amplified Bible renders this verse, "You have ascended on high. You have led away captive a train of vanquished foes; You have received gifts of men, yes, of the rebellious also, that the Lord God might dwell there with them."

It was the custom in biblical times for an army to return home from victory following its leader in triumph. After the triumphal procession with the captives and spoils that had been taken, the military leader would distribute gifts, which included the spoils. The Apostle Paul would have been well acquainted with this custom and in Ephesians would have been referring to the victory of Christ in defeating all His foes and then giving gifts to His own people.

Christ's triumph over His foes is mentioned in Colossians 2:15: "And having spoiled principalities and powers, He made a shew of them openly, triumphing over them in it." He "spoiled" principalities and powers in the sense that He stripped Satan and his evil hosts of their power. He exposed them openly, having triumphed over them in His death on the cross. The "in it" of verse 15 refers to the cross, mentioned in verse 14. Concerning Colossians 2:15, the noted Bible scholar Matthew Henry commented that Christ conquered those who had conquered us, such as sin, the Devil and death.

Hebrews 2:14,15 also tells of Christ's triumph: "Forasmuch then as the children are partakers of flesh and blood, he also himself likewise took part of the same; that through death he might destroy him that had the power of death, that is, the devil; and deliver them who through fear of death were all their lifetime subject to bondage." The word translated "destroy" does not mean Satan was annihilated; rather, it reveals his power was broken. At the cross, Christ broke the power of Satan, and Satan himself will eventually be confined to the lake of fire (Rev. 20:10).

From Colossians 2:15 and Hebrews 2:14,15 we see that the time of Christ's triumph was when He died on the cross for the sin of the world. Philippians 2 tells us that Christ "became obedient unto death, even the death of the cross. Wherefore God also hath highly exalted Him, and given Him a name which is above every name: that at the name of Jesus every knee should bow, of things in heaven, and things in earth, and things under the earth; and that every tongue should confess that Jesus Christ is Lord, to the glory of God the Father (vv. 8-11). Christ has triumphed over all Satanic powers, and although He is not recognized by everyone as Lord now, the time will come when He will be.

Thus it seems that when Ephesians 4:8 refers to Christ's leading "captivity captive," it is referring to the time when He triumphed over His enemies at the cross. And having triumphed, He "gave gifts unto men."

The context of Ephesians 4 is how believers are prepared to effectively serve Christ. First, they must be delivered from Satan's power, by which he disrupts their progress, and second, they must be given gifts to enable them to properly function in the Body of Christ.

Before Jesus ascended to the Father, He told His disciples what was about to happen, explaining to them that He would give them another "Comforter" (John 14:16), referring to the Holy Spirit. He told them, "He shall teach you all things, and bring all things to your remembrance whatsoever I have said unto you" (v. 26). Jesus also said, "When he is come, he will reprove the world of sin, and of righteousness, and of judgment. He shall glorify me: for he shall receive of mine, and shall shew it unto you" (16:8,14).

Let us look at the order of events. First, Christ died on the cross, which was not only the means of our salvation but was also the deathblow to Satan and his power. Although Satan attempts to get people to fear him, believers are instructed, "Submit yourselves therefore to God. Resist the devil, and he will flee from you" (James 4:7). Christ spoiled

Satan's power so believers can be victorious in the spiritual warfare (Eph. 6:11-17). Second, Christ descended into hades, the place of the departed dead. Third, Christ rose from the dead, thereby proving the validity of all He had said. Fourth, He ascended to the Father, thereby giving proof of His entry into eternal exhaltation. Fifth, He sent the Holy Spirit to indwell those who know Him as Saviour. Through the Holy Spirit, Christ triumphantly lives in the Church, which is His Body. While He was on earth Jesus said, "I will build my church; and the gates of hell [hades] shall not prevail against it" (Matt. 16:18). Christ had gained the victory at the cross and nothing or no one would be able to overpower the Church.

Christ lives triumphantly in and through His Church and through the Spirit distributes gifts to believers. A central passage of Scripture on gifts for individuals is I Corinthians 12, which we have discussed.

Gifted Men Given

In Ephesians 4, however, the subject is not gifts given to men but gifted men who are given to the Church. Having spoken of Christ's ascension, Paul then added that he "gave some, apostles; and some, prophets; and some, evangelists; and some, pastors and teachers" (v. 11).

Jesus had received men from the Father and now He was giving them to the Church. In Jesus' prayer of intercession He said, "I have manifested thy name unto the men which thou gavest me out of the world: thine they were, and thou gavest them me; and they have kept thy Word" (John 17:6). He also said, "I pray for them: I pray not for the world, but for them which thou hast given me: for they are thine. And now I am no more in the world, but these are in the world, and I come to thee. Holy Father, keep through thine own name those whom thou hast given me, that they may be one, as we are. While I was with them in the world, I kept them in thy name: those that thou gavest me I have kept, and none of them is lost, but the son of perdition; that the scripture might be fulfilled" (vv. 9,11,12).

These that Christ received from the Father He gave to the Church as apostles, prophets, evangelists, pastors and teachers. All of the Persons of the Trinity are involved because the Father is calling out a people for His name, Christ is forming the Body, and the Spirit is preparing each believer for his particular ministry.

The "apostles" and "prophets" of Ephesians 4:11 were gifted men in the first century of the Church. Inasmuch as we have their writings in the Scriptures, we still benefit from these gifted men that were given to the Church. It was through them that the doctrinal foundation of the Church was laid. We no longer have apostles and prophets in this New Testament sense.

The word "evangelists" refers to those who are gifted in proclaiming the Good News; that is, the gospel. Christ has given to the Church men gifted as evangelists, and He especially blesses their ministry of proclaiming the message of the gospel. However, even though not all are gifted evangelists, each believer is to "do the work of an evangelist" (II Tim. 4:5). Those gifted in other areas are to be faithful in witnessing for Christ and encouraging others to place their faith in Christ alone.

One of the great needs of missions today is for those with the gift of evangelism to take the gospel to all parts of the world. Through these gifted men, the Holy Spirit convinces others of sin and draws them to the Saviour.

Christ has also given to the Church "pastors and teachers" (Eph. 4:11). Pastors are shepherds of God's flock. They are those whom God has especially gifted to deal with the problems of His children, to encourage and comfort them, and to build them up in the Christian faith by teaching God's Word. Because of the construction in the original language, the pastor-teacher gift seems to be considered a combined gift.

The Lord not only gifts His people but chooses the place of their service. Absolutely nothing in Christ's service is left to mere human judgment.

Chapter 15

The Purpose of the Gifts

(Eph. 4:12-16)

Ephesians 4:11 lists some of the gifted men Christ has given to His Church, and verses 12-16 reveal Christ's purpose in giving them.

Verse 12 says, "For the perfecting of the saints, for the work of the ministry, for the edifying of the body of Christ." The word translated "perfecting" means "strengthening" or "making fit." The verb form of this word means "to furnish completely, to complete, to equip, to prepare."

The Amplified Bible translates verse 12, "His intention was the perfecting and the full equipping of the saints (His consecrated people), [that they should do] the work of ministering toward building up Christ's body (the church)."

Equipping the Saints

The addition of a comma after the word "saint" in the King James Version has obscured the true meaning of the passage. The first two clauses should be read as one thought because together they give Christ's first purpose in giving gifted men to His Church. The gifted men are for the equipping of the saints to do the work of the ministry. This reveals that the gifted men are not commissioned by the Lord to do all the work of the Church; rather, they are to teach the Word to believers and to train them to do the work of the ministry.

It is common today to single out a group of individuals and call them "ministers." However, this sometimes implies that only they are responsible for the work of the ministry.

But according to the Word of God each believer is a minister and is to have a vital part in the ministry. Paul told believers, "All things are of God, who hath reconciled us to himself by Jesus Christ, and hath given to us the ministry of reconciliation" (II Cor. 5:18). Every Christian has been reconciled to God and has a ministry of taking the message of reconciliation to others. No believer can escape this responsibility.

The responsibility of every believer is clearly set forth in I Corinthians 12, which we have examined concerning gifts. This chapter reveals that each believer has a responsibility in the Body of Christ. Paul said, "God set the members every one of them in the body, as it hath pleased him" (v. 18). Verses 27,28 tell how individual believers fit into the Body of Christ: "Now ye are the body of Christ, and members in particular. And God hath set some in the church, first apostles, secondarily prophets, thirdly teachers, after that miracles, then gifts of healings, helps, governments, diversities of tongues."

Notice that in this list is the gift of "helps," indicating that God has uniquely gifted some believers in assisting others. Also, "governments" indicates the gift of administration. Not everyone is gifted to be an evangelist, pastor or teacher. The entire Body of Christ has the same life and is bound together for service.

From Ephesians 4:11 we see that the responsibility of the gifted men God has given to the Church is to equip the saints to do the work of the ministry. From other Scriptures we have seen that every believer has a responsibility in the Body of Christ. Although there are some that are called to lead in special ways, all believers are to have a ministry to others. What a shame it is that there are some believers who do not see that they share the responsibility of ministering to others; rather, they are still depending on others to minister to them. Such a tragic situation is seen in the Book of Hebrews, where believers were told, "For when for the time ye ought to be teachers, ye have need that one teach you again which be the first principles of the oracles of God; and are become such as have need of milk, and not of strong meat. For every one that useth milk is unskilful in the word of righteousness: for he is a babe. But strong meat belongeth to them that are of full age, even those who by reason of use have their senses exercised to discern both good and evil" (5:12-14). Chapter 6 continues the same subject when it says, "Therefore leaving the principles of the doctrine of Christ, let us go on unto perfection [maturity]; not laying again the foundation of repentance from dead works, and of faith toward God" (v. 1). Each believer should desire to become more mature so he can better minister to the needs of others.

Building Up the Body

From Ephesians 4:12, we also see that the gifted men are to equip the saints "for the edifying of the body of Christ." To "edify" is to "build up." The Body of Christ itself is built up as individuals trust Christ as Saviour and become part of the Body. Also, those in the Body are built up in various ways. First, believers are to be filled with the Spirit, as Paul mentioned later in his letter to the Ephesians (5:18). Second, the Body of Christ is built up by individual believers' exercising their gifts. Paul told believers, "But unto every one of us is given grace according to the measure of the gift of Christ" (4:7). Also, Paul said, "Having then gifts differing according to the grace that is given to us, whether prophecy, let us prophesy according to the proportion of faith; or ministry, let us wait on our ministering: or he that teacheth, on teaching; or he that exhorteth, on exhortation: he that giveth, let him do it with simplicity; he that ruleth, with diligence; he that showeth mercy, with cheerfulness" (Rom. 12:6-8).

The Length of Ministry

From Ephesians 4:13 we learn how long the ministry mentioned in verse 12 is to continue: "Till we all come in the unity of the faith, and of the knowledge of the Son of God, unto a perfect man, unto the measure of the stature of the fulness of Christ." Notice the four things mentioned in this verse.

First, the ministry of equipping the saints to do the work of the ministry and of edifying the Body of Christ is to continue "till we all come in the unity of the faith." With the word "we" Paul included himself with other believers. No believer is excluded from this responsibility of expressing unity which is in keeping with the positional unity we have in Christ.

Second, the ministry is to continue until we come in the unity "of the knowledge of the Son of God." The word translated "knowledge" means "full knowledge." Paul was not referring to the time of salvation, when a person comes to "know" Christ by placing his faith in Him as Saviour; rather, Paul was referring to the Church's getting to know Christ better until it comes to a full knowledge of Him. Just as in the marriage relationship, couples get to know each other better as they live together, so believers should be learning to know Christ better as the days and years go by.

Paul was constantly concerned that he might know Christ better. Paul said, "That I may know him, and the power of his resurrection, and the fellowship of his sufferings, being made conformable unto his death" (Phil. 3:10).

Third, Ephesians 4:13 indicates the ministry of gifted men must continue until we each come to be "a perfect man." The word translated "perfect" means "mature." The work of the ministry is for the maturing of the saints. The Amplified Bible says, "That [we might arrive] at really mature manhood—the completeness of personality." As we have seen from Hebrews 5:12-14, one becomes mature by knowing the Word of God and applying it to daily living.

Fourth, the ministry is to continue until we all come to "the measure of the stature of the fulness of Christ." The Amplified Bible renders this phrase "the measure of the stature of the fullness of the Christ, and the completeness which is found only in Him."

This fourfold description of what we are to be becoming in Christ is emphasized in other Scriptures. First John 3:2,3 says, "Beloved, now are we the sons of God, and it doth not yet appear what we shall be: but we know that, when he shall appear, we shall be like him; for we shall see him as he is. And every man that hath this hope in him purifieth himself, even as he is pure." Ephesians 1:5 says that God has "predestinated us unto the adoption of children by Jesus Christ." As we saw from our study of this verse, the "adoption" refers to our position in Christ with all the privileges and responsibilities as mature sons.

What God is wanting to accomplish in our lives at the present time is seen from Romans 8:29. The preceding well-known verse says "that all things work together for good to them that love God, to them who are the called according to his purpose." Verse 29 reveals what the Father wants to accomplish by working all things together for good: "For whom he did foreknow, he also did predestinate to be conformed to the image of his Son." The Father is using everything that comes into our lives to make us more like His Son, Jesus Christ.

In his desire to know Christ better in order to be more like Him, Paul never considered himself to have reached the ultimate. He said, "Not that I have already obtained it, or have already become perfect, but I press on in order that I may lay hold of that for which also I was laid hold of by Christ Jesus. Brethren, I do not regard myself as having laid hold of it yet; but one thing I do: forgetting what lies behind and reaching forward to what lies ahead, I press on toward the goal for the prize of the upward call of God in Christ Jesus." (Phil. 3:12-14, NASB). No wonder Paul prayed for believers "to know the love of Christ, which passeth knowledge, that ye might be filled with all the fulness of God" (Eph. 3:19).

Importance of Spiritual Growth

Paul was very concerned about the growth of believers into what they ought to be in Christ. Ephesians 4:14,15 reveals the extreme importance—even necessity—of spiritual growth. Verse 14 states the importance negatively and verse 15 states it positively.

Paul said, "That we henceforth be no more children, tossed to and fro, and carried about with every wind of doctrine, by the sleight of men, and cunning craftiness, whereby they lie in wait to deceive." (v. 14). The Amplified Bible renders this verse, "So then, we may no longer be children, tossed [like ships] to and fro between chance gusts of teaching, and wavering with every changing wind of doctrine, [the prey of] the cunning and cleverness of unscrupulous men, (gamblers engaged) in every shifting form of trickery in inventing errors to mislead."

Our attention must be focused on Christ and His Word if we are going to keep from being tossed about like ships on violent waves of the sea. It is not enough just to know what someone else teaches; we need to study the Bible personally and apply it to the circumstances we face in daily living. There needs to be a continual searching of the Scriptures so that our faith stands on the Word of God instead of the word of men.

Ephesians 4:14 reveals there are different winds of doctrine; that is, false teachings. We must be careful that we don't spend all of our energies bracing ourselves against one false teaching, only to be overtaken from a different direction by another false teaching.

Because man's old nature is so corrupt, some will even use religious issues to mislead others. Believers must be on their guard so they are not taken in "by the sleight of men, and cunning craftiness." Everyone who claims to speak for God is not necessarily doing so; thus, we are again brought back to the Scriptures to analyze a person's work, or activity, in the light of the Scriptures.

Satan is the master of deception. In the Garden of Eden he appeared to Eve in the form of a serpent (Gen. 3) and was able to deceive her into eating the forbidden fruit.

Those who serve false gods are actually serving Satan, and they are being used by him to demonstrate his power and ability to deceive. The magicians of Egypt (Ex. 7, 8) were used by Satan to perform miracles to imitate the miracles performed by servants of the true God—Moses and Aaron. When Moses and Aaron went before Pharoah to plead for him to let the Israelites leave Egypt, he refused. This gave rise to a contest of miracles between Aaron and the Egyptian magicians. Aaron threw down his rod and "it became a serpent" (7:10). Pharoah then called his wise men and sorcerers and "they also did in like manner with their enchantments. For they cast down every man his rod, and they became serpents" (vv. 11,12).

This incident shows that not all miracles are from God. But even at that time, God's power was shown to be greater than Satan's. The Bible says that after the rods of Aaron and

the magicians of Egypt had become serpents, "Aaron's rod
swallowed up their rods" (v. 12).

Another time when Moses and Aaron were before
Pharoah, God told Aaron to strike the dust of the land so
that it would become lice throughout Egypt. Aaron did so
and the dust "became lice in man, and in beast; all the dust
of the land became lice throughout all the land of Egypt"
(8:17). The magicians tried "with their enchantments to
bring forth lice, but they could not" (v. 18). The servants of
Satan were not able to imitate this miracle of God through
Aaron. They were so astounded by Aaron's miracle that they
told Pharoah, "This is the finger of God" (v. 19).

During the coming Tribulation, Satan will deceive the
world through his miracle working and the persons whom he
energizes to do his will. The key figure of the Tribulation, the
Antichrist, is described as one "whose coming is after the
working of Satan with all power and signs and lying
wonders" (II Thess. 2:9). When Jesus was on earth, He told
of this time: "For there shall arise false Christs, and false
prophets, and shall shew great signs and wonders; insomuch
that, if it were possible, they shall deceive the very elect"
(Matt. 24:24).

Because miracles can be performed by both God and
Satan, believers are told, "Believe not every spirit, but try the
spirits whether they are of God: because many false prophets
are gone out into the world" (I John 4:1). This passage
continues by telling how to try the spirits: "Hereby know ye
the Spirit of God: Every spirit that confesseth that Jesus
Christ is come in the flesh is of God: and every spirit that
confesseth not that Jesus Christ is come in the flesh is not of
God" (vv. 2,3).

Notice that the test concerns the Person of Christ.
Included in this test is the teaching concerning His preexistence and incarnation. He existed before He was born
of a virgin to live on earth. In his gospel, John said, "In the
beginning was the Word, and the Word was with God, and the
Word was God. And the Word was made flesh, and dwelt
among us, (and we beheld his glory, the glory as of the only
begotten of the Father,) full of grace and truth" (1:1,14).
Those who deny that Jesus Christ is God and that He came in
the flesh are not of God.

It should also be remembered that His incarnation implies His Saviourhood, for He took upon Himself flesh that He might die for the sin of the world (I John 2:2). So the questions we should ask concerning a person or a group to determine if they are really representing God are: What do they believe about Christ's preexistence? about His incarnation? about His death for sin? about His resurrection?

It is easy for people to be swept up in a movement that emphasizes miracles yet does not hold scriptural views on the Person and work of Christ. People in such a movement are deluded by Satan, and instead of being of God they are "false prophets [who] are gone out into the world" (I John 4:1).

The teaching of Ephesians 4 is that gifted men have been given to the Church to keep people from being led into error. Having shown the necessity of spiritual growth from a negative standpoint in verse 14, Paul then showed the positive side: "But speaking the truth in love, may grow up into him in all things, which is the head, even Christ (v. 15). We are to speak "the truth in love." How sad it has been, and how devastating have been the results, when the truth has been spoken without love. Our lives should be characterized by love while we "grow up into him in all things." Here again we see the New Testament's emphasis on the importance of advancing in the knowledge of Christ and of growing in grace.

Concerning Christ, Paul said, "From whom the whole body fitly joined together and compacted by that which every joint supplieth, according to the effectual working in the measure of every part, maketh increase of the body unto the edifying of itself in love" (v. 16). In this verse, Paul likened the whole company of believers to a growing body in which every part is active in its effort to build up the whole to maturity. There ought not to be spiritual deterioration but rather "increase." The increase is attained only as believers fulfill their responsibilities to each other in the Body of Christ. The Amplified Bible renders this verse, "For because of Him the whole body (the church, in all its various parts closely) joined and firmly knit together by the joints and ligaments with which it is supplied, when each part (with power adapted to its need) is working properly (in all its functions), grows to full maturity, building itself up in love."

Chapter 16

The Conduct of the Believer as a New Man

(Eph. 4:17-32)

The appeal of Ephesians 4:1-16 is made to the Church united—all believers in Christ. The appeal of verses 17-32 is made to individual believers, for each to live according to his new position in Christ. The manifestation of Christ through his life should correspond to the inner regeneration of the Holy Spirit which he has experienced. The appeal, then, is based on the premise that individually we are to express outwardly what we are inwardly in Christ. Here again we see that what one does comes from what he is—the doing must come from the being.

How Not to Live

In this section Paul first tells believers how they are not to live: "This I say therefore, and testify in the Lord, that ye henceforth walk not as other Gentiles walk, in the vanity of their mind, having the understanding darkened, being alienated from the life of God through the ignorance that is in them, because of the blindness of their heart: who being past feeling have given themselves over unto lasciviousness, to work all uncleanness with greediness" (vv. 17-19).

The seriousness of Paul's appeal is seen in that he identifies himself with Christ: "This I say therefore, and testify in the Lord" (v. 17). Paul saw himself as an ambassador for Christ (II Cor. 5:20), and now he was pleading with the believers—in Christ's behalf—to live lives pleasing to Him. It grieves the Lord when we have Him as our life but do not allow Him to live in and through us as He desires.

The Scriptures call for a complete separation from the old, unregenerate life. Believers are exhorted, "Be ye not unequally yoked together with unbelievers: for what fellowship hath righteousness with unrighteousness? and what communion hath light with darkness? and what concord hath Christ with Belial? or what part hath he that believeth with an infidel? and what agreement hath the temple of God with idols? for ye are the temple of the living God; as God hath said, I will dwell in them, and walk in them; and I will be their God, and they shall be my people. Wherefore come out from among them, and be ye separate, saith the Lord, and touch not the unclean thing; and I will receive you" (II Cor. 6:14-17).

Paul was concerned that believers "henceforth walk not as other Gentiles walk" (Eph. 4:17). The word translated "henceforth" means "no more" or "no longer." It is a time word and emphasizes in this verse that certain action is to stop now, not sometime in the future.

The word "walk" refers to the way a person lives—what he does and where he goes. It is a good figure for the Christian life, because a person walks a step at a time. This is the way a Christian is to live for the Lord—one step at a time, in dependence on Him.

Paul was concerned that believers make a sharp turn in their walk and never again live as they did before they knew Christ as Saviour. Salvation is an immediate, complete change from spiritual death to spiritual life, and the believer is to evidence this change in the way he lives. Of course, there will be many changes in the individual that are not apparent to the casual observer, but there should be several outer evidences of the complete change that has taken place.

Paul appealed to believers not to walk as other Gentiles walk and then gave a description of man's old nature and the practices that stem from that nature. It's a description of what a person is like apart from Jesus Christ. Paul exhorted believers not to walk "in the vanity of their mind" (v. 17). This is a reference to the folly, emptiness and futility of the unregenerate person. In writing to the Corinthians, Paul said, "But the natural man receiveth not the things of the Spirit of God: for they are foolishness unto him: neither can he know them, because they are spiritually discerned" (I Cor. 2:14).

This verse reveals that without the regenerative work of God, a person is not able to comprehend spiritual truths.

Writing to the Romans, Paul referred to unbelievers when he said, "Because that, when they knew God, they glorified him not as God, neither were thankful; but became vain in their imaginations, and their foolish heart was darkened. Professing themselves to be wise, they became fools" (1:21,22).

In Ephesians 4:17 Paul was instructing believers to never again let their lives be characterized by what they were like before they came to Christ. Verse 18 further describes what they were like: "Having the understanding darkened, being alienated from the life of God through the ignorance that is in them, because of the blindness of their heart." Notice from this verse that unbelievers are without light and without life. By contrast, believers are the light of the world and have spiritual life from the Lord Jesus Christ. Furthermore, verse 19 indicates the unbeliever has no spiritual sensitivity: "Who being past feeling have given themselves over unto lasciviousness, to work all uncleanness with greediness." They are callous to the things of God. Paul referred to such people in I Timothy 4:2: "Speaking lies in hypocrisy; having their conscience seared with a hot iron." Thus we see that the unbeliever is morally degenerate, even though he may do many things that society approves.

How to Live

Having told in Ephesians 4:17-19 how not to live, Paul then gave instructions in verses 20-24 as to how the believer *is* to live.

Verses 20,21 reveal that Christ calls for a different kind of life for the believer. "But ye have not so learned Christ; if so be that ye have heard him, and have been taught by him, as the truth is in Jesus." Paul reminded believers that living like other Gentiles was not what they had learned from Christ. Christ's kind of life is mentioned in several Scriptures. Jesus Himself said, "I do nothing of myself; but as my Father hath taught me, I speak these things" (John 8:28). He said to the Father, "I have glorified thee on the earth: I have finished the work which thou gavest me to do" (17:4). These statements show what Christ meant when He said, "I came down from heaven, not to do mine own will, but the will of him that sent me" (6:38). This is the life of Christ—living to please the Father.

Having received Christ as Saviour, we have received His life. As we allow Him to have His way in our lives, the characteristics of His life will be seen in us. Paul emphasized that Christ lives within the believer when he said, "I am crucified with Christ: nevertheless I live; yet not I, but Christ liveth in me" (Gal. 2:20). So let us make Paul's words ours—that "Christ shall be magnified in my body, whether it be by life, or by death. For to me to live is Christ, and to die is gain" (Phil. 1:20,21).

The Amplified translates Ephesians 4:17: "So this I say and solemnly testify in [the name of] the Lord [as in His Presence], that you must no longer live as the heathen (the Gentiles) do in their perverseness—in the folly, vanity and emptiness of their souls and the futility—of their minds." Paul was emphasizing to the Ephesian believers that the teaching they had from Christ was that their lives would be drastically different after salvation from what it was like before salvation.

Those who receive Christ as Saviour are indwelt by the Holy Spirit and He continues to teach them about Christ. When Jesus told of the coming of the Holy Spirit, He said, "But the Comforter, which is the Holy Ghost, whom the Father will send in my name, he shall teach you all things, and bring all things to your remembrance, whatsoever I have said unto you" (John 14:26). Jesus also said, "I have yet many things to say unto you, but ye cannot bear them now. Howbeit when he, the Spirit of truth, is come, he will guide you into all truth: for he shall not speak of himself; but whatsoever he shall hear, that shall he speak: and he will shew you things to come" (16:12,13). Thus we see that all truth centers in the Person of Jesus Christ and His Word. He Himself said, "I am the way, the truth, and the life" (14:6).

Our Part in Sanctification

God's part in our sanctification is that He has placed us in Christ because of our faith in Christ as Saviour. The first three chapters of Ephesians tell of the position we have in Christ. Ephesians 4:22-24 reveals our part in sanctification. These verses state: "That ye put off concerning the former conversation the old man, which is corrupt according to the deceitful lusts; and be renewed in the spirit of your mind; and that ye put on the new man, which after God is created in righteousness and true holiness."

Verses 22-24 call on the believer to "put off" (v. 22), "be renewed" (v. 23) and "put on" (v. 24).

It is important to realize that Paul was reminding believers that their way of life, or practice, should be in line with their position. Paul was calling for present conformity to a position which had been accomplished in the past. Reference to their position was made in verses 20,21: "But ye have not so learned Christ; if so be that ye have heard him, and have been taught by him, as the truth is in Jesus."

Believers are told to "put off concerning the former conversation the old man, which is corrupt according to the deceitful lusts" (v. 22). Positionally, the old man was crucified when we received Christ. Romans 6 tells of this. Verse 3 says, "Know ye not, that so many of us as were baptized into Jesus Christ were baptized into his death?" Verse 6 says, "Knowing this, that our old man [was] crucified with him, that the body of sin might be [rendered powerless], that henceforth we should not serve sin." Verse 12 says, "Let not sin therefore reign in your mortal body that ye should obey it in the lusts thereof."

Since the power of the sin nature has been broken, we should make our practice conform to our position by no longer doing those things that characterized us before salvation. Ephesians 4:22-24 is the meeting point between what God has already accomplished on our behalf and what our part is in conforming to that which He has done. We are to put off the things of our unregenerate life just as we would take off clothes, and we are to put on the things of the regenerate life as we would put on clothes. It must be understood, of course, that the power which enables us to do this is the indwelling Holy Spirit. The unregenerate man does not have power to put off the characteristics of his life; it is only after receiving Christ as Saviour that he has the desire and the power to put off these things. The old man is that which we were because of Adam; the new man is that which we are because of Christ. The old man can do nothing that merits God's approval either in salvation or daily living; the new man always has God's approval because of the imputed righteousness of Christ.

Practicing Righteousness, Not Sin

Inasmuch as the new man is the nature which we have from Christ, it is impossible for this nature to sin. A passage of Scripture bearing on this subject is I John 3:6-10. Some have misunderstood the teaching of this passage because of the way it is translated in the King James Version. However, the Greek tenses clarify the meaning that is intended. Verse 6 says, "Whosoever abideth in [Christ] sinneth not: whosoever sinneth hath not seen him, neither known him." Both of the Greek words translated "sinneth" are in the Greek present tense, which emphasizes continuous action. So what is involved here is not a single act of sin but a practice of sin. The person who knows Christ as Saviour does not practice sin. On the other hand, the one practicing sin does not know Jesus Christ as Saviour.

Verse 7 says, "Little children, let no man deceive you: he that doeth righteousness is righteous, even as he is righteous." The word for "doeth" is in the Greek present tense. The one who practices righteousness must first be righteous; that is, only by knowing Christ as Saviour and inheriting a new nature is one enabled to live a righteous life. The Bible says, "For he hath made him to be sin for us, who knew no sin; that we might be made the righteousness of God in him" (II Cor. 5:21). Because we have been made righteous, we are able to practice righteousness.

First John 3:8 says, "He that committeth [practices] sin is of the devil; for the devil sinneth from the beginning. For this purpose the Son of God was manifested, that he might destroy the works of the devil."

Perhaps the verse in this passage that has brought the most confusion because of the way it is translated is verse 9: "Whosoever is born of God doth not commit sin; for his seed remaineth in him: and he cannot sin, because he is born of

God." The word "commit" in this verse refers to practicing sin, or habitually sinning. Also, the words "he cannot sin" mean "he cannot practice sin." Of course, the new nature a person receives at the time of salvation cannot sin at all because that nature is the righteousness of Christ. But the key emphasis of this verse is that the person who knows Christ as Saviour does not practice sin as a way of life.

The believer, however, will commit occasional acts of sin because he still has a sin nature. So believers are told, "My little children, these things write I unto you, that ye sin not. And if any man sin, we have an advocate with the Father, Jesus Christ the righteous" (2:1). Jesus Christ is at the right hand of the Father interceding for believers. The one who knows Christ as Saviour will not practice sin as a way of life. But when he commits an act of sin, Jesus Christ intercedes for him because Christ has paid the penalty for his sin. The believer's responsibility in this wonderful provision is to confess his sin (I John 1:9).

First John 3:10 says, "In this the children of God are manifest, and the children of the devil: whosoever doeth [practices] not righteousness is not of God, neither he that loveth not his brother." This passage reveals what takes place in a person's life when he receives Christ as Saviour. He is given a new nature that gives him the desire to please Christ rather than practice sin.

God always takes the initiative in our salvation and walk. Before He asks or expects us to act, he has already acted. This is seen from Romans 5:8: "But God commendeth his love toward us, in that, while we were yet sinners, Christ died for us." This is also the message of John 3:16. Inasmuch as God has acted in providing salvation, our responsibility is to receive Jesus Christ as personal Saviour and then live according to the position we have in Him.

Our need is to put our position into practice. By faith, we must count on the fact that we have died to sin and are now free to live lives pleasing to God. What God has made true for us positionally, He now longs to make real for us experientially. However, He can do this only as we cooperate with Him. We are not push-button robots; God will not override our wills and force us to do what is right. God first gives us everything essential to living the life and then gives us the desire and power to do so. Our lives should be an expression of Christ in us.

Unconditional Renunciation

In order to carry out the putting off of the old man, the renewing of the spirit of the mind, and the putting on of the new man (Eph. 4:22-24), there must be an unconditional renunciation of the sin that characterized a person's life before salvation. The believer now has new motivation to please Christ by doing those things fitting to his position in Christ.

This new motivation is seen from II Corinthians 5:17: "Therefore if any man be in Christ, he is a new creature [creation]: old things are passed away; behold, all things are become new." The context of this passage particularly refers to motivation: "For the love of Christ constraineth us" (v. 14). The believer has a new motivation because of his relationship with Christ, who lives within him and gives him the desire to live a righteous life.

The renunciation of the old life must be clear cut. Christ said, "If any man will come after me, let him deny himself, and take up his cross daily, and follow me" (Luke 9:23). The way the Apostle Paul put off his former manner of life is seen from Philippians 3:7: "But what things were gain to me, those I counted loss for Christ." Paul took a positive stand; he made a definite decision that determined his forward progress. Paul's desire was to please Jesus Christ in everything. This is evident from his words, "I press toward the mark for the prize of the high calling of God in Christ Jesus" (v. 14).

Paul also said that the believer should "be renewed in the spirit of [his] mind" (Eph. 4:23). This is comparable to Paul's statement in Romans 12:2: "And be not conformed to this world: but be ye transformed by the renewing of your mind, that ye may prove what is that good, and acceptable, and perfect, will of God." Before salvation, a person's mind thinks according to the world system. After salvation, a person has "the mind of Christ" (I Cor. 2:16), which enables him to discern spiritual truths. The believer's mind is renewed as he thinks upon the Word of God and in this way thinks God's thoughts.

Not only are believers to put off the corruptness characterizing their former life, and to renew their minds, but they are also to "put on the new man, which after God is created in righteousness and true holiness" (Eph. 4:24). It must be understood that a person does not become right with God by putting on certain things; rather, it is because he has salvation that he is to do certain things that reveal his position in Christ. The "new man" to which Paul referred is not obtained by a process but by receiving Christ as Saviour. The new man is what a person is because of his new spiritual nature.

In Ephesians 4:24 the words "is created" should read "has been created." It is because the person is already a new creation in Christ that he is urged to live accordingly. Hebrews 12 reveals that sometimes it is necessary for God to chasten us so that we will see the need of living according to our position. Every believer is told, "My son, despise not thou the chastening of the Lord, nor faint when thou art rebuked of him: for whom the Lord loveth he chasteneth, and scourgeth every son whom he receiveth" (vv. 5,6). God wants our lives to reveal the holiness unto which we were created. Therefore, He chastens us "for our profit, that we might be partakers of his holiness" (v. 10).

The Ephesians, the same as anyone else, did not become new creations of God by self-reformation or by imitating Christ but by placing their faith in Christ alone as their Saviour. This Paul indicated when he wrote: "And you hath he quickened [made alive], who were dead in trespasses and sins. For by grace are ye saved through faith; and that not of yourselves: it is the gift of God: not of works, lest any man should boast" (Eph. 2:1,8,9).

Ephesians 4:24 says that the new man has been "created in righteousness and true holiness." Romans 10:10 says, "For with the heart man believeth unto righteousness." This is referring to the righteousness God places on the account of all those who receive Jesus Christ as Saviour. First Corinthians 1:30 says, "But of him are ye in Christ Jesus, who of God is made unto us wisdom, and righteousness." This is what we are in Christ. He who created us in righteousness and gave us a perfect position wants us to glorify Him in our daily walk. Therefore, by an act of faith we must claim our position in Christ. We must take a definite stand once and for all, but we also must renew our stand daily as we live for Him. When we examine the armor of the believer mentioned in Ephesians 6, we will see the importance of using the shield of faith and the sword of the Spirit, praying constantly. In a practical sense, this shows the importance of the daily devotional life—regularly getting into the Word of God and talking to Him in prayer. Colossians 3:1,2 reminds us, "If ye then be risen with Christ, seek those things which are above, where Christ sitteth on the right hand of God. Set your affection on things above, not on things on the earth."

Note the progression in the Book of Ephesians. First we are told that Christ has "chosen us in him before the foundation of the world, that we should be holy and without blame before him in love" (1:4). Then we are told that our new man, or new self, has been "created in righteousness and true holiness" (4:24). Then we are told that Christ desires to present the Church to Himself, "not having spot, or wrinkle, or any such thing; but that it should be holy and without blemish" (5:27). This progression of thought reveals how God continues to work in believers to make their practice more like their position in Christ.

Chapter 17

Characteristics of the New Man

(Eph. 4:25-32)

Having told believers to put off the characteristics of their former life and to put on characteristics that are becoming to their position of righteousness and holiness, Paul listed several specifics in Ephesians 4:25-32. In this way, he left no doubt concerning the things to which he referred. His list provides a portrait of what the new man in Christ should be like.

The first word of verse 25, "Wherefore," relates this section to what Paul had just written. It shows the specific steps a believer should take to make his conduct correspond with his position in Christ. This is not an exhaustive list, but it details many of the most basic areas where believers face problems.

"Wherefore putting away lying, speak every man truth with his neighbour: for we are members one of another" (v. 25). The Greek word translated "putting away" is an aorist participle better translated "having put off." Although lying would have been a characteristic of the person without salvation, Paul urges the believer to put off lying once and for all and, having put it off, to practice telling the truth. Paul's reason for this is "For we are members one of another." We have seen previously in Ephesians that believers are to edify and help mature each other. A lie never edifies another member of the Body, and certainly it does not help mature another member.

Lying has many variations. Deception is a lie, even though perhaps no word is spoken. Hypocrisy—the false assumption of an appearance of virtue—is a lie. Misrepresentation is also a lie, even though many truths may

186

be involved. False pretentions and professions have absolutely no place in the believer's life because he serves Christ, who is "truth" (John 14:6). All of these things were put off positionally when we received Christ as Saviour; now we need to put off these things in practice.

Lying, in all of its forms, originates with Satan. Jesus told a group of people, "Ye are of your father the devil, and the lusts of your father ye will do. He was a murderer from the beginning, and abode not in the truth, because there is no truth in him. When he speaketh a lie, he speaketh of his own: for he is a liar, and the father of it" (John 8:44).

No form of lying has any place in the believer's life. Notice that the Scriptures make no allowances for situation ethics, which says that sometimes lying is not wrong because of the results it achieves. According to God's Word, lying is always wrong and the believer should refuse to lie in any way.

Be Angry, But Don't Sin

Paul also urged believers, "Be ye angry, and sin not: let not the sun go down upon your wrath" (Eph. 4:26). What does this verse mean? Is it possible to be angry and not sin? From this verse we must conclude that this is a possibility. The Amplified Bible renders this verse, "When angry, do not sin; do not ever let your wrath—your exasperation, your fury or indignation—last until the sun goes down."

So we see the wording of this verse indicates that sometimes anger is not sin. When Jesus Christ was on earth, He was sometimes angry with others. One time when He was about to heal the withered hand of a man, He was being watched by those who wanted to accuse Him for healing on the Sabbath. The Bible says, "And when he had looked round about on them with anger, being grieved for the hardness of their hearts, he saith unto the man, Stretch forth thine hand. And he stretched it out: and his hand was restored whole as the other" (Mark 3:5). Yet the Scriptures say of Christ, "In him is no sin" (I John 3:5). Therefore, this incident of anger was not sin.

Verse 31 of Ephesians 4 says concerning wrath and anger, "Let all bitterness, and wrath, and anger, and clamour, and evil speaking, be put away from you, with all malice." In the light of this verse it is reasonable to ask when anger is a sin and when it is not a sin.

From the Scriptures it is apparent that we should be angry with sin and come to hate that which would separate us from God or cause loss of fellowship. This means there will be times when we will hate what others do because it goes contrary to the Word of God. Such anger may be referred to as "righteous indignation." However, when self becomes projected into the matter it is possible for a believer to sin, at least in his attitude, toward others. In verse 26 Paul was warning against permitting smoldering fires of resentment to remain in anyone's heart: "Let not the sun go down upon your wrath." We should make it our practice never to retire without first being sure that we have confessed known sin of actions and attitudes "for the wrath of man worketh not the righteousness of God" (James 1:20).

Jesus was angry with those who withstood God. He called the Pharisees and Sadducees a "generation of vipers" (Matt. 3:7). The scribes and Pharisees He called "hypocrites" (23:14). On another occasion He made a whip of small ropes and drove the money changers from the temple (John 2:13-16).

Although the Lord Jesus Christ was able to be angry without sinning, it is difficult for us. That is why Paul gave the command as he did in Ephesians 4:26. Our anger should be stirred when God's name is taken in vain or when He is blasphemed, but we must be careful that we do not sin in the way we react to these incidents. If we speak unkind words or are embittered toward others, we have sinned and it needs to be confessed to the Lord.

We need to confess the moment we sin, but especially we must make sure that if our anger has caused us to sin, we have confessed it before going to sleep. God has promised to forgive when we confess our sins to Him: "If we confess our sins, he is faithful and just to forgive us our sins, and to cleanse us from all unrighteousness" (I John 1:9).

Paul's words "and sin not" (Eph. 4:26) serve as a reminder that we must be very careful how we relate to those who do not please God by what they say and do. We must make sure that we do not become filled with bitterness and resentment, for these are sin and break our fellowship with God.

Give Satan No Opportunity

Verse 27 says, "Neither give place to the devil." This means we should never give the Devil an opportunity or occasion to act against us. Not confessing one's sin at least by nightfall gives the Devil such an opportunity. The reason for this is that if we do not confess it by the end of one day, we are more likely to put it off in succeeding days and our hearts will become hardened to that sin. This gives the Devil the opportunity he needs to use this sin against us and to make it harder for us to confess it and return to fellowship with God.

Believers are reminded to be careful "lest Satan should get an advantage of us: for we are not ignorant of his devices" (II Cor. 2:11). If we give him opportunity, Satan will make us less concerned about maintaining fellowship with God.

Paul told the Corinthians, "But I fear, lest by any means, as the serpent beguiled Eve through his subtilty, so your minds should be corrupted from the simplicity that is in Christ. And no marvel; for Satan himself is transformed into an angel of light" (11:3,14). So all believers need to heed Paul's admonition, "Put on the whole armour of God, that ye may be able to stand against the wiles of the devil" (Eph. 6:11). Each of us needs to check his heart to make sure that what began as holy indignation has not turned into personal resentment. If it has, it needs to be confessed to the Lord. And if what we have said or the way we have said it has been wrong, we need to go to the person to whom we said it and apologize.

Don't Steal

Paul next commanded, "Let him that stole steal no more: but rather let him labour, working with his hands the thing which is good, that he may have to give to him that needeth" (Eph. 4:28).

Just as there are various forms of lying, so also there are various forms of stealing. One of the prominent forms mentioned in the Scriptures is stealing from God: "Will a man rob God? Yet ye have robbed me" (Mal. 3:8). The context of this passage reveals the people had robbed God in not bringing their tithes to Him. But, someone asks, was not this written to those under the Law? Yes, but we who are under grace should not do less than those who were under Law. The Law required that a person do certain things, but under grace the believer has Christ in him to motivate him and to make effective what is done. Philippians 2:13 tells us, "For it is God which worketh in you both to will and to do of his good pleasure."

As well as having obligations to God, the believer has an obligation to others. Paul viewed himself as a debtor to others, with a responsibility to take the gospel to them (Rom. 1:14). This includes not only going personally to share the gospel with others, but also giving of one's means so that others are able to go with the gospel. Romans 13:8 reveals that our responsibility is to "owe no man any thing, but to love one another." Let us be sure that we are paying this debt of love to others as well as paying our debts for what we have purchased.

It is well for us to remember that God has set us apart for a particular purpose. After salvation, we are to be ambassadors for the Lord Jesus Christ (II Cor. 5:18-20); this is one of the chief purposes that God has for believers on earth. He has appointed us to go with the gospel: "Ye have not chosen me, but I have chosen you, and ordained you, that ye should go and bring forth fruit" (John 15:16). Inasmuch as God has made us responsible to proclaim the gospel, it is important that we be faithful in this regard.

Our values are put into proper perspective when we recognize that we have been redeemed by Jesus Christ and really owe everything to Him. Believers are told, "What? know ye not that your body is the temple of the Holy Ghost which is in you, which ye have of God, and ye are not your own? For ye are bought with a price: therefore glorify God in your body, and in your spirit, which are God's" (I Cor. 6:19,20). We were bought with the price of the shed blood of the Lord Jesus Christ. Having received Him as Saviour, our concern should be to please Him, not ourselves. As we have seen from Ephesians 2:10, we are saved to do good works:

"For we are his workmanship, created in Christ Jesus unto good works, which God hath before ordained that we should walk in them." God has even given us enabling grace so that we might serve Him: "Unto every one of us is given grace according to the measure of the gift of Christ" (4:7). Therefore, it is exceedingly important that we consider the various aspects of our relationship with God and be sure that we are not stealing from Him.

In our relationships with others, we need to be sure that we do not steal from them. We need to be honest in business transactions and be faithful in giving service for which we are paid. If we are paid for a full day's work, we steal from our employer if we do not give him a full day's work. Even such a relatively small matter as taking too long on coffee break is a way of stealing from one's employer. The Bible says, "Provide things honest in the sight of all men" (Rom. 12:17). Each believer needs to examine himself to be sure that he is not stealing from God or others. The Bible says, "Wherefore we labour, that, whether present or absent, we may be accepted of him. For we must all appear before the judgment seat of Christ; that every one may receive the things done in his body, according to that he hath done, whether it be good or bad" (II Cor. 5:9,10). We cannot expect to be rewarded by the Lord if we have stolen time and money that should have been spent for Him.

In contrast to stealing, Paul said, "But rather let him labour, working with his hands the thing which is good, that he may have to give to him that needeth" (Eph. 4:28). Notice that there is a purpose for the work, and that purpose is that the believer might be able to help others. The Christian is one who should genuinely care about others; and the more he cares, the more he wants to give to help them in their need.

Speak 'No Corrupt Communication'

Paul continued with his list that portrayed what the new man in Christ should be like when he said, "Let no corrupt communication proceed out of your mouth, but that which is good to the use of edifying, that it may minister grace unto the hearers" (v. 29). Our conversation should be pleasing to

God and beneficial to others. Of course, speech reveals what
is in the heart. Paul is talking here about the new man, whose
speech should reveal the righteousness in his heart. Inasmuch
as the believer also has a sin nature, he has to choose whether
his speech will be characterized by sin or by holiness.

Previously in the chapter, Paul said, "Walk not as other
Gentiles walk, in the vanity of their mind" (v. 17). Paul also
said concerning conversation, "There must be no indecency,
silly talk or suggestive jesting, for they are unbecoming.
There should be thanksgiving instead" (5:4, Williams). So the
Christian is forbidden to tell shady stories or tell jokes with
sensual meanings.

James had much to say about speech: "For in many
things we offend all. If any man offend not in word, the same
is a perfect [mature] man, and able also to bridle the whole
body. Behold . . . the ships, which though they be so great,
and are driven of fierce winds, yet are they turned about with
a very small helm, whithersoever the governor listeth. Even so
the tongue is a little member, and boasteth great things.
Behold, how great a matter a little fire kindleth! And the
tongue is a fire, a world of iniquity: so is the tongue among
our members, that it defileth the whole body, and setteth on
fire the course of nature; and it is set on fire of hell"
(3:2,4-6).

In speaking of the difficulty of controlling the tongue,
James said, "But the tongue can no man tame; it is an unruly
evil, full of deadly poison. Therewith bless we God, even the
Father; and therewith curse we men, which are made after
the similitude of God. Out of the same mouth proceedeth
blessing and cursing. My brethren, these things ought not so
to be" (vv. 8-10).

The Bible says we are to present our "members as
instruments of righteousness unto God" (Rom. 6:13). Rather
than presenting our tongues to sin, we Christians should
present our tongues to the Lord, to use them in honoring
Him. This doesn't mean that we always have to be saying
something about God, but it does mean that whatever we say
should be pleasing to Him. One of the key purposes of the
conversation of believers is that of "edifying" others (Eph.
4:29). This calls for conversation that is constructive. We
must not let our tongues be mouthpieces for the old nature

but for the new nature. The characteristics of the old man are to be put off (v. 22), and the characteristics of the new man are to be put on (v. 24). Certainly, there is no place for malicious gossip in the rightful use of the Christian's tongue.

Don't Grieve the Spirit

Concerning the Holy Spirit, Paul told believers, "And grieve not the holy Spirit of God, whereby ye are sealed unto the day of redemption" (v. 30). Notice, however, that even if the believer grieves the Spirit, the Spirit does not leave him, because the believer is sealed with the Spirit "unto the day of redemption." During Old Testament times the Holy Spirit did not indwell all believers; rather, He came upon some for special service and left them after the service was accomplished. David's prayer, "Take not thy holy Spirit from me" (Ps. 51:11), reveals he was afraid God would remove the Spirit from him, which would mean an end to his being especially used by God.

The New Testament teaching concerning the Holy Spirit is altogether different. A believer receives the Holy Spirit at the time of salvation, for believers are "sealed with that holy Spirit of promise, which is the earnest of our inheritance until the redemption of the purchased possession, unto the praise of his glory" (Eph. 1:13,14). The Holy Spirit was given on the Day of Pentecost, and in referring to this future event, the Lord Jesus said, "I will pray the Father, and he shall give you another Comforter, that he may abide with you for ever; even the Spirit of truth; whom the world cannot receive, because it seeth him not, neither knoweth him: but ye know him; for he dwelleth with you, and shall be in you" (John 14:16,17).

The time of "the redemption of the purchased possession" (Eph. 1:14) is the same as "the day of redemption" (4:30). First Thessalonians 4:16,17 refers to the day of redemption: "For the Lord himself shall descend from heaven with a shout, with the voice of the archangel, and with the trump of God: and the dead in Christ shall rise first: then we which are alive and remain shall be caught up together with them in the clouds, to meet the Lord in the air: and so shall we ever be with the Lord."

Although the Spirit's indwelling is not affected when a believer grieves the Spirit, the filling (controlling) of the Spirit is affected. Ephesians 5:18 commands believers, "Be not drunk with wine, wherein is excess; but be filled with the Spirit." This filling of the Spirit characterizes every believer who has confessed his known sin. When sin enters the believer's life, the control of the Spirit is broken. The believer can return to this control only by confessing his sin.

In addition to Ephesians 4:30 telling us not to "grieve . . . the holy Spirit," I Thessalonians 5:19 tells us not to "quench . . . the Spirit." Grieving the Spirit and quenching the Spirit are closely related. When the Spirit is exercising His ministry in our lives, such as guiding us, and we refuse to heed His guidance, this is quenching, or suppressing, Him, which grieves Him. The Holy Spirit indwells us to produce the Christ-life in us. Concerning the coming of the Holy Spirit, Jesus said, "He shall glorify me: for he shall receive of mine, and shall shew it unto you. All things that the Father hath are mine: therefore said I, that he shall take of mine, and shall shew it unto you" (John 16:14,15). When we refuse to have our lives molded more into the image of Christ, we quench the Spirit and grieve Him because this is what He is endeavoring to do in our lives.

We also grieve the Holy Spirit by unbelief—not trusting Him to perform His work of convicting, teaching and guiding. We grieve Him by trying to live the Christian life in our own strength rather than depending on Him, which is walking in the Spirit (Gal. 5:16). We need to yield ourselves to Him by being sensitive to His work and doing as He prompts us to do. It is He who activates and motivates our wills so that we want to please Jesus Christ in all we do. Let us not quench and grieve Him in this vital ministry.

The Believer's Responsibilities

Verses 31, 32 of Ephesians 4 are similar to verses 22, 24 of the same chapter in that Paul stated negative aspects in one verse and positive aspects in another. In verse 31 Paul instructed believers, "Let all bitterness, and wrath, and anger, and clamour, and evil speaking, be put away from you, with all malice."

The first thing mentioned that needs to be put away is "bitterness." What a shame it is that we Christians can so easily become guilty of bitterness. This is the product of hurt feelings that turn into resentment. Bitterness can be found in the home, the church and the business; but wherever it is, it is to "be put away." We do this by confessing our sin to the Lord and then depending on Him to grant us victory in the particular problem in the future. Regardless of the mental and spiritual agony we experience, and no matter how justified we think we are in feeling as we do, we must make sure we are in fellowship with the Lord and have attitudes that please Him. We must forgive others even as Christ has forgiven us.

"Wrath, and anger" are also to be put away. This was discussed in connection with verse 26. Paul also mentioned "clamour," which means "crying out, shouting" and is translated by some as "loud threats" and "yelling." This is typical of those who do not get their own way and is certainly typical of the world in general. But the believer is not to be like the world.

Next, Paul listed "evil speaking." This refers to slanderous talk. The Christian should have no part in destroying another person's character. When the temptation comes to say something that would be slanderous to another, it is to be "put away." Here again it is a matter of saying No to sin and Yes to what pleases Christ. The clue to how this is done is seen from the first word of this verse "let." It is accomplished by the power of the indwelling Holy Spirit. By an act of the will, the believer is to say No to that which is wrong and then rely on the Holy Spirit for the power to overcome the temptation. The word translated "let" actually means "to carry off" or "to take away" and this is what the Holy Spirit will do as we rely on Him. James 4:6,7 tells us, "But he giveth more grace. Wherefore he saith, God resisteth the proud, but giveth grace unto the humble. Submit yourselves therefore to God. Resist the devil, and he will flee from you." We need to confess to the Lord that we cannot handle a particular situation on our own and then count on Him to give us the strength to overcome.

Notice that "all" of each of those things Paul mentioned in Ephesians 4:31 is to be put away—there is to be a thorough, spiritual housecleaning. The Holy Spirit gives no ground to evil, and the believer is to say No to all sin.

But notice that Paul did not stop with the negative aspects; he also gave positive things for the believer to do. The believer must replace the bad with good. "And be ye kind one to another, tenderhearted, forgiving one another, even as God for Christ's sake hath forgiven you" (v. 32). It is not enough to meet the negative requirements; one must also meet the positive requirements. We see this from I John 3:14,15: "We know that we have passed from death unto life, because we love the brethren. He that loveth not his brother abideth in death. Whosoever hateth his brother is a murderer: and ye know that no murderer hath eternal life abiding in him." We may not hate someone, but do we really love them? To avoid being hateful, we must be full of love. First John 4:10,11 tells us, "Herein is love, not that we loved God, but that he loved us, and sent his Son to be the propitiation for our sins. Beloved, if God so loved us, we ought also to love one another."

The first positive action spoken of in Ephesians 4:32 is to be "kind one to another." Being kind is more than merely doing good deeds; it results from being in right relationship with Jesus Christ. Kindness should be evidenced to others in every aspect of life. To be "tenderhearted" is to be compassionate. Christ is our greatest example of showing compassion, and we need to study His life, remembering that He indwells us to live that same kind of life in and through us.

We are also to be "forgiving." Notice the extent to which we should forgive one another: "Even as God for Christ's sake hath forgiven you." "If God so loved us, we ought also to love one another" (I John 4:11). The measure of Christ's work in our behalf is used because this same Christ now lives in us, to live His life through us.

Chapter 18

The Believer and the World

(Eph. 5:1-14)

Ephesians 4 is directed mostly to the believer in his relationships with God and with fellow believers. Now we turn our attention to Ephesians 5, which tells what kind of relationship the believer should have to the world. This chapter continues to paint a portrait of what the believer's walk should be like.

Follow God

Verse 1 says, "Be ye therefore followers of God, as dear children." The word "therefore" connects this verse with the last verse of the preceding chapter: "Be ye kind one to another, tenderhearted, forgiving one another, even as God for Christ's sake hath forgiven you" (4:32). In the light of this, believers are to be "followers of God, as dear children" (5:1). Here the word "followers" means "imitators." Unbelievers are sometimes told to follow Christ as an example, but such instruction is fruitless because they cannot follow Him as an example unless they know Him as Saviour. It is only His life within an individual that enables that individual to live a life pleasing to God. Notice that even here the statement is qualified: "as dear children." Paul was telling believers, not unbelievers, to be imitators of God.

Paul also said, "And walk in love, as Christ also hath loved us, and hath given himself for us an offering and a sacrifice to God for a sweetsmelling savour" (5:2). Here again, Christ is our example in the matter of love. God is the standard as to how His children should love. First John 4:16 says, "God is love; and he that dwelleth in love dwelleth in

197

God, and God in him." Christ said, "As the Father hath loved me, so have I loved you: continue ye in my love. This is my commandment, That ye love one another, as I have loved you" (John 15:9,12). God is love, and His every thought, word and act expresses love.

Does the standard of God's love seem too high to attain? Not if you remember what the first three chapters of Ephesians tells us we have in Christ. Have you prayed for the eyes of your understanding to be enlightened, as Paul did in his first prayer (1:18)? Have you prayed that these truths might become a reality in your life, as Paul did in his second prayer (3:19)?

Having received Jesus Christ as Saviour, we have been born of the Holy Spirit and have become members of God's family. We have become partakers in, or sharers of, the divine nature (II Pet. 1:4), and the essence of the divine nature is love. It is the kind of love that loves even when there is no response, always seeking the highest good for the other person. That God loved us when there was no response is evident from Romans 5:8: "But God commendeth his love toward us, in that, while we were yet sinners, Christ died for us." But it can be said that because of our having received Jesus Christ as Saviour, "the love of God is [now] shed abroad in our hearts by the Holy Ghost which is given unto us" (v. 5). Since it is His love that is in our hearts, we are able to attain God's standard of love by letting Christ live His life in us as He desires. The expression of this love in us is one of the strongest proofs that we really are the children of God (I John 4:7-16).

From incidences in Christ's earthly life, we see that His love was the kind that caused Him to give Himself to others. In the Garden of Gethsemane, when Judas and a garrison of soldiers came after Him, He willingly let Himself be taken captive (John 18:2-14). On the cross, He had words of concern for His mother—that she be taken care of by John, for one of the thieves being crucified with Him—that he would be in Paradise with the Lord, and for the executioners—that they might be forgiven. Even His death revealed His love for others, for Christ died for *us* (Rom. 5:8). It is this very same Person who lives in us and expresses

His life through us, as we accept by faith His indwelling us and then give ourselves to obey Him.

As we mature in the Christian life, becoming more like Christ by our obedience to Him, His characteristics will be more evident in our lives. Philippians 2:5 says, "Let this mind be in you, which was also in Christ Jesus." As we allow the Lord to work in us, we will become experientially what we are potentially.

When Paul urged believers to "walk in love" (Eph. 5:2), he was emphasizing that our life is lived one step at a time. As we rely on the Lord for the step we are now taking, we need not worry about the steps that are ahead. Of course, Paul was referring to a person's way of life. First John 3:18 says, "My little children, let us not love in word, neither in tongue; but in deed and in truth." It is easy to talk, but it is costly to walk.

We must be rightly related to Jesus Christ and live in a way pleasing to Him if we really want to be effective. There are things we may desire to do that may not be wrong in themselves, but we will have to refuse to do many of these things as we seek to accomplish what we believe Christ has set for the goal of our lives.

A life that pleases Christ includes surrendering to Him. It is a surrendering of our wills to Christ's will to do that which pleases Him. We are to "give up" serving ourselves and are to present ourselves to Christ to carry out His will.

Forsake Sin

Paul said, "But fornication, and all uncleanness, or covetousness, let it not be once named among you, as becometh saints" (v. 3). "Fornication" refers to sexual sins of all kinds and "uncleanness" refers to impurity. These characterize unbelievers, but believers are not to be guilty of them nor even to focus their talk on such matters. "Covetousness" refers to greediness. The person who does not know God is characterized by greediness because all he has is what this world can give him. But this is not true of the believer, and he is not speaking worthy of his position in Christ when his talk evidences greed. It is extremely difficult for the twentieth-century believer to be free of greed because of living in a world that is so materialistically minded. But this shows how important it is that we keep our minds focused on the Scriptures, which cause us to realize that eternal matters are more important than temporal matters. By the words "let it not be once named among you" Paul did not seem to be forbidding Christians to even discuss these problems; rather, he was forbidding them to talk about these things as interested parties.

The list continues: "Neither filthiness, nor foolish talking, nor jesting, which are not convenient: but rather giving of thanks" (v. 4). Here, Paul continues to deal with conversation. "Filthiness" refers to that which is base or shameful, no doubt referring to that which is obscene and immoral in conduct as well as conversation. Here again, it is extremely difficult for Christians to resist being carried away with the world in this regard. The values of the world system are becoming lower and lower, but for the one who desires to please Christ there is no place for obscene conduct or conversation.

"Foolish talking" refers to an artfully phrased manner of speaking so that the words have double meanings, especially immoral meanings. Some people cannot be witty without using suggestive phrases. Christians can spoil their testimonies with such shameful conversation.

"Jesting" has to do with witty speech as the instrument of sin. In this regard it is similar to "foolish talking." Jesting can be a joke at the expense of a person being talked to or about. God says this kind of speech is out for the believer. It is not "convenient"; that is, such things are not becoming to the believer's position in Christ. Instead, there should be the "giving of thanks." This is the fitting characteristic for the child of God.

The Bible says, "In every thing give thanks: for this is the will of God in Christ Jesus concerning you" (I Thess. 5:18). Some wonder what the will of God is for their lives, and they often overlook this specific directive to give thanks in everything. Our hearts should be full of praise to God, who has provided salvation and all that we need to live victoriously.

The sins mentioned in Ephesians 5:3,4 were common sins in Noah's day when "God saw that the wickedness of man was great in the earth, and that every imagination of the thoughts of his heart was only evil continually" (Gen. 6:5). The Bible says, "For the coming of the Son of Man will be just like the days of Noah. For as in those days which were before the flood they were eating and drinking, they were marrying and giving in marriage, until the day that Noah entered the ark, and they did not understand until the flood came and took them all away, so shall the coming of the Son of Man be" (Matt. 24:37-39, NASB).

People of Noah's day were living only for the pleasures of the time without any concern for God, and that seems to also be the characteristic of our day. This is especially evidenced in much of the current secular literature, which reflects the moral corruptness of our times.

In Ephesians 5:5 Paul declared the destiny of those who prefer sin to fellowship with God: "For this ye know, that no whoremonger, nor unclean person, nor covetous man, who is an idolator, hath any inheritance in the kingdom of Christ and of God." Paul was not saying that it is impossible for such people to be saved; rather, he was saying that those who habitually practice such things reveal they have not received Christ as Saviour. That such people can be saved if they will receive Christ as Saviour is evident from I Corinthians 6:11. Having given a list of those who cannot inherit the kingdom of God, Paul told the Corinthians, "And such were some of you: but ye are washed, but ye are sanctified, but ye are justified in the name of the Lord Jesus, and by the Spirit of our God."

Paul cautioned believers, "Let no man deceive you with vain words: for because of these things cometh the wrath of God upon the children of disobedience" (v. 6). While it is "man" who deceives, it is Satan who uses unregenerate people, and even carnal Christians, to deceive others. The word translated "vain" means "empty." People deceive others by using empty words that make groundless arguments and thereby justify sin.

It is prominent today to say that sin is really sickness. By changing the terminology people are being deceived into thinking that very little, if anything, is sin. But we must not forget that God's attitude toward sin has not changed. Although He is a God of love, He will someday pour out His

wrath against sin in this world and will separate from Him
eternally those who have not faced their sin and received
Christ as Saviour. This is why Paul said, "For because of
these things cometh the wrath of God upon the children of
disobedience" (Eph. 5:6). But until this time, mankind will
continue being deceived by Satan, whom Christ described as
"a liar, and the father of it" (John 8:44).

But as to the deeds of the children of disobedience, Paul
said, "Be not ye therefore partakers with them" (Eph. 5:7).
Those who know Christ as Saviour must take a definite stand
against the world system. As believers we have been
translated out of the dominion of darkness into the kingdom
of God's Son (Col. 1:13); therefore, we ought not to be
joined with those who do not know and love the Lord.

'Walk as Children of Light'

Thus, all of this leads up to verse 8, which I consider to
be the key verse of Ephesians 5:1-14: "For ye were
sometimes darkness, but now are ye light in the Lord: walk
as children of light."

Here we see two kingdoms in contrast, the kingdom of
light and the kingdom of darkness. Notice Paul says that
before salvation believers "were . . . darkness," not just living
in darkness. Upon salvation, however, the same people are
"light."

Subjects of Satan are subjects of darkness. John 3:19,20
says, "And this is the condemnation, that light is come into
the world, and men loved darkness rather than light, because
their deeds were evil. For every one that doeth evil hateth the
light, neither cometh to the light, lest his deeds should be
reproved."

Contrasting the kingdom of darkness and the kingdom of
light, Paul said, "Be ye not unequally yoked together with
unbelievers: for what fellowship hath righteousness with
unrighteousness? and what communion hath light with
darkness?" (II Cor. 6:14). First John 1:5-7 also tells of light
and darkness: "This then is the message which we have heard
of him, and declare unto you, that God is light, and in him is
no darkness at all. If we say that we have fellowship with
him, and walk in darkness, we lie, and do not the truth: but

if we walk in the light, as he is in the light, we have fellowship one with another, and the blood of Jesus Christ his Son cleanseth us from all sin."

Because we have been placed into the kingdom of light by receiving Christ as Saviour, we are to live in a way becoming to that position. We should not be living as if we were the children of darkness. From the characteristics Paul mentioned in Ephesians 5, we see that those who live in darkness have a conduct and a conversation that are morally corrupt. No wonder Paul warns the child of God, who is "light in the Lord," not to have any part in doing those things that characterize the children of darkness.

Ephesians 5:9 shows the characteristics that will be evident when believers walk in the light: "For the fruit of the Spirit is in all goodness and righteousness and truth." Evidence from Greek manuscripts indicate that the word "Spirit" should be "light." This also fits the context as it explains the results of walking in the light. Notice that these results are referred to as "fruit" in contrast to the "works" of darkness (v. 11). The light has positive moral fruit—goodness, righteousness and truth—in contrast to the products of darkness, which are all degrading and destructive.

Notice particularly the threefold fruit of the light. "Goodness" is an active and positive display of kindness toward others. It will encourage believers in the faith and will bring unbelievers under conviction of sin. God uses our lives to show unbelievers their lack and to draw them to Himself. God desires for "all men to be saved, and to come unto the knowledge of the truth" (I Tim. 2:4). This same truth is emphasized in II Peter 3:9, where we are told that the Lord is "not willing that any should perish, but that all should come to repentance."

This shows us that when we are faced with a decision concerning a particular matter, the question is not just whether it will harm us but whether it will help attract others to Christ or tend to repel them from Him. Concerning other believers we need to ask ourselves if various matters encourage them or discourage them in their walk with the Lord.

The Bible says, "Whatsoever ye do in word or deed, do all in the name of the Lord Jesus, giving thanks to God and the

Father by him. And whatsoever ye do, do it heartily, as to
the Lord, and not unto men" (Col. 3:17,23). Concerning
being a stumbling block to weaker Christians through the
eating of meat offered to idols, Paul said, "But meat
commendeth us not to God: for neither, if we eat, are we the
better; neither, if we eat not, are we the worse. But take heed
lest by any means this liberty of your's become a
stumblingblock to them that are weak" (I Cor. 8:8,9). Even
though it was technically all right to eat such meat, Paul said,
"If meat make my brother to offend, I will eat no flesh while
the world standeth, lest I make my brother to offend"
(v. 13). Paul wanted to encourage and strengthen other
believers rather than do anything that might hinder their
spiritual growth. He had strong words for those who might be
stumbling blocks to others: "But when ye sin so against the
brethren, and wound their weak conscience, ye sin against
Christ" (v. 12).

"Righteousness" is another aspect of the fruit of the light
(Eph. 5:9). Righteousness is a moral integrity that is
irreproachable. It is ultimate rightness. Christ is the righteousness of the believer because Christ is in the believer
to produce light through him. Of course, Christ cannot sin
because He is God, but the believer sins when he fails to put
Christ first in his life. When we fail we are to confess our sin
to God, who has promised to forgive when we confess
(I John 1:9).

Because the believer has the righteous life of Christ
within him, the believer is able to live righteously. We are
told to "prove all things; hold fast that which is good.
Abstain from all appearance [form] of evil" (I Thess.
5:21,22). It is important that we have a clear conscience
before God. Paul was able to say, "I have lived in all good
conscience before God until [up to] this day" (Acts 23:1).
He also said, "Herein do I exercise myself, to have always a
conscience void of offence toward God, and toward men"
(24:16).

The third aspect of the fruit of light is "truth" (Eph.
5:9). We are to be totally sincere with no pretense, no
compromise, and no secret alliances with evil. We are to crave
reality and should welcome the scrutiny of our Lord. Such
was the case with David, who prayed, "Search me, O God,

and know my heart: try me, and know my thoughts: and see
if there be any wicked way in me, and lead me in the way
everlasting" (Ps. 139:23,24). David realized that God could
look into his heart and see everything there. And David
wanted God to do so to be sure there was nothing there
displeasing to Him. We can walk in the light only as we have
this same attitude and then confess anything that God, who
is light, exposes to us as being displeasing to Him (see I John
1:5-7).

In Ephesians 5:10 Paul says that believers are to be
"proving what is acceptable unto the Lord." The word
translated "proving" has reference to testing for the purpose
of approving. One translator renders this, "You must approve
what is pleasing to the Lord" (Williams). Having determined
what is of God, we are to put ourselves at His disposal to
have it worked out in our lives. The Bible urges believers,
"Present your bodies a living sacrifice, holy, acceptable unto
God, which is your reasonable service. And be not conformed
to this world: but be ye transformed by the renewing of your
mind, that ye may prove what is that good, and acceptable,
and perfect, will of God" (Rom. 12:1,2). We should be
constantly approving that which is acceptable to God and
demonstrating it by our behavior.

We ought never to measure ourselves by others, for only
Christ is the true standard of righteousness. The question
ought never to be, Is everyone else doing it? Rather, we
should ask, Is it acceptable to the Lord? It is to the Lord that
we must someday give account, not to others (II Cor.
5:9,10).

Paul told believers, "And have no fellowship with the
unfruitful works of darkness, but rather reprove them" (Eph.
5:11). Again we see that there must be an abrupt turnabout
by the one who has received Christ as Saviour; he is to have
nothing to do with the sins that characterize the unregenerate.

First John 1:5-7 says, "This then is the message which we
have heard of him, and declare unto you, that God is light,
and in him is no darkness at all. If we say that we have
fellowship with him, and walk in darkness, we lie, and do not
the truth: but if we walk in the light, as he is in the light, we
have fellowship one with another, and the blood of Jesus

Christ his Son cleanseth us from all sin." Notice that walking in the light is the same as being in fellowship with God. Sin breaks fellowship with God, so believers are told, "If we confess our sins, he is faithful and just to forgive us our sins, and to cleanse us from all unrighteousness" (v. 9). The confession of sin restores fellowship with God, and the believer is again walking in the light.

Notice that in Ephesians 5:11 there are both negative and positive aspects. Negatively, the believer is to "have no fellowship with the unfruitful works of darkness." Positively, the believer is to "reprove them." So we see that it is not enough just to refrain from sin; we must also "reprove" it. The "works of darkness" must be exposed and expelled as light expels darkness. We must remember, however, that we are to manifest the fruit of the Spirit while exposing sin. Christians also have a responsibility toward other believers who sin. Once sin has occurred, we should be more concerned about recovery than condemnation, and we should do nothing that would be unchristlike in attitude or action toward those involved. Galatians 6:1 says, "Brothers, if anybody is caught in the very act of doing wrong, you who are spiritual, in the spirit of gentleness must set him right; each of you continuing to think of yourself, for you may be tempted too" (Williams).

As we expose sin, we see from II Timothy 4:2 that we are to do it by means of the Word of God: "Preach the word; be instant in season, out of season; reprove, rebuke, exhort with all longsuffering and doctrine." The basis of reproof must always be the Bible, which is the Word of God. Second Timothy 3:16 says, "All scripture is given by inspiration of God, and is profitable for doctrine, for reproof, for correction, for instruction in righteousness." Personal opinion is not sufficient when rebuking sin; God's Word must be the criterion for truth. In exposing the works of darkness, it is not necessary that we become moral detectives or spiritual spies. Rather, when sin is evident, we are to deal with it; when it is not, we do not need to go hunting for it. But especially we must not close our eyes to sin or remain silent when we see it. Open sin needs to be reproved openly, but nothing is gained by publicizing secret sin. In dealing with sin, however, our purpose should be to eliminate it, not publicize it.

Concerning the acts of unbelievers, Paul said, "For it is a shame even to speak of those things which are done of them in secret. But all things that are reproved are made manifest by the light: for whatsoever doth make manifest is light" (vv. 12,13). The works of darkness are revealed by light. John 3:19-21 says, "And this is the condemnation, that light is come into the world, and men loved darkness rather than light, because their deeds were evil. For every one that doeth evil hateth the light, neither cometh to the light, lest his deeds should be reproved. But he that doeth truth cometh to the light, that his deeds may be made manifest, that they are wrought in God."

Believers are "children of light" (v. 8), and they should live in a way that their words and actions cause others to look at themselves and become aware of their sin. Matthew 5:16 says, "Let your light so shine before men, that they may see your good works, and glorify your Father which is in heaven."

A godly life is a reproof to people who hold to selfishness and sin. When Paul was falsely criticized he said, "As for me, myself, it is of very little concern to me to be examined by you or any human court; in fact, I do not even examine myself. For although my conscience does not accuse me, yet I am not entirely vindicated by that. It is the Lord Himself who must examine me. So you must stop forming any premature judgments, but wait until the Lord shall come again, for He will bring to light the secrets hidden in the dark and will make known the motives of men's hearts, and the proper praise will be awarded each of us" (I Cor. 4:3-5, Williams). We are to deal with sin, not question the motives of others. Others may sometimes question our motives, and although we cannot always please others, we must make sure that our motives are right before the Lord.

Observe Stephen's response to those who criticized and eventually killed him. He was a man "full of faith and power" (Acts 6:8). His countenance brought conviction to his enemies, for they "saw his face as it had been the face of an angel" (v. 15). He boldly described the condition of his antagonists: "Ye stiffnecked and uncircumcised in heart and ears, ye do always resist the Holy Ghost: as your fathers did, so do ye" (7:51). The Bible says, "Now when they heard this, they were cut to the quick, and they began gnashing their teeth at him. But being full of the Holy Spirit, he gazed intently into heaven and saw the glory of God, and Jesus standing at the right hand of God; and he said, 'Behold, I see the heavens opened up and the Son of Man standing at the right hand of God.' But they cried out with a loud voice, and covered their ears, and they rushed upon him with one impulse. And when they had driven him out of the city, they began stoning him, and the witnesses laid aside their robes at the feet of a young man named Saul. And they went on stoning Stephen as he called upon the Lord and said, 'Lord Jesus, receive my spirit!' And falling on his knees, he cried out with a loud voice, 'Lord, do not hold this sin against them!' And having said this, he fell asleep" (vv. 54-60). Even though they were stoning him, Stephen prayed for them to be forgiven. What a display of God's love!

In considering all that is involved when we "walk as children of light" (Eph. 5:8), we must remember that we can do this only as we "walk in the Spirit" (Gal. 5:16). Some misunderstand what it means to depend on the Spirit in daily living. The impression of some is that the believer does nothing; he just commits himself to the Spirit and the Spirit does everything through him.

Believers are not automatons, however. Every person has intellect, emotions and a will. This will is not obliterated when a person comes to Christ. By an act of the will the believer is to present himself to Christ to carry out His will. The question is not whether a person has a will or not; it is whether he's using his will to carry out the will of Christ or to please himself.

The Holy Spirit is the source of power in the believer's life, but the believer must make certain decisions before this power will be effective. A parallel can be drawn to an automobile's power steering. All the power that is needed is available in the equipment, but it does not steer the automobile on its own. The driver must decide whether or not to move the steering wheel and when he does move it, there is power available to carry out the decision he has made. So, when believers make the decision to say No to sin and Yes to those things which please Christ, the power of the Holy Spirit is available to make this decision effective.

Because many believers do not live as they should, Paul said, "Awake thou that sleepest, and arise from the dead, and Christ shall give thee light" (Eph. 5:14). This is a reference from Isaiah 60:1,2, which Paul applies here to believers in the church who need to be shocked out of their spiritual slumber. Paul was wanting believers to become sensitive to their responsibility of walking as children of light. It is a shame when believers live as if they are spiritually asleep. It is as if they are dead and unable to respond to the real issues involved. Because we must all give account someday to the Lord, it is important that we become spiritually awake to the need of pleasing Him in our daily lives. We need to be awake to the fact that the Lord may return at any time.

Concerning the return of the Lord, I Thessalonians 5:4-8 says, "But ye, brethren, are not in darkness, that that day should overtake you as a thief. Ye are all the children of light, and the children of the day: we are not of the night, nor of darkness. Therefore let us not sleep, as do others; but let us watch and be sober. For they that sleep sleep in the night; and they that be drunken are drunken in the night. But let us, who are of the day, be sober, putting on the breastplate of faith and love; and for an helmet, the hope of salvation."

Written to believers, Ephesians 5:14 assures each one that when he awakes from his sleep, "Christ shall give thee light." We receive further light concerning His will only as we conform our lives to the light we already have.

Chapter 19

The Spirit-Filled Believer

(Eph. 5:15-21)

Because of the subtle works of darkness and the importance of being a witness for the Lord, Paul said, "See then that ye walk circumspectly, not as fools, but as wise" (Eph. 5:15).

The word translated "see" means "to look, to consider, to take heed." It was as if Paul was waving a sign before them that said, "Stop, look and listen." Paul wanted believers to make a thorough check of the way they were living to be sure they were walking as they should be. Paul wanted them to make sure they were walking "circumspectly," which means "looking around" or "being cautious." The Greek word Paul used means "accurately" or "exactly." One of the reasons believers should live carefully is that unbelievers are observing them. To live carefully, believers must have an intelligent purpose in living. If we do not have such a purpose, our lives will not be as effective as the Lord desires.

Paul's purpose in living is seen in I Corinthians 2:2: "For I determined not to know any thing among you, save Jesus Christ, and him crucified." To the Philippians, he wrote: "According to my earnest expectation and my hope, that in nothing I shall be ashamed, but that with all boldness, as always, so now also Christ shall be magnified in my body, whether it be by life, or by death. For to me to live is Christ, and to die is gain" (1:20,21). Paul's desire was to know Christ intimately and to make Him known to others. This should be the desire of every believer.

In urging believers to live carefully, Paul again used the word "walk" (Eph. 5:15). As we have seen, this emphasizes living a step at a time and in this case may well have been

210

Paul's way of saying, "Pick your way very carefully." The
Christian life is a walk composed of individual steps, and it is
necessary to rely on the Lord for each step. One serious
misstep can greatly affect a person's life. For instance, a
believer who goes contrary to the Scriptures and marries an
unbeliever may regret it for years to come. We need to pick
our way carefully among the hazards of life, and we can be
sure the Lord will guide us as we seek His wisdom. When I
was traveling in a foreign country, I saw something that
reminded me of the need for Christians to walk carefully.
Surrounding a compound of buildings, a wall of brick and
stone had been built. The wall was topped by a layer of
cement, which had imbedded in it pieces of broken glass that
had been placed in the cement while it was soft. These jagged
pieces protruded to keep intruders from climbing over the
wall. I saw a cat walking gingerly on this wall, very carefully
placing his feet between the sharp pieces of glass. So also,
Christians need to walk carefully to avoid the many hazards
of life.

A successful walk yesterday does not necessarily guar-
antee a successful walk today. There are various and
unexpected snares and pitfalls in the Christian pathway, and
nothing would please Satan more than for the believer to rely
on his own wisdom so that he would be spiritually injured
and be a poor testimony to others. We especially need to be
careful of the so-called little sins such as manner of speech,
choice of companions, use of time, the kind of literature we
read, and styles of dress. Each believer needs to decide
whether a particular thing pleases the Lord, affects himself
adversely, or is a hindrance to the spiritual progress of others.

Some unbelievers refuse to respond to the gospel when
they hear it, but as they see believers living consistent,
Christ-honoring lives, they are attracted to Him. In I Peter
3:1,2 believing wives are instructed how to win their
unbelieving husbands to Christ: "In the same way, you wives,
be submissive to your own husbands so that even if any of
them are disobedient to the word they may be won without a
word by the behavior of their wives, as they observe your
chaste and respectful behavior" (NASB). The same principle
is true in other relationships of life.

In urging believers to live carefully, Paul said, "Not as
fools, but as wise" (Eph. 5:15). Literally, this phrase should
read: "Not as unwise but as wise." The unwise take the path
of least resistance; the wise depend on the Lord to show
them the right path. The unwise have their eyes on what is
around them; the wise have their eyes on God. The unwise
rely on their own wisdom; the wise rely on Christ's wisdom.
We need to heed the words of Proverbs 3:5,6: "Trust in the
Lord with all thine heart; and lean not unto thine own
understanding. In all thy ways acknowledge him, and he shall
direct thy paths." The Bible says, "But unto them which are
called, both Jews and Greeks, Christ the power of God, and
the wisdom of God" (I Cor. 1:24). Verse 30 of this chapter
says that "Christ . . . is made unto us wisdom."

Believers need to frequently read the first two chapters of
I Corinthians to be reminded that God's wisdom is different
than that of man and that God's wisdom can be known only
by the spiritual man. "But he that is spiritual judgeth all
things, yet he himself is judged of no man. For who hath
known the mind of the Lord, that he may instruct him? But
we have the mind of Christ" (2:15,16). The wisdom of Christ
is sufficient for every situation. This especially needs to be
seen as it relates to the home. Whether the believer is a wife
witnessing to an unsaved husband or a child who is the only
Christian in the family, Christ gives wisdom in how to
effectively witness when the believer relies on Him. This is
also true for parents who have rebellious children. As the
parents rely on the Lord, He will give them wisdom and will
help them to control their tempers as they deal with difficult
problems.

'Redeeming the Time'

Paul also instructed believers to be "redeeming the time,
because the days are evil" (Eph. 5:16). The Christian who
lives wisely is one who redeems the time. Colossians 4:5
emphasizes the same truth: "Walk in wisdom toward them
that are without, redeeming the time." "Redeeming the
time" is "making the most of opportunities." The believer is
to buy up opportunities as he serves the Lord. Just as
commercially one watches for a good buy, so believers must

be alert to opportunities and to the best use of time. The word "redeeming" is a translation of the Greek word that emphasizes buying out of the marketplace.

Whereas Ephesians 5:16 emphasizes "buying up" the time, it also emphasizes "buying back" the time at the cost of self-denial. We need to check ourselves regarding our attitude toward time. Time and opportunities lost can never be redeemed. Past time is irretrievable, and future time is not yet available, so it is important we concentrate on using present time to the greatest profit.

Parents with children at home must especially concentrate on the present, because soon these children will be ready to leave home for college, work or marriage. It is easy for parents to worry about the failures of the past or to be concerned about the future and not to have the spiritual ministry at the present that they should have. It also must be realized that the child who is open to these truths today may not be as open in the days to come, so we need to buy up the opportunities presently available.

Every day God gives us opportunity, as children of light, to exhibit His grace. It is important that we take advantage of opportunities to demonstrate God's love. Inasmuch as most unbelievers will not read the Scriptures, it is important that they see God revealed in our lives. Paul told the Corinthians, "Ye are our epistle [letter] written in our hearts, known and read of all men" (II Cor. 3:2). As others "read" our lives, are they seeing the "goodness and righteousness and truth" (Eph. 5:9) of God? If we are careless with time and do not make the most of our opportunities, we cannot expect to be an effective witness for the Lord. How refreshing it is to occasionally hear someone say, "If I ever become a Christian, I want to be like that Christian." But how sad it is to also hear it said, "If he is a Christian, then I don't want to be one."

As days, weeks, months and years pass, we come closer to the return of Christ for His Church. It is important for us to realize that even if His return should be after our lifetime, the time we have in which to serve the Lord is relatively short—every moment counts. As one gets older he begins to think about how few years he may have left to serve Christ.

But whether they be many or few, the important thing is that the believer uses the years to count for God.

As one views world conditions, he sees moral corruption becoming worse and atheistic thinking becoming more prevalent. The political system of Communism is furthering atheistic thinking at the present, but in the future there will be the religious system of the apostate church. As Paul urged Timothy to make the most of his opportunities to proclaim the Word, he explained, "For the time will come when they will not endure sound doctrine; but after their own lusts shall they heap to themselves teachers, having itching ears; and they shall turn away their ears from the truth, and shall be turned unto fables" (II Tim. 4:3,4).

Inasmuch as "the days are evil" (Eph. 5:16), Paul said, "Wherefore be ye not unwise, but understanding what the will of the Lord is" (v. 17). Although our Christian walk may be filled with great difficulties, there is no excuse for carelessness or neglect of our duty. We must remember that God never requires a walk without making full provision for it. This is why we need to understand "what the will of the Lord is." Paul was concerned that believers know the will of the Lord. He told the Colossians, "For this cause we also, since the day we heard it, do not cease to pray for you, and to desire that ye might be filled with the knowledge of his will in all wisdom and spiritual understanding" (1:9). Paul urged the Romans to "prove what is that good, and acceptable, and perfect, will of God" (12:2).

In the first three chapters of Ephesians, God has clearly given us the fundamentals of His will and purpose for us.

To walk in the will of God, we must walk in the whole truth of God's Word. We must remember that it is impossible to have a thorough understanding of God's will without a systematic, prayerful study of God's Word under the careful instruction of the Holy Spirit, whose ministry it is to open our spiritual eyes. The Holy Spirit enlightens us as we study the Word of God. Paul prayed for believers, "That the God of our Lord Jesus Christ, the Father of glory, may give unto you the spirit of wisdom and revelation in the knowledge of him: the eyes of your understanding being enlightened" (Eph. 1:17,18). Christ promised, "But the Comforter, which is the Holy Ghost, whom the Father will send in my name, he shall teach you all things, and bring all things to your remembrance, whatsoever I have said unto you" (John 14:26).

Believers who redeem the time are those who set aside at least some time every day to study and think deeply on God's Word. A believer who does not make this his practice is not living wisely, as the Scripture commands (Eph. 5:15).

The Spirit-Filled Inner Walk

The key verse of Ephesians 5:15-21 is verse 18: "And be not drunk with wine, wherein is excess; but be filled with the Spirit." The entire Book of Ephesians emphasizes the fullness of the triune God—Father, Son and Spirit. Various verses on the subject are: "That ye might be filled with all the fulness of God" (3:19); "Till we all come . . . unto the measure of the stature of the fulness of Christ" (4:13); "Be filled with the Spirit" (5:18).

The Filling and Its Results

Every believer is indwelt by the Holy Spirit, but not every believer is filled with the Holy Spirit. Christ told believers that when the Holy Spirit came He would be "in you" (John 14:17). From Ephesians we have seen that believers have been "sealed with that holy Spirit of promise" (1:13) and that they "are sealed unto the day of redemption" (4:30). The Spirit never ceases to indwell the believer. Romans 8:9 says, "Now if any man have not the Spirit of Christ, he is none of his." However, as has been mentioned, even though the Spirit indwells every believer, not every believer is filled with the Spirit. The clue to what is meant by being "filled" with the Spirit is seen in the first part of verse 18: "Be not drunk with wine, wherein is excess." The drunk person is under the control of intoxicating drink. In contrast to this, believers are to be controlled by the indwelling Holy Spirit.

Being filled with the Holy Spirit is not receiving more of the Spirit; rather, it is the Spirit's possessing more of us. We are filled with the Holy Spirit when we yield to Him the master key that unlocks every department of our lives.

Galatians 5:16 says, "Walk in the Spirit, and ye shall not fulfil the lust of the flesh." As we submit to the influence of the Spirit in our lives, we will be in His control, rather than being controlled by the desires of the flesh. Verse 25 says, "If we live in the Spirit, let us also walk in the Spirit." As we live a step at a time, being sensitive to the Spirit's leading, the Spirit will motivate us to please God and will empower us for service. Galatians 5:17 indicates the Holy Spirit takes up the battle in our behalf against the selfish "flesh."

Ephesians 1:3 reveals that God has provided everything we need: "Blessed be the God and Father of our Lord Jesus Christ, who hath blessed us with all spiritual blessings in heavenly places in Christ." The Father gave the Son in order that we might have all we need, and both the Father and the Son gave the Spirit to make these things effective in our lives (John 14:26; 15:26). Therefore, yielding to the Holy Spirit's control is essential if we are to benefit from all that God has for us. As we submit to the control of the Holy Spirit, the flesh-life recedes and the Christ-life becomes evident in the fullness of power.

When a believer sins, his fellowship with God and the filling of the Spirit is disrupted. He is restored to fellowship and the control of the Spirit, not by praying for fellowship or for the Spirit, but by confessing his sins. When confession is made, God forgives (I John 1:9) and the believer is again under the control of the Holy Spirit. The filling of the Spirit is important for more than just service; it is needed for every aspect of the Christian life. As the believer is controlled by the Spirit, he will be effective in service, for what he does will result from what he is.

Negative and Positive Contrasts

Ephesians 5:18 presents a negative and positive contrast. The Amplified Bible translates this verse, "And do not get drunk with wine, for that is debauchery; but ever be filled and stimulated with the (Holy) Spirit."

Drunkenness is clearly condemned in the Scriptures. Proverbs says, "Wine is a mocker, strong drink is raging: and whosoever is deceived thereby is not wise. Be not among winebibbers; among riotous eaters of flesh: for the drunkard and the glutton shall come to poverty: and drowsiness shall clothe a man with rags" (20:1; 23:20,21). The word translated "excess" in Ephesians 5:18 means "wastefulness" and implies a wasting away to destruction.

The negative and the positive in verse 18 show the battle that goes on in a believer's heart. He must decide whether he is going to yield to the desires of the old nature or to the desires of the new nature. The old nature is from Adam, and its power over us was broken when we received Christ as Saviour (Rom. 6:6). The new nature is from Christ, because at salvation we were "made the righteousness of God in him" (II Cor. 5:21) and became "partakers of the divine nature" (II Pet. 1:4). The new nature is Christ in the believer. Paul said, "I am [have been] crucified with Christ: nevertheless I live; yet not I, but Christ liveth in me" (Gal. 2:20). Having received this new nature, believers are to "put on" those things that are becoming to it (Eph. 4:24).

The two natures of the believer are in conflict with each other: "For the flesh [old nature] lusteth against the Spirit, and the Spirit against the flesh: and these are contrary the one to the other: so that ye cannot do the things that ye would" (Gal. 5:17). But as the believer says No to the old nature and Yes to the new nature (Christ), he is under the control of the Spirit and will not "fulfil the lust of the flesh" (v. 16).

The drunkenness mentioned in Ephesians 5:18 is the result of the appetites of the flesh. Drunkenness robs one of self-control, produces counterfeit pleasure, and destroys the power of the mind and the will to function normally. It causes a person to lose his physical and mental equilibrium, making it difficult for him to cope with routine living. It can lead to immorality because it breaks down restraint.

On the other hand, being filled with the Spirit produces the Christ-life in and through the believer. Being filled with the Spirit gives the believer greater self-control because he has placed himself under the control of the Holy Spirit. The filling of the Spirit produces lasting joy; it invigorates one's whole being with new life. The heart, mind and will are strengthened to fulfill the divine purpose. Moral purity results from being filled with the Spirit. Such a believer's conversation is pleasing to the Lord because his life is separated unto the Lord. God desires that every believer be controlled by the Spirit, for this should be the normal Christian life—life on the highest plane.

The drunken man cannot hide his drunkenness—his walk and his talk betray him. Neither can the Spirit-filled man conceal his condition—his separated walk and sanctified talk reveal he is under the control of the Holy Spirit.

A Continual Filling

The ministry of the Spirit is referred to elsewhere in the Scriptures in connection with thirst. "In the last day, that great day of the feast, Jesus stood and cried, saying, If any man thirst, let him come unto me, and drink. He that believeth on me, as the scripture hath said, out of his belly shall flow rivers of living water. (But this spake he of the Spirit, which they that believe on him should receive: for the Holy Ghost was not yet given; because that Jesus was not yet glorified)" (John 7:37-39).

For the Christian to remain Spirit-filled, he must keep on thirsting and keep on drinking the living water. Every believer is commanded, "Be filled with the Spirit" (Eph. 5:18). Therefore, it is not the responsibility and privilege of only a few favored Christians. It is not an emotional, ecstatic experience or a once-for-all act; it is a relationship with the Holy Spirit that produces joy in the believer's life. A radiant heart and an enhanced comprehension of the Scriptures result from confession of sin and being in the control of the Holy Spirit.

The Greek word translated "be" in Ephesians 5:18 is in a tense that emphasizes continual action. Thus the phrase can read: "Be constantly filled" or "Be being filled." However, just as obedience is not a once-for-all act, neither is the filling of the Spirit. A believer should always be obedient, but when his fellowship with the Lord is interrupted by disobedience, it is to be confessed so the believer will be restored to fellowship. God desires the believer to continually be filled with the Spirit, but sometimes a believer takes himself out of the Spirit's control by yielding to appetites of the flesh. Upon confession of his sin, however, the Spirit again takes control of his life. Thus we see that the filling of the Spirit is a daily, continuous matter.

When we are filled with the Spirit, our lives will evidence the fruit of the Spirit: "Love, joy, peace, longsuffering, gentleness, goodness, faith, meekness, temperance" (Gal. 5:22,23). This fruit is automatically produced in our lives as we are filled with the Spirit. If we are not revealing the fruit of the Spirit, it is because we are not filled with the Spirit.

Key to Sustaining the Spirit-Filled Life

Ephesians 5:19-21 reveals that the key to sustaining the Spirit-filled life is the living Word of God. Verse 19 says, "Speaking to yourselves in psalms, and hymns and spiritual songs, singing and making melody in your heart to the Lord."

In my Christian life, the Psalms have been a special blessing. Psalm 1 has been a favorite and I have gone to the first three verses of this Psalm many times: "Blessed is the man that walketh not in the counsel of the ungodly, nor standeth in the way of sinners, nor sitteth in the seat of the scornful. But his delight is in the law of the Lord; and in his law doth he meditate day and night. And he shall be like a tree planted by the rivers of water, that bringeth forth his fruit in his season; his leaf also shall not wither; and whatsoever he doeth shall prosper."

From these verses we see the importance of the believer's meditating on the Scriptures. The Amplified Bible renders verse two, "But his delight and desire are in the law of the Lord, and on His law—the precepts, the instructions, the teachings of God—he habitually meditates (ponders and studies) by day and by night." We are to think on the Scriptures during the day and even in the nighttime when we awake.

When we do this, we will be fruitful and grow to maturity like a tree planted by water. Second Timothy 3:16 tells us concerning the Word of God, "Every Scripture is God-breathed—given by His inspiration—and profitable for instruction, for reproof and conviction of sin, for correction of error and discipline in obedience, and for training in righteousness [that is, in holy living, in conformity to God's will in thought, purpose and action]" (Amplified).

This is what the Word of God is and does; no believer can live an effective spiritual life without it. It was Jesus who said, "It is the spirit that quickeneth [makes alive]; the flesh profiteth nothing: the words that I speak unto you, they are spirit, and they are life" (John 6:63). Jesus Himself is spoken of in the Gospel of John as the "Word": "In the beginning was the Word, and the Word was with God, and the Word was God. And the Word was made flesh, and dwelt among us" (1:1,14). Jesus is the living Word and now it is the written Word of God, the Bible, that communicates Him to us. The Bible is the only infallible basis for knowing about Jesus Christ. Thus we see that the written Word does something for the believer that no other book can do.

Jesus told believers, "Now ye are clean through the word which I have spoken unto you. If ye abide in me, and my words abide in you, ye shall ask what ye will, and it shall be done unto you" (15:3,7).

Because the Word of God is so tremendously important to our spiritual lives, our spiritual effectiveness depends on our maintaining a daily time of meditating on the Scriptures, frequently called a "devotional time." Psalm 119 clarifies what the Word can mean to us. The person who is filled with the Spirit will be living in God's Word.

A parallel verse to Ephesians 5:19 is Colossians 3:16: "Let the word of Christ dwell in you richly in all wisdom; teaching and admonishing one another in psalms and hymns and spiritual songs, singing with grace in your hearts to the Lord." Notice the close relationship between being filled with the Spirit and centering our thoughts on the Word of God—the results are similar because the Spirit of God takes the message of the Bible and produces the peace and joy of God in our lives.

A Song in the Heart

Notice, too, that the Spirit-filled believer has a song in his heart: "Singing and making melody in your heart to the Lord" (Eph. 5:19). From this we see that the Spirit-filled life is not only the holiest life but also the happiest. This is the result of being in fellowship with God, which comes from walking in the light as He is in the light (I John 1:7).

The Spirit-filled Christian can have a song in his heart even in the midst of extremely difficult circumstances. Circumstances gave no hope to Paul and Silas when they were thrown into prison, but "at midnight Paul and Silas prayed, and sang praises unto God" (Acts 16:25). Spirit-filled Christians have something to sing about and circumstances cannot rob them of that song.

Notice from Ephesians 5:20 that the singing and making melody is to be done "to the Lord." In order for music to edify believers, it needs to be pleasing to the Lord. We have seen that believers are built up spiritually through the Word, which implies that the music needs to meet scriptural standards also. This would apply to both the words of the songs and the music accompanying the words. Let us be sure as we "sing to the Lord" that the words do not convey a message contrary to the teachings of the Scriptures. As to the kind of music involved, it is hard to make a statement that sufficiently covers this complex field. However, the Scriptures indicate that "God is not the author of confusion, but of peace" (I Cor. 14:33). Therefore, the kind of music sung to the Lord should magnify Him by bringing comfort to people's lives rather than confusion and tumult. The Christian should have nothing to do with music that fosters unwholesome revelry.

The singing and making melody does not necessarily need to be done audibly; the important thing is that these are present "in your heart" (Eph. 5:19). Even though we may not have the ability to sing or play instruments for others, our hearts should be filled with praise to the Lord. We do not have to produce sound—the Lord can hear the melody in our hearts.

Thank God for Everything

Believers are also to be "giving thanks always for all things unto God and the Father in the name of our Lord Jesus Christ" (Eph. 5:20). Notice that it is not only giving thanks "always" but also giving thanks for "all things." Only a Spirit-filled believer can do this. This does not mean that we are to enjoy suffering, but it does mean that we are to rejoice because we know God is going to do something in our lives through the suffering. Romans 8:28 says that "all things work together for good to them that love God, to them who are the called according to his purpose." Observe that it is as all things work together in our lives that they accomplish good for us.

Philippians 4:6-8 gives us valuable instruction about thanksgiving: "Stop being worried about anything, but always, in prayer and entreaty, and with thanksgiving, keep on making your wants known to God. Then, through your union with Christ Jesus, the peace of God, that surpasses all human thought, will keep guard over your hearts and thoughts. Now, brothers, practice thinking on what is true, what is honorable, what is right, what is pure, what is lovable, what is high-toned, yes, on everything that is excellent or praiseworthy" (Williams).

Such thanksgiving is obviously impossible for the natural man and even for the carnal Christian, but it is not impossible for the Spirit-filled man. Make it a practice to thank the Lord for everything. This is a sure way of victory over the Devil because he fears a thankful Christian. Thanksgiving is also an expression of faith; if we believe what God says, we will be thankful for His Word, and this will express our faith to others. When the Lord has revealed that it is His will to do a particular thing, let us thank Him ahead of time for the victory that will be eventually won. This is an expression of our faith in God.

Believers are also to be "giving thanks always . . . in the name of our Lord Jesus Christ" (v. 20). Because the name of Christ represents all that He is, and because Christ obtained for us everything we need, He is the only One through whom we can claim anything from God. Notice also the title "Lord." This emphasizes the sovereignty of Jesus Christ and the fact that He is to be the Master of our lives. The Master-servant relationship of Jesus Christ and the believer is the basis for all other relationships. Many specific relationships are mentioned in the following verses of Ephesians and will be considered later.

Paul also told believers, "Submitting yourselves one to another in the fear of God" (v. 21). The word translated "submitting" refers to one person's being under another. In biblical times the word was used mostly as a military term, in the sense of "to rank under." Believers are to be concerned about edifying the Body of Christ and should be characterized by the attitude of ranking under others rather than ranking over them. Observe that it is to be done "in the fear of God." Because of our reverence for the Lord, we are to gladly subject ourselves to those under whom we serve.

No believer lives a spiritually isolated life. Together, we are members of Christ's Body (v. 30) and have responsibilities to each other. Ephesians 4:25 says, "We are members one of another." Therefore, Spirit-filled believers treat fellow Christians as they would treat themselves. We are not to be domineering, but recognizing that Christ is the Lord of all, we are to have a submissive spirit.

As we mutually desire to do the will of God, the Holy Spirit will give us a harmonious relationship with each other. We are to submit ourselves to others "in the fear of God," which is a reverential fear lest we displease or dishonor God. Because of all that Christ has done for us, our desire should be to please Him in everything we do. As we submit ourselves to Him and to others, the Devil is given no opportunity in our lives. Ephesians 4:27 tells believers, "Neither give place to the devil." First Peter 5:5-9 says, "Likewise, ye younger, submit yourselves unto the elder. Yea, all of you be subject one to another, and be clothed with humility: for God resisteth the proud, and giveth grace to the humble. Humble yourselves therefore under the mighty hand of God, that he may exalt you in due time: casting all your care upon him; for he careth for you. Be sober, be vigilant; because your adversary the devil, as a roaring lion, walketh about, seeking whom he may devour: whom resist stedfast in the faith, knowing that the same afflictions are accomplished in your brethren that are in the world."

God gives the grace that is needed to resist the temptation to disrupt the harmony of believers: "But he giveth more grace. Wherefore he saith, God resisteth the proud, but giveth grace unto the humble. Submit yourselves therefore to God. Resist the devil, and he will flee from you" (James 4:6,7). When we maintain this kind of relationship with Christ, through the Holy Spirit, we have the proper basis for the various relationships in life, some of which are mentioned in Ephesians 5.

Chapter 20

The Believer's Married Life
(Eph. 5:22-33)

Having said that believers are to be "submitting [themselves] one to another in the fear of God" (Eph. 5:21), Paul proceeded to discuss the marriage relationship.

In Ephesians 5:22-33 Paul was not speaking to unbelievers but to believers. No unsaved person has the power within himself to do what Paul here instructs. The home is the first divine institution brought into existence. The second such institution is the Church. In Ephesians 5 the Church—with its sacred relationships—is used to explain what the marriage relationship should be like for believers, thus lifting marriage to its highest level.

The bonds between Christ and the Church illustrate the sacred bonds of the marriage relationship. The bonds between Christ and the Church are arranged, ordained and perfected in heaven. So also is the marriage relationship of believers. But for marriage to be what God desires, both partners must not only be believers in Christ but also be controlled by the Holy Spirit. It is to such people that the Book of Ephesians is addressed: "To the faithful in Christ Jesus" (1:1).

As we have seen previously, when such high standards are set by God, He makes provision for maintaining them. That provision is our position in Christ. In the first three chapters of Ephesians the Church is revealed as the Body of Christ; in chapter 5 it is revealed as the Bride of Christ. The Church is first seen as an intimate part of Christ and is then revealed as the Bride, who must become more like the Bridegroom. Romans 8:29 reveals that God wants us "to be conformed to the image of his Son," and He works in our lives to that end.

As Christ's Body, the Church is to become like Him, but He—as its Head—takes all the responsibility of providing everything needed for her well-being and performance.

Ephesians 5:22 says, "Wives, submit yourselves unto your own husbands, as unto the Lord." To be able to submit oneself to another requires self-denial. This, of course, is important for everyone because Christ said, "If any man will come after me, let him deny himself, and take up his cross daily, and follow me" (Luke 9:23). Notice it is not a denial of things, it is a denial of self. Rather than assert our rights, we are to be willing to put others first. Believers are told, "Let nothing be done through strife or vainglory; but in lowliness of mind let each esteem other better than themselves. Look not every man on his own things, but every man also on the things of others" (Phil. 2:3,4).

We are to think in the same way the Lord Jesus thought: "Let this mind be in you, which was also in Christ Jesus" (v. 5). The way Jesus thought is explained in this passage as it tells how He left the throne of the Father to come to the earth in order to die on the cross for us. As we think on what Christ did for us, we will be motivated to be more considerate of others.

The Wife's Responsibility

The words "submit yourselves" (Eph. 5:22) do not appear in the better Greek manuscripts but are understood from verse 21. Together, these verses literally read: "Submitting yourselves one to another in the fear of God. Wives to their own husbands as to the Lord." The Amplified Bible renders Ephesians 5:22-24, "Wives, be subject—be submissive and adapt yourselves—to your own husbands as [a service] to the Lord. For the husband is head of the wife as Christ is the Head of the church, Himself the Savior of [His] body. As the church is subject to Christ, so let wives also be subject in everything to their husbands."

Notice that the word "obey" is not specifically used in connection with the wife although obedience is implied in subjection. The word "obey" is the key word used in regard to children's relationship to their parents (6:1). Although obedience is implied, the main emphasis in the subjection of a wife to her husband is that of her being under him in God's line of authority. Peter also wrote to wives to "be in subjection to your own husbands" (I Pet. 3:1). The word translated "subjection" here and "submitting" in Ephesians 5:21 has to do with one ranking under another.

God's line of authority is revealed in I Corinthians 11: "The head of every man is Christ; and the head of the woman is the man; and the head of Christ is God" (v. 3). The order of authority, then, from the top down, is: Father, Son, man, woman. This does not mean that the wife is inferior to her husband in capabilities or capacities, but it does mean that as far as the line of authority is concerned she ranks under him.

Whenever two or more persons are to work closely together in harmony, there must be an order of recognized authority. While Christ was on earth, He did nothing on His own but was in subjection to the Father. He said, "The words that I speak unto you I speak not of myself: but the Father that dwelleth in me, he doeth the works" (John 14:10). This was not a degrading relationship, and neither does it need to be degrading for a wife to be in subjection to her husband.

The submission of Christian wives to their husbands is based on the intimate, vital relationship: "Your own husbands." Notice also that wives are to submit to their own husbands "as unto the Lord" (v. 22). This reveals that a wife's submission to her husband involves more than the marriage relationship; it is indicative of her submission to the Lord. The wife who rebels at having her husband be the head of the family is actually rebelling against the Lord. This would be the same as the Church rebelling against Christ.

When a Christian wife submits to her husband, the Lord accepts this as submission to Himself and He rewards accordingly. There are temporal rewards of present joy and peace in the marriage relationship and eternal rewards for being faithful to Christ.

Ephesians 5:23 gives the reason the wife should be in subjection to her husband: "For the husband is the head of the wife, even as Christ is the head of the church: and he is the saviour of the body." The wife's subjection to her husband is put on the highest plane possible as it is parallel to the relationship of Christ and the Church. Here we see that the headship of the husband is a divine appointment, not something man has devised. Just as the Father gave Christ to be the Head of the Church (1:22,23), so He has given the husband to be the head of the wife (5:23). "Therefore," Paul said, "as the church is subject unto Christ, so let the wives be to their own husbands in every thing" (v. 24).

The Husband's Responsibility

As a Christian wife, do you feel that you have been too severely dealt with? Do you think that more is required of you than should be reasonably expected? Then notice God's instructions to husbands. This will help you to see that there is mutual responsibility and that the husband bears the greater responsibility because he stands as the head of the marriage relationship, even as Christ is Head of the Church.

"Husbands," the Bible says, "love your wives, even as Christ also loved the church, and gave himself for it" (v. 25). This reveals that a wife's subjection is not a slavish obedience to the whims and fancies of an unreasonable and selfish husband; rather, it is the joyous subjection of loyalty to one who loves her as Christ loved the Church. A wife will not find it difficult to submit to a husband who loves her in this way. All of this, of course, requires a marriage that honors God. Thus, believers are told, "Be ye not unequally yoked together with unbelievers" (II Cor. 6:14).

Notice the extent to which husbands are to love their wives: "Even as Christ also loved the church" (Eph. 5:25). So what Christ is in His love relationship to the Church, the husband is to the wife. There is no allowance here for a husband to be domineering and inconsiderate of his wife. The husband himself is under the headship of Christ, for the Bible says that "the head of every man is Christ" (I Cor. 11:3). This, of course, makes Christ the head of both the man and the woman, and this is true in His relationship with them as "the head over all things to the church" (Eph. 1:22).

The husband and wife are first to have the mutual joy of being in right relationship with Christ, then they are to be in relationship to each other as described in Ephesians 5. There is no license for the husband to ask the wife to do anything only to please himself. He is to be in right relationship with Christ, and this dramatically affects his relationship with his wife. The fact that husbands are to love their wives as Christ loved the Church reveals that Christian marriage has a heavenly pattern.

When Paul told husbands, "Love your wives" (5:25), the word he used for love was *agapao*. This is the kind of love that originates with God Himself. It is a love that loves even when there is no response. This is the word used in John 3:16: "For God so loved the world, that he gave his only begotten Son." Revealing that God loved even when there was no response from us, Romans 5:8 says, "But God commendeth his love toward us, in that, while we were yet sinners, Christ died for us." This is the kind of love that is "shed abroad in our hearts by the Holy Ghost" (v. 5) when we are in right relationship to God.

The expression of such a love is not possible for those who do not know Jesus Christ as Saviour because this love comes from Christ, who indwells the believer. This is why Paul prayed for believers "to be strengthened with might by his Spirit in the inner man; that Christ might dwell in your hearts by faith; that ye, being rooted and grounded in love. . . ." (Eph. 3:16,17).

When the husband loves his wife with this kind of love, she will find it a joy to submit herself to him. Christ's love knows no bounds; He loves not thinking of what He can get but of what He can give. It is this kind of self-sacrificing love that is the fruit of the Spirit (Gal. 5:22).

There were other words for "love" available to Paul to use, if he had cared to, in saying that husbands ought to love their wives. There was *eros*, which was predominantly used in referring to physical love. Eventually this word became associated with the lower side of love, especially in regard to passion. It is from this word that we derive "erotic," which means "of, devoted to, or tending to arouse sexual love or desire." This word is not once used in the Bible.

Another word common in Paul's time was *storge*, which had mostly to do with affection in the family relationship. It was mainly used in referring to love of parents for their children and children for their parents.

Paul used this word in Romans 12:10, where it is translated "be kindly affectioned . . . to." He also said that this kind of love will be lacking in the last days, when men will be "without natural affection" (II Tim. 3:3).

Another common word for love was *phileo*, which emphasized a fondness or affection and is perhaps best seen in the reciprocal relationship of friendship.

But Paul, writing by the inspiration of the Holy Spirit, chose none of the above in commanding husbands to love their wives. He chose *agapao*, which emphasized the highest kind of love.

Inasmuch as husbands are to love their wives "as Christ also loved the church" (Eph. 5:25), the Scriptures explain how much He loved the Church. He "gave himself for it; that he might sanctify and cleanse it with the washing of water by the word, that he might present it to himself a glorious church, not having spot, or wrinkle, or any such thing; but that it should be holy and without blemish" (vv. 25-27).

Concerning these verses, Dr. C. I. Scofield said, "Christ's love-work for the church is threefold: past, present, future: (1) For love He gave Himself to redeem the church (v. 25); (2) in love He is sanctifying the church (v. 26); (3) for the reward of His sacrifice and labour of love He will present the church to Himself in flawless perfection, 'one pearl of great price' (v. 27; Mt. 13.46)" (*Scofield Reference Bible*, p. 1254).

Having explained how much Christ loved the Church, Paul said, "So ought men to love their wives as their own bodies. He that loveth his wife loveth himself. For no man ever yet hateth his own flesh; but nourisheth and cherisheth it, even as the Lord the church: for we are members of his body, of his flesh, and of his bones" (v. 28-30).

From these verses we see the personal aspect inasmuch as husbands are to love their wives "as their own bodies" (v. 28). As it is natural for a person to be concerned about himself, it should be natural for the Christian husband to love his wife. Love causes the husband to protect his wife and provide for her every need as Christ protects and provides for the Church (v. 29).

Loving his wife in this way means the husband will take his place as the head of the home. He will not force his wife, by his lack of leadership, into a position that is not rightfully hers nor—in most cases—desired by her. J. Allan Petersen of

Family Concern, Inc., has said, "When we as husbands and fathers don't assume our rightful place of leadership and responsibility, it will pass by default to our wives. We will have a matriarchal society, and it will be no one's fault but our own. Juvenile court judges, marriage counselors and psychologists all agree that the increases in drug abuse, sexual immorality, homosexuality and crime among young people is a direct result of the breakdown in the family. And that breakdown is caused in an overwhelming majority of cases by the failure of fathers to be real men" (*Stop, Love and Listen*, p. 44).

The words "we are members of his body, of his flesh and of his bones" (v. 30) are similar to the words spoken by Adam after the woman was created: "This is now bone of my bones, and flesh of my flesh: she shall be called Woman, because she was taken out of Man" (Gen. 2:21-23). Christ's Body, the Church, was brought into existence on the Day of Pentecost and derives its life from His death, burial and resurrection. The Church is related to Christ for He is the Head of it (Eph. 1:22,23). This relationship provides the illustration for what the husband-wife relationship should be.

Sacred Implications of Christian Marriage

The Bible says, "For this cause shall a man leave his father and mother, and shall be joined unto his wife, and they two shall be one flesh" (5:31).

From this verse we see that marriage is an intimate and permanent union. The permanency of marriage has almost been forgotten in the 20th century. People need to be asked as Christ asked those when He was on earth, "Have you not read, that He who created them from the beginning made them male and female, and said, 'For this cause a man shall leave his father and mother, and shall cleave to his wife; and the two shall become one flesh'? Consequently they are no more two, but one flesh. What therefore God has joined together, let no man separate" (Matt. 19:4-6, NASB). Thus we see that marriage was never intended to be dissolved.

Having referred to what was said in Genesis 2:24 (Eph. 5:31), Paul said, "This is a great mystery: but I speak concerning Christ and the church" (v. 32). The Christian is obligated to hold marriage sacred and indissoluble since it reveals the mystery of Christ and the Church. Will Christ ever divorce the Church? No. Nothing will hinder His relationship with it because He has obligated Himself to protect and provide for it. He said, "I will build my church; and the gates of hell shall not prevail against it" (Matt. 16:18).

Neither can the Church separate itself from Christ. Concerning believers, Jesus said, "I give unto them eternal life; and they shall never perish, neither shall any man pluck them out of my hand. My Father, which gave them me, is greater than all; and no man is able to pluck them out of my Father's hand" (John 10:28,29). Since the Church cannot sever its relationship with Christ, this indicates that God never desires wives to sever their relationships with their husbands. To violate these principles is to violate the sacredness of the relationship of marriage and of Christ's relationship to the Church.

Paul concluded his instructions to husbands and wives with these words: "Nevertheless let every one of you in particular so love his wife even as himself; and the wife see that she reverence her husband" (Eph. 5:33). Here we see again the mutual obligation in the marriage relationship: the husband is to "love his wife even as himself," and the wife is to "reverence her husband." The original word translated "reverence" means "fear," but the context indicates it is to be a "reverential fear." The wife is to be respectful of her husband's position in the line of God's authority, and the husband is to love his wife as he loves himself.

In an unregenerate society it is to be expected that there would be little respect for God's line of authority. Such is the case in the United States today. Women are asserting their rights and in many cases they are justified, but in many other instances what they are gaining is counterbalanced by what they are losing. In His infinite wisdom, God has established an arrangement that is for our greatest good and His glory. To go against what God has established is to invite eventual destruction of the marriage relationship itself. The wife who fails to submit to her husband cannot expect him to love her as the Scriptures command. So also, the husband who refuses to accept his position of headship in the home and to love his wife as he should cannot expect his wife to willingly submit.

They disrupt the relationship that must exist for the greatest benefit to all on a long-range basis.

The first woman who stepped out of her position of submission to her husband was Eve. She listened to Satan, who invited her to act independently of her husband, and she was deceived. However, Adam deliberately chose to follow his wife in her sin and thereby, as the head of the race, plunged all of mankind into sin. The Bible says, "For Adam was first formed, then Eve. And Adam was not deceived, but the woman being deceived was in the transgression" (I Tim. 2:13,14).

In this day of relatively easy divorce, marriage has been lowered to the level of a civil contract that can be broken at will. It is understandable that unbelievers view marriage in this light, but it is deplorable that an increasing number of Christians are going the divorce route. This evidences not only unfaithfulness to the marriage vows but also unfaithfulness to Christ. When a married couple submit themselves to Christ, He gives them the wisdom and strength to cope with problems that arise in the marriage relationship. How regrettable it is, however, that even Christians are sometimes more concerned about pleasing themselves than they are about pleasing their marriage partners, or especially Christ. We desperately need to get back to the principles of marriage as revealed in the opening chapters of Genesis. Because God's eternal plan and purposes for husband and wife were a foreshadowing of the Church, it is little wonder that Satan hates the opening chapters of Genesis and influences so many to reject them. We need to search our hearts to be sure we are not rebelling against the principles God has established concerning the marriage relationship.

Chapter 21

Children and Parents

(Eph. 6:1-4)

Having said what the husband and wife relationship should be, Paul then stated what the relationship should be between children and parents.

"Children, obey your parents in the Lord: for this is right" (Eph. 6:1). Obedience is presented here, not as just desirable, but as a command of God. This command involves both children, who are to obey, and parents, who are to exercise loving authority in the family. Although this relationship should be true in any family, it reaches its highest plane only in families that know Christ as Saviour and Lord. When parents live as Paul commanded in 5:22,23, it is not difficult for children to respect them.

There must be unity between the parents if their children are going to know what is expected in order to willingly obey. This means that one parent should never correct the other parent in the presence of the children, especially when it concerns the discipline of the children. This only frustrates the children and makes it possible for them later to pit one parent against the other in endeavoring to get their own way. When children see sharp division of opinion in matters of discipline, it causes them to lose respect for one or both parents. Therefore, parents must be agreed in their basic principles of rearing their children and support each other in the decisions that are made.

The situation should be avoided where the wife says, "It's all right with me, but go ask your father," or where the husband says, "It's all right with me, but go ask your mother." The parents should either agree ahead of time or one should make the decision and the other should not reverse it after it has been made.

Sometimes parents do not have an opportunity to discuss a matter ahead of time, and a decision is made by one partner that the other partner thinks is wrong. The decision should not be discussed in front of the child. It should be discussed later so the parents are agreed on what the decision should be the next time a similar problem arises. In cases of discipline, it may sometimes be necessary to delay discipline until the parents can agree on what should be done.

Regardless of how unreasonable parents may seem, children are commanded to obey them "in the Lord" (6:1). The words "in the Lord" refer to children being in the Lord. In order to obey "in the Lord" children must have received Christ as Saviour so that they are in Christ. These words do not mean that children are to analyze what their parents request to see if the command is scriptural. Obedience is a duty of children. It is assumed that the parents involved are those who have met the requirements of the previous chapter; thus, the entire family is "in the Lord." A saved child expresses his obedience to the Lord by being obedient to his parents, the Lord's representatives in the family.

When a Christian home has a wife who takes her place in loving subjection to her husband and a husband who loves his wife as previously described, there will be created an atmosphere that will make it possible for children to obey their parents from love and respect instead of from compulsion and fear.

Ephesians 6:1 says that children should obey their parents, "for this is right." That is, it is right before God, who is the creator of the universe and everything in it.

It is a fundamental principle that God's universe obeys Him. He has set the planets in motion in their prescribed courses and has established laws by which everything functions. Because of this, it can be said that everything obeys God, whether it is the rolling waves of the sea, the blowing wind, or flowers that grow to beautify the landscape. All are functioning according to established laws of God.

Even the Son of God Himself, while living on earth, obeyed his parents. The Bible says that after He had discourses with the teachers of law in the temple, "He went down with them [his parents], and came to Nazareth, and was subject unto them" (Luke 2:51).

From all of this it is apparent that if we are to please the Lord we must be obedient to Him, and if children are to please the Lord they must be obedient to their parents. Children are also told, "Honour thy father and mother; which is the first commandment with promise; that it may be well with thee, and thou mayest live long on the earth" (Eph. 6:2,3). Here, Paul was making reference to Exodus 20:12, "Honour thy father and thy mother: that thy days may be long upon the land which the Lord thy God giveth thee." Although the commandment in Exodus was specifically spoken to the children of Israel, who were on their way to the Promised Land, Paul applies it to children living in the Church Age.

Ephesians 6:4 describes the spiritual responsibility that parents have to their children: "And, ye fathers, provoke not your children to wrath: but bring them up in the nurture and admonition of the Lord." The word "fathers" does not just refer to the father of the family; it is used here in the sense of "parents." But since the father has the primary responsibility, it is important that he take more time for his children than most fathers are accustomed to taking. The father stands in God's place in the home, and as such he is to be the leader in the spiritual life of the family.

Negative and Positive Commands

Verse 4 gives both a negative and a positive command to parents concerning their children. Negatively, they are commanded, "Provoke not your children to wrath." Positively, they are commanded, "Bring them up in the nurture and admonition of the Lord."

The word translated "provoke" means "to irritate" or "to arouse to resentment." Colossians 3:21 says, "Fathers, provoke not your children to anger, lest they be discouraged." Parents discourage their children and unnecessarily irritate them by unreasonable demands, a dictatorial manner, nagging, faultfinding and harsh criticism.

Instead of provoking the children, parents are to "bring them up in the nurture and admonition of the Lord" (Eph.

6:4). Another translation reads: "Bring them up in the discipline and instruction of the Lord" (NASB). Thus, the parents' responsibility is to teach their children the proper things and see to it that these truths are carried out in daily living.

All of this is to be done in and of the Lord, because the principles for training must come from the Lord. Parents should keep the Bible in hand as they train their children; that is, parents must be sure that they are studying the Word of God so they are following the proper principle for training their children.

Hebrews 12:9,10 draws a distinction between the disciplining of earthly fathers and the disciplining of the Heavenly Father: "Furthermore we have had fathers of our flesh which corrected us, and we gave them reverence: shall we not much rather be in subjection unto the Father of spirits, and live? For they verily for a few days chastened us after their own pleasure; but he for our profit, that we might be partakers of his holiness."

Parents are held responsible by God for the lives they bring into the world, and God expects them to wisely train their children according to principles revealed in His Word.

Child training begins at birth. It is in the child's formative years, when he bends easily like a sapling, that the most can be done by parents. But if they wait until the child is older, and like a tree whose trunk is hard and set, they will find it is too late to begin training him.

It is normal for children to want their parents to ease the restrictions on them. Children will sometimes say, "Why can't we be like our friends? They have a lot more freedom than we do." In a Christian family the children will sometimes cite other Christian families as examples as a special plea for them to get their way in a particular matter. It is at times like these that parents need to be considerate of their children's feelings and endeavor to explain to their children why they have certain limitations. Each family has its own guidelines, and the children must be helped to see that even though they had no choice of the family into which they were born, they are responsible to follow the guidelines of their family. They need to be helped to realize that their submission to their parents is pleasing to God and He will reward them for it. This is difficult for children to see and understand, but if their parents are patient with them and if the children are concerned about pleasing the Lord, they will eventually see this principle.

Parents are responsible to live lives pleasing to the Lord before their children. Parents must not give the impression that they are infallible; it must be obvious to the children that the parents are seeking the Lord's wisdom and that they confess their failures to the Lord. As parents live in fellowship with the Lord and with each other, their children will see this and respect them for it and will eventually express their gratitude when they have homes of their own. When children are grown they should be able to look back on their home lives and remember their father and mother for the happy and wholesome relationship they had rather than for their cross words and inconsiderate attitude toward each other. The children will be able to do this if each partner gives this matter the proper place in the marriage relationship now.

We are to consider our children a heritage from God and their training as an investment in life. We must remember that the training of our children is more important than obtaining possessions. To provide the kind of training our children need, we may have to sacrifice financially. However, we will not call it a "sacrifice" if it benefits our children and makes them more effective in years to come. More important than the amount of money you have available to spend today is the investment you have made in the lives of your children.

If we train our children "in the nurture and admonition of the Lord," our sons will be able to take their places as the heads of their homes and our daughters will be the kind of wives and mothers that please the Lord.

Proverbs 31 extols the wife who pleases the Lord: "Who can find a virtuous woman? for her price is far above rubies. The heart of her husband doth safely trust in her, so that he shall have no need of spoil. She will do him good and not evil all the days of her life. She riseth also while it is yet night, and giveth meat to her household, and a portion to her maidens. She layeth her hands to the spindle, and her hands hold the distaff. She stretcheth out her hand to the poor;

yea, she reacheth forth her hands to the needy. She openeth her mouth with wisdom; and in her tongue is the law of kindness. She looketh well to the ways of her household, and eateth not the bread of idleness. Her children arise up, and call her blessed; her husband also, and he praiseth her. Many daughters have done virtuously, but thou excellest them all. Favour is deceitful, and beauty is vain: but a woman that feareth the Lord, she shall be praised. Give her of the fruit of her hands; and let her own works praise her in the gates" (vv. 10-12,15,19,20,26-31).

Proverbs instructs parents, "Train up a child in the way he should go: and when he is old, he will not depart from it" (22:6). This involves training that begins at birth and continues until the child leaves your home to establish his own.

The first 20 years of a person's life are crucial to his effectiveness in succeeding years. One expert has estimated that 90 percent of a person's habits are formed during these years. The American Council on Alcohol Problems says that two-thirds of today's alcoholics began drinking while of high school age. These early years are also crucial spiritually. Numerous reports indicate that between 80 and 90 percent of those who receive Christ as Saviour do so during their teenage years or earlier.

All of these things emphasize how important it is for parents to properly train their children. Above all, we are to train them in the truths of the Word of God. What a child believes when he has finished college largely depends on what he was taught during his formative years. True, he may come up against teaching in college that will cause him to be uncertain about spiritual realities for a time, but if the truths of God's Word have been effectively communicated to him in the formative years, he will not become spiritually shipwrecked.

Training involves at least three elements: education, example and discipline. Education is the process of transmitting to a child the knowledge and experiences of humanity. We must also communicate to them spiritual principles—such as, God blesses those who obey and He withholds His blessings from those who disobey.

We also train by example, as we have previously discussed. Children learn from others and this is especially true in the home. It is normal for children to imitate their parents, so it is exceedingly important that parents are living in a way pleasing to the Lord.

Training also includes discipline, which may be defined as "that method of training whereby we seek to make doing right pleasant and doing wrong unpleasant." This involves correction as well as reward.

There are many reasons for the decline of proper training today—such as a low view of family life—but one of the main reasons is the decreasing value that has been placed on spiritual training. Families are not spending as much time together nor as much time studying God's Word. Personal standards of living have become so high that frequently mother and father must both work for an income. This keeps them so busy that it is difficult for them to have a home life where they spend time with the children, and the children suffer in the process.

If we want our children to have spiritually effective lives in the future, we must train them now. By training a generation of born-again children, we can greatly affect the future of other families, the church, society, and even the nation. The path of least resistance will not produce what our children will need in the future. We must invest in the lives of our children, and we can be sure that our investment will bring eternal dividends. However, if we are negligent in our responsibility to properly train our children, we can also be sure that society will be in even greater disruption in the future. As Edmund Burke, a British statesman, wrote: "The only thing necessary for the triumph of evil is for good men to do nothing."

Chapter 22

Servants and Masters

(Eph. 6:5-9)

Spirit-filled believers are instructed in Ephesians not only how to live in relationship to their married partners and to their children, but also how they should live in their work relationships.

Ephesians 6:5-8 instructs servants how to live with regard to their masters, and verse 9 tells masters how they should live with regard to their servants.

Paul said, "Servants, be obedient to them that are your masters according to the flesh, with fear and trembling, in singleness of your heart, as unto Christ" (v. 5). Paul was actually addressing these remarks to Christian slaves, inasmuch as the word translated "servants" means "slaves." Paul was not condoning slavery, but he was giving principles to help Christian slaves to know how to please Christ in their relationship with their masters. That they were Christian slaves is evident from the words "as unto Christ." The principles found here are applicable to any employee-employer relationship.

The key word for servants is the same as for children—"obedience." God is the God of order, and throughout the Scriptures we see the importance of the line of authority. There was confusion among the nation of Israel during a certain period in Old Testament times, because "in those days there was no king in Israel: every man did that which was right in his own eyes" (Judges 21:25).

Just as the wife expresses her submission to the Lord by submitting to her husband, the husband his submission to the Lord by loving his wife, and the children their submission to the Lord by obeying their parents, so servants show their

240

submission to the Lord by obeying their masters. Of course, these masters are only "according to the flesh" because every believer's ultimate Master is Jesus Christ. The Christian master himself is a servant of Christ.

Paul wrote that servants are to obey their masters "with fear and trembling." That is, they are to be concerned that they not willfully neglect their responsibility to their masters, which would amount to robbing their masters and making themselves chargeable to God. The Master of all believers is God, and believers are told, "Work out your own salvation with fear and trembling" (Phil. 2:12). Notice that salvation is not something to be worked "for" but to be worked "out." Servants need to be aware of their weaknesses and make sure they are not chargeable to their masters by being poor workers.

As far as the service of the Lord is concerned, the Christian servant is to do his work not only as to the Lord but in the Lord's strength. Philippians 2:13 reveals, "It is God which worketh in you both to will and to do of his good pleasure." Servants are to serve their masters "in singleness of . . . heart" (Eph. 6:5). This refers to motive for service. The Christian servant has the main desire to please the Lord in all things, which includes pleasing his earthly master.

Paul said that servants were to be obedient, "not with eyeservice, as menpleasers; but as the servants of Christ, doing the will of God from the heart" (v. 6). The Christian servant should desire to please the Lord, not just his employer. This means he must be faithful in doing the right kind of work and giving a full day's work for a full day's pay. Only when he willingly does this will he be "doing the will of God from the heart."

Verse 7 further emphasizes that Christian servants are to be most concerned about pleasing the Lord: "With good will doing service, as to the Lord, and not to men." The Amplified Bible translates verses 6,7: "Not in the way of eyeservice—as if they were watching you—and only to please men; but as servants (slaves) of Christ, doing the will of God heartily and with your whole soul; rendering service readily with goodwill, as to the Lord and not to men."

The most menial task may—even must—be done "as to the Lord." And when it is, drudgery is turned to joy.

We must remember that the Lord never overlooks the smallest thing that is ultimately done to please Him—He rewards even a cup of water given in His name (Matt. 25:35,40). When we serve others because we love Christ, He accepts this as a service done directly for Him.

Although employers are prone to overlook many good things employees do, the Lord sees all and rewards all. However, as employers we should make it our concern to know how our employees are doing and to commend them for doing well, even as Christ will someday reward the believer for doing well.

When employees want to please their employers in order to please Christ, their work takes on a new perspective. Each Christian employee should be motivated by the desire to please Christ in everything. The desire of all Christians should be the same as that expressed in II Corinthians 5:9: "Wherefore we labour, that, whether present or absent, we may be accepted of him." The reason this is so important is given in the following verse: "For we must all appear before the judgment seat of Christ; that every one may receive the things done in his body, according to that he hath done, whether it be good or bad [worthless]." The Lord takes everything we do into consideration. He views the service we give to our employers as service we give Him. Paul told servants they should serve with goodwill "knowing that whatsoever good thing any man doeth, the same shall he receive of the Lord, whether he be bond or free" (Eph. 6:8). Paul was saying it makes no difference whether a person is a slave or not; he is rewarded by the Lord for any good thing he does. Another way to render this verse is, "Knowing that for whatever good any one does, he will receive his reward from the Lord, whether he is slave or free" (Amplified). Even if one's earthly employer does not treat him according to what he deserves, he can be sure that his heavenly Master will not have the same failure.

I remember so well a dear Christian brother, John Paton, who is now with the Lord. He was my editorial assistant for several years, and his task was primarily to edit my radio messages for book form. He did an excellent job of putting the spoken word into written form. One day I said to him, "John, you do such a good job of editing my messages; in fact, you make it look as if I'm a good writer. But you don't get any credit for it. The readers don't realize the work you have done." He smiled, pointed to heaven and said, "Brother Epp, I know who keeps the books."

Regardless of whether or not your work is seen by the public, remember that the Lord sees it and will reward you accordingly. May each of us labor in such a way that we will someday hear Him say, "Well done, thou good and faithful servant: thou hast been faithful over a few things, I will make thee ruler over many things: enter thou into the joy of thy lord" (Matt. 25:21).

The Lord does not expect us to serve without rewards. Even Old Testament saints realized there were rewards for faithfully serving the Lord. Of Moses it is said, "Choosing rather to suffer affliction with the people of God, than to enjoy the pleasures of sin for a season; esteeming the reproach of Christ greater riches than the treasures in Egypt: for he had respect unto the recompence of the reward" (Heb. 11:25,26).

From Matthew 25:21 we see that the Lord is going to reward by giving privileges of ruling. But the way a believer gains this reward is by being faithful. As we faithfully serve in what God has given us to do now, He will reward us and give us more responsibility in the future. The important question is, How faithful are we in pleasing the Lord in that which He has given us to do now? We may be sure that the Heavenly Master keeps a good account and that He gives good rewards.

Having given instructions to servants, Paul then told masters, "And, ye masters, do the same things unto them, forbearing threatening: knowing that your Master also is in heaven; neither is there respect of persons with him" (Eph. 6:9). The Amplified Bible translates this verse: "You masters, act on the same [principle] toward them, and give up threatening and using violent and abusive words, knowing that He Who is both their Master and yours is in heaven, and that there is no respect of persons—no partiality—with Him."

Here we see the so-called golden rule of doing unto others as you would have them do unto you. Just as the servant is to give his best to the master because of his desire to please Christ, so the master should give his servant the best treatment because of his desire to serve Christ. Philippians

2:3 says, "Let nothing be done through strife or vainglory; but in lowliness of mind let each esteem other better than themselves." The servant is to esteem his master better than himself, and the master is to esteem the servant better than himself. The master should not use harsh, violent language nor intimidate his servant; rather, he should inspire his servant by his own example. Employers are given good advice in Romans 12:9. One translation states it this way: "If your department is the direction of others' labors, stimulate them by your own enthusiasm for the work. Let there be no pretense about your love" (Way).

Masters are reminded to be careful to have their servants' interests in view because their "Master also is in heaven" (Eph. 6:9). Christ is Master of both the servant and the earthly master. This should cause those who have responsibility over others to exercise it with all caution, because they themselves must someday give account to the Heavenly Master.

Concerning the Heavenly Master, Paul said, "Neither is there respect of persons with him." Jesus Christ is partial to no one. Earthly masters and servants stand on the same basis before Him. He does not judge by earthly standards but by heavenly ones. Thus it is important that we heed the words of Colossians 3:23,25: "And whatsoever ye do, do it heartily, as to the Lord, and not unto men; but he that doeth wrong shall receive for the wrong which he hath done: and there is no respect of persons." God is omniscient—He knows the acts and the motives of every person. Let us then make it our desire to please Jesus Christ in everything, living according to our position in Him.

Chapter 23

The Believer's Spiritual Conflict
(Eph. 6:10-20)

There are three lines of truth unfolded in the Book of Ephesians. Each is an outgrowth of the other. First, there is the teaching of the believer's exalted position in Jesus Christ, as set forth in the first three chapters of Ephesians. Everyone who has received Christ as Saviour has this perfect position. The teaching concerning this position reveals what Christ has done for the believer.

Second, the Book of Ephesians concerns the believer's spiritual walk on this earth, based on his exalted position in Christ. This subject is emphasized in the last three chapters of Ephesians through verse 9 of chapter 6. This passage tells of what Christ wants to accomplish in the believer's "walk," or life.

Third, the Book of Ephesians concludes with teaching about the believer's spiritual conflict. Here Christ is seen working *through* the believer.

Some ask, Why the conflict? Why end the epistle on a battlefield?

Perhaps it seems strange that after the book reveals the lofty position each believer has in Christ and the noble walk that every believer is to have, it then dwells on warfare. Throughout Ephesians we have noted that Christ has won the victory for the believer. Chapter 4 tells us that "he led captivity captive" (v. 8); that is, He led captive those who held us captive. So if we are victorious in Him, why the conflict?

It is a characteristic of believers to want to remain "on the mountaintop." This was true of Peter when he, along with James and John, witnessed the Transfiguration of the

Lord on the mountaintop. They not only saw Christ in all of His glory, but they also saw Moses and Elijah talking with Him. It was such a thrilling experience that Peter said to the Lord, "It is good for us to be here: if thou wilt, let us make here three tabernacles; one for thee, and one for Moses, and one for Elias [Elijah]" (Matt. 17:4). But this was not to be done; they had to return to the valley. One cannot stay on the mountaintop; he must return to the duties of life to serve Jesus Christ in these activities also.

Reasons for Spiritual Conflict

There are three reasons why a believer can expect—and must be prepared for—a spiritual conflict as he lives for the Lord. First, believers must be prepared for spiritual warfare because there is a traitor in the camp. This traitor is the "flesh," which is the old nature. The old nature is not eradicated when a person receives Christ as Saviour, so there is a spiritual struggle between the old nature and the new nature in the life of each believer.

Galatians 5:17 says, "For the flesh lusteth against the Spirit, and the Spirit against the flesh: and these are contrary the one to the other: so that ye cannot do the things that ye would." Here we see the flesh opposing the liberty we have in Christ. The flesh always seeks to bring us into bondage to its desires. Satan entices us through the flesh. Jesus had to rebuke Peter one time and say, "Simon, Simon, behold, Satan hath desired to have you, that he may sift you as wheat: but I have prayed for thee, that thy faith fail not" (Luke 22:31,32).

Satan is the enemy of our souls; he is envious of our salvation in Christ and especially seeks to destroy our allegiance to Christ. Satan trails believers and tries to take advantage of them. The Bible tells us, "Be sober, be vigilant; because your adversary the devil, as a roaring lion, walketh about, seeking whom he may devour: whom resist stedfast in the faith" (I Pet. 5:8,9).

A second reason there is spiritual conflict is that the believer is a member of the Body of Christ. From the time that God pronounced the curse on Satan in the Garden of Eden, Satan has sought to destroy Christ. Therefore, anyone associated with Christ—especially a part of His Body—is subject to Satan's attack. There are many instances recorded throughout the Scriptures when Satan sought to destroy Christ. When Christ took upon Himself a body to be born among men to die for their sin, Satan sought to destroy Him as a baby. Herod served Satan's purpose when he decreed that all the children in Bethlehem and surrounding areas, two years old and under, should be killed (Matt. 2:16). However, because God is wiser than Satan, Jesus escaped death because Mary and Joseph had been instructed to take Him out of the country.

Later, when Satan tried to entice Jesus to sin, he challenged Christ to throw Himself down from a pinnacle of the temple, but Christ responded, "Thou shalt not tempt the Lord thy God" (4:7). When Jesus was on the cross, Satan no doubt thought he was victorious in having Christ put to death, but Christ rose from the dead and thereby proved that He had conquered Satan. Christ then ascended to the Father, beyond the realm of Satan.

Inasmuch as Satan can no longer attack Christ Himself, Satan attacks the Body of Christ which is the Church. The mystical Body of Christ, made up of all believers, is within the reach of Satan even though Christ Himself is not. However, the Body of Christ will ultimately be victorious, for Christ said, "I will build my church; and the gates of hell shall not prevail against it" (16:18).

A third reason there is spiritual conflict for believers is that God's plan and purpose include the fact that Christ will someday rule the world in righteousness. Because this refers to a future time, this might be referred to as a "dispensational" reason for spiritual conflict. As the Apostle John told of a vision he had had of Christ's return to earth, he said, "And I saw heaven opened, and behold a white horse; and he that sat upon him was called Faithful and True, and in righteousness he doth judge and make war" (Rev. 19:11). Acts 17:31 prophesies, "Because he [God] hath appointed a day, in the which he will judge the world in righteousness by that man whom he hath ordained; whereof he hath given assurance unto all men, in that he hath raised him from the dead." This verse reveals that the Father has delegated all judgment to the Son. This means—and Satan knows this—that there will be a final reckoning with the powers of evil, which will result in their—and Satan's—ultimate destruction. In Revelation 1:18 Christ says, "I am he that liveth, and was dead; and, behold, I am alive for evermore, Amen; and have the keys of hell and of death." Revelation 20:10 tells of the final doom of Satan: "And the devil that deceived them was cast into the lake of fire and brimstone, where the beast and the false prophet are, and shall be tormented day and night for ever and ever."

Inasmuch as believers are to share with Christ in His reigning and judging, we are laid open to the attacks of Satan at the present time. Satan and his messengers claim this world as their own; thus, those of us who will eventually sit in judgment over them are laid open to conflict. Satan is well aware that God's program is closing in on him and for this reason he directs much of his attention to harassing the Church. Even though Satan is at work, the Holy Spirit is at present restraining evil. Second Thessalonians 2:7 says, "For the mystery of lawlessness is already at work; only he who now restrains will do so until he is taken out of the way" (NASB). This restraining work of the Holy Spirit, through believers, has been going on ever since the Day of Pentecost when the Church came into existence. But it is evident we are being brought ever nearer to the final conflict.

Therefore, as Paul wrote his letter to the Ephesians, his final remarks concerning the believer's warfare were necessary and right on target. Believers ought not to be controlled by fear because of this warfare. Rather, we should remember the words of Matthew 16:18: "I will build my church; and the gates of hell shall not prevail against it"; of John 16:33: "In the world ye shall have tribulation: but be of good cheer; I have overcome the world"; and of I John 4:4: "Greater is he that is in you, than he that is in the world."

The Christian does not need to live in constant fear of Satan and his emissaries. Romans 8:31 assures us, "If God be for us, who can be against us?" Paul was writing to believers and the word "if" has the meaning of "since." That is, those of us who have received Jesus Christ as Saviour know that God is for us because Paul has told us this in the preceding passages. Therefore, since God is for us no one is able to stand against us. Paul further explained, "He that spared not his own Son, but delivered him up for us all, how shall he not with him also freely give us all things?" (v. 32). This is where we stand! This is our position in Christ. Thus Paul said, "Who shall lay anything to the charge of God's elect? It is God that justifieth. Who is he that condemneth? It is Christ that died, yea rather, that is risen again, who is even at the right hand of God, who also maketh intercession for us" (vv. 33,34).

The Devil cannot effectively charge us with something now because, having believed in Jesus Christ as Saviour, we have been justified—declared righteous. Though the Devil may bring accusations, Jesus Christ is at the right hand of the Father interceding for us. The Lord Jesus Christ has paid the full penalty for our sin so the Devil—or anyone else—is not able to bring condemnation on us.

Provision for Victory

With these truths in mind concerning our position in Christ, let us now focus our attention on Ephesians 6:10-20. This passage refers to the spiritual warfare in which every believer is involved. It reveals the source of the strength and the equipment we have that enable us to be victorious. We must understand clearly the principles by which this warfare is to be waged. There are certain conditions that must be met if we are to personally experience the victory that Christ has already accomplished for us. It is important to recognize that victory is assumed. Christ has defeated Satan and has won the victory for us. Therefore, our responsibility is to live according to our victorious position and not to suffer defeat at the hands of the Enemy, who has already been defeated. We are to take our stand against any onslaught of the Enemy because he has no chance to defeat us as long as we recognize our position in Christ.

Victory for the believer is the valid promise on which everything else is based. This is seen from Romans 8:35-39. In this passage Paul asked the question, "Who shall separate us from the love of Christ?" (v. 35). After mentioning some things that could be considered possibilities, Paul gave this resounding answer: "Nay, in all these things we are more than conquerors through him that loved us" (v. 37). How can we be more than conquerors? This will be revealed as we examine Ephesians 6:10-20. How wonderful it is to know that nothing "shall be able to separate us from the love of God, which is in Christ Jesus our Lord" (Rom. 8:39).

Paul also reminded the Corinthians of the victory we have in Christ: "But thanks be to God, which giveth us the victory through our Lord Jesus Christ" (I Cor. 15:57). "Now thanks be unto God, which always causeth us to triumph in Christ" (II Cor. 2:14). Ephesians 6:10-20 reveals God's all-sufficient provision for such total victory.

Chapter 24

The Believer's Strength for the Conflict
(Eph. 6:10)

Having told us of our position in Christ and the necessity to put this into practice, Paul said, "Finally, my brethren, be strong in the Lord, and in the power of his might" (Eph. 6:10). From this verse we see that all the power of heaven is at our disposal. This power is available because of our position in Christ that Paul described in the first three chapters of Ephesians. It is only from our position in Christ that the battle can be successfully waged. It's a position of faith—taking God at His Word and trusting Him to do what He said He will do.

This same principle is seen throughout the Scriptures. When the Israelites entered the land of Canaan, God told Joshua, "There shall not any man be able to stand before thee all the days of thy life: as I was with Moses, so I will be with thee: I will not fail thee, nor forsake thee. Be strong and of a good courage: for unto this people shalt thou divide for an inheritance the land, which I sware unto their fathers to give them" (Josh. 1:5,6). Notice that the God of Moses was the God of Joshua, and He is our God also. Again God told Joshua, "Be strong and of a good courage; be not afraid, neither be thou dismayed: for the Lord thy God is with thee whithersoever thou goest" (v. 9).

The word "finally" in Ephesians 6:10 indicates Paul's final word concerning the believer's walk. Paul said, "Be strong in the Lord." Notice he did not say that we are to take our strength *from* the Lord but that we are to be strong *in* the Lord. We are to recognize our position in Christ and live accordingly. As we do this, we will be continuously empowered by the Lord for any conflict. It is important to see that we do not just take our place at the side of the Lord but that our place of strength is in the Lord. Having received Him as Saviour, we are in Him and He is our strength. The word "in" is the key word in the Book of Ephesians. The book reveals how each member of the Body of Christ has its strength in Christ. This is why Paul could say in Philippians 4:13, "I can do all things through Christ which strengtheneth me."

Christ Is Lord

Notice the title "Lord" in Ephesians 6:10. The more common title used throughout Ephesians in referring to the second Person of the Trinity is "Christ." His full title is "Lord Jesus Christ." Each of these three words has a special emphasis. "Jesus" is His earthly name for it was given to Him at birth and has to do with His work of redemption. The angel of the Lord told Joseph, "She [Mary] shall bring forth a son, and thou shalt call his name Jesus: for he shall save his people from their sins" (Matt. 1:21). The name "Christ" is His heavenly name. This is the name Andrew used when he told his brother, " 'We have found the Messiah,' which translated means Christ" (John 1:41, NASB). It has to do with His heavenly work and also His return as the Messiah. In emphasizing our position because of salvation, the Bible most frequently uses the heavenly name, "Christ." This is seen in Galatians 2:20: "I am crucified with Christ: nevertheless I live; yet not I, but Christ liveth in me: and the life which I now live in the flesh I live by the faith of the Son of God, who loved me, and gave himself for me."

The title "Lord" not only reveals His position within the Trinity—He is God—but designates that He is our Master. Remember what Jesus told His disciples: "You call me Teacher, and Lord; and you are right; for so I am" (John 13:13, NASB). Because Jesus Christ is God, He is to be the Master, or Lord, of our lives.

The title "Lord" also reveals the power of Jesus Christ. Referring to the time He will return to earth to destroy His enemies and to establish His kingdom, the Bible says, "And he hath on his vesture and on his thigh a name written, King of Kings, and Lord of Lords" (Rev. 19:16). This is what Jesus is to the believer. He has not only atoned for our sins, but He has overcome our foes by His mighty power. Through death, He has broken Satan's power so that we need not be defeated by him.

This we see in Hebrews 2:14,15: "Since then the children share in flesh and blood, He Himself likewise also partook of the same, that through death He might render powerless him who had the power of death, that is, the devil; and might deliver those who through fear of death were subject to slavery all their lives" (NASB). The same truth is emphasized in Colossians 2:14,15: "Blotting out the handwriting of ordinances that was against us, which was contrary to us, and took it out of the way, nailing it to his cross; and having spoiled principalities and powers, he made a shew of them openly, triumphing over them in it." (Also compare Ephesians 1:19-23 with 4:8).

Christ's resurrection put Him in a position of authority, far above all principalities and powers (Phil. 2:9-11). Because He has all power we are to be "strong in the Lord" (Eph. 6:10), for He is the victorious One. As we think of Him, we must see Him as the Conqueror He is and ourselves as having been raised to the place of conqueror in Him. In Ephesians 2:5,6, Paul wrote that God "even when we were dead in sins, hath quickened us together with Christ, (by grace ye are saved;) and hath raised us up together, and made us sit together in heavenly places in Christ Jesus."

As we have seen, the events in the Book of Joshua illustrate beautifully many of the truths of the Ephesians. Just as Joshua had to recognize the Captain of the Lord's host, so we believers must recognize Christ as the Lord of our lives. Joshua had entered the land of Canaan and before him was the territory that was to be conquered. It seemed almost impossible that the Israelites would be able to take the land as God had promised. But then there appeared a man before him with a drawn sword and Joshua said to him, "Art thou for us, or for our adversaries?" (5:13). The man answered, "Nay; but as captain of the host of the Lord am I now come" (v. 14). Joshua immediately prostrated himself before the man, recognizing him as an appearance of the Lord, and asked, "What saith my lord unto his servant?" The Lord then gave Joshua orders. So we too must recognize Christ as our

Lord and expect Him to guide us and be our strength in battle.

The Book of Joshua presents Jesus Christ as Lord. As the Israelites stood on the border of the Promised Land, the Lord appeared to them as the Conqueror. Joshua had to learn that he could do all things through the Lord, who strengthens believers. The Lord had told Joshua, "Every place that the sole of your foot shall tread upon, that have I given unto you, as I said unto Moses" (1:3). But when the Lord appeared to Joshua, as recorded in chapter 5, He was saying in effect, "I've promised you this land but you must follow Me if you are to take it, for only then will I enable you to take it."

We must remember that the Promised Land is not symbolic of heaven but of abundant life. It was a place filled with conflict, but victory was had as the people took God at His word and lived in obedience to Him. The battles fought in Canaan were won supernaturally. This is evident from events such as the conquering of Jericho. The Israelites marched around Jericho once each day for six days, and on the seventh day they marched around the city seven times. "And it came to pass at the seventh time, when the priests blew with the trumpets, Joshua said unto the people, Shout; for the Lord hath given you the city" (6:16).

Identification With Victory

Many other instances revealed the supernatural working of God in behalf of His people. We must remember that the God of Joshua's time is our God too, that His power has not diminished, and that is available to us through faith. We must not only view Christ as our Captain, having seen Him as the Conqueror, but we must also identify ourselves with Him in His victory. The key to victory is that we must take our position with Christ as a co-victor. We will experience victory on a daily basis as we have faith in Him. Remember, that the evidence of faith is action based on that faith. A faith that does not produce action is not a genuine faith. We must show ourselves partners in the victory.

The account in the tenth chapter of Joshua shows how Joshua required the Israelites to identify themselves with the position of victors. After a great battle, during which Joshua commanded the sun to stand still, he returned to his Gilgal camp. However, the Bible says, "But these five kings fled, and hid themselves in a cave at Makkedah" (v. 16). Joshua commanded that huge stones be placed at the mouth of the cave to prevent the kings from escaping while the Israelites continued to fight their enemies. Then, returning to the cave, Joshua commanded that the kings be brought before him. The mouth of the cave was opened and the kings of Jerusalem, Hebron, Jarmuth, Lachish and Eglon stood before Joshua. The Bible says, "When they brought out those kings unto Joshua, that Joshua called for all the men of Israel, and said unto the captains of the men of war which went with him, Come near, put your feet upon the necks of these kings. And they came near, and put their feet upon the necks of them. And Joshua said unto them, Fear not, nor be dismayed, be strong and of good courage: for thus shall the Lord do to all your enemies against whom ye fight" (vv. 24,25). The placing of their feet on the necks of their enemies was the symbol of victory for the conquerors of Joshua's day. Joshua required that his captains of war do this to identify themselves in this victory and reminded them that the Lord would give them victory over all their enemies.

We also have a victorious position, which Christ has obtained for us. The fact that God has "raised us up together, and made us sit together in heavenly places in Christ Jesus" (Eph. 2:6) does not mean that we have been physically transported to a heavenly position; rather, by faith we are in this place of victory.

Jesus Christ has completely conquered the enemy, but the enemy will continue to harass us until we take our position of victory with Christ. It is as in a physical battle where the one at the top of the hill has the advantage. Christ is at the top of the hill because He has conquered Satan, and we can be victorious over Satan only as we take our position with Christ.

We must act by faith on the basis of our position in Christ. Beware of those who talk of living by faith as if there is absolutely nothing the believer does. Some give the impression that the believer becomes totally passive and that God does everything apart from the will and personality of the believer. God does accomplish the victory, but He does it in and through the believer. We must not rely on self-effort, but neither are we to be guilty of laziness or disobedience in following the Lord. The Lord does not override our wills, but as we place our faith in Him and live accordingly, He will give us victory. God not only does the work in and through us but He even gives us the desire to do His will: "For it is God who is at work in you, both to will and to work for His good pleasure" (Phil. 2:13, NASB). The preceding verse indicates that we are to work out through our lives what God works in us. This calls for obedience, and only when we are obedient will we be powerful in the Lord.

Source of Confidence

The account of I Samuel 17 illustrates the importance of trusting in the Lord rather than in human resources. This passage of Scripture tells how the giant Goliath and the Philistines were challenging the army of Israel. Goliath bargained with the Israelites to choose a man to fight against him, and the army of the winner would be considered victorious over the other army. No one in the army of Israel was willing to accept the challenge. When young David came looking for his brothers, he learned of Goliath's challenge and offered to fight him himself. At first no one would take David seriously because he was such a young man and Goliath was a veteran of warfare.

David recounted for King Saul how he had killed a lion and a bear while he was keeping his father's sheep, and he was confident that the Lord would deliver Goliath into his hand, just as He had the wild animals. Saul agreed to let David fight Goliath, but before he sent David out he gave him his armor. Trying on Saul's armor, David realized he would be unable to fight Goliath while wearing this armor because he was not used to it. The armor is a reminder of man-made protection in warfare. David's past victories had been because of trust in the Lord, not because of trusting in man-made armor.

Saul was a man of weak faith; his confidence was almost entirely in the armor. David was a man of strong faith; his confidence was in God.

David's confidence in God was evident from what he said to Goliath after he had taken five smooth stones and met Goliath at the place of battle: "Thou comest to me with a sword, and with a spear, and with a shield: but I come to thee in the name of the Lord of hosts, the God of the armies of Israel, whom thou hast defied. This day will the Lord deliver thee into mine hand" (vv. 45,46). David told Goliath that all of this was to be so "that all the earth may know that there is a God in Israel. And all this assembly shall know that the Lord saveth not with sword and spear: for the battle is the Lord's, and he will give you into our hands" (vv. 46,47).

How could David be so sure? He had learned that confidence in the Lord is never misplaced. In the words of Ephesians 6, David was "strong in the Lord, and in the power of his might" (v. 10).

The great need today is for believers to be "strong in the Lord." This is not a matter of progressive attainment; rather, it is a matter of occupying one's victorious position that Christ has already gained for us. As we recognize these truths and live accordingly, our faith will become more courageous for we will see God work in our lives. But it is important to remember that we need to take our position with Christ before we begin battle. Jesus Christ has already triumphed over our foes; therefore, we need to take our position with Him in the place of victory. Just as there was no question in David's mind before the battle but what God would give the victory, there should be no question in the believer's mind because Christ has already accomplished the victory. The real victory over Goliath was won before David ever went to meet him in the valley; our victory in spiritual warfare has been won by Christ before we enter the battle.

The conflict does not consist in fighting *for* a victory with the Lord's help. We do not need to ask the Lord to help us to gain a victory, since He has already gained the victory. We do not fight *for* victory but *from* a position of victory in Christ. This is the character of our spiritual conflict. Because Christ has already accomplished the victory, the enemy has already been dislodged from his stronghold and is a conquered foe (Heb. 2:14; Col. 2:15).

The Lord Is Our Strength

Not only has the Lord accomplished the victory for us, but He also indwells and strengthens us. Because He indwells us, it is more than our getting our strength from Him; it is that He Himself *is* our strength.

The Bible indicates the believer is in a place of victory and that his responsibility is to hold his position, not to attempt to gain it. Ephesians 6:11,13 emphasizes that we are to "stand" and "withstand." This is holding our position in Christ.

Revelation 2:25,26 provide an illustration of this. To the Church of Thyatira, the Lord Jesus Christ said, "But that which ye have already hold fast till I come. And he that overcometh, and keepeth my works unto the end, to him will I give power over the nations." Here we see that to overcome is to maintain one's position. The Lord Jesus Christ told the Church at Philadelphia, "Behold, I come quickly: hold that fast which thou hast, that no man take thy crown. Him that overcometh will I make a pillar in the temple of my God" (3:11,12). There is no substitute for the strength and power that is ours because of our position in Christ. From Ephesians 6 we see that the believer is made fit with inner strength before he is offered outer equipment, or armor. This armor is valuable only as our minds and wills are properly adjusted by our faith relationship to the Lord Jesus Christ.

Ephesians 6:10 says, "Be strong in the Lord, and in the power of his might." The words "be strong" can be translated "be strengthened." Here Paul used the Greek present tense so it has the meaning of "be continually strengthened." First Corinthians 16:13 says, "Be on the alert, stand firm in the faith, act like men, be strong" (NASB).

Ephesians 6:10 contains three Greek words that emphasize different aspects of power, or strength. The word translated "be strong" means "to make strong, to endue with strength." It portrays a person clothing himself with strength as one puts on a garment. As we have seen, it is used in a tense which emphasizes continuous action. Also notice that it is a command—for us to "be strong in the Lord."

The word translated "power" refers to manifested power. This word was often used of a power that depends on another's power—in this case it is the believer's power that depends on the power of Christ.

The word translated "might" refers to a special enduement of power. The believer is endued with power from Christ, and because Christ lives in the believer, He really is the believer's power. Colossians 1:27 refers to this when it says, "Christ in you, the hope of glory." Verse 29 says, "For this I labor [unto weariness], striving with all the superhuman energy which He so mightily enkindles and works within me" (Amplified). This refers to the same power mentioned in Ephesians 1:19: "The exceeding greatness of his power to us-ward who believe, according to the working of his mighty power."

Chapter 25

The Believer's Foes and Their Methods
(Eph. 6:11,12,16)

The primary foe of believers is referred to in Ephesians 6:11, which records Paul's command, "Put on the whole armour of God, that ye may be able to stand against the wiles of the devil." The Devil himself, also known as "Satan," is the believer's main enemy.

From this we see that even though the world system and the flesh are enemies of the believer, the key figure in the spiritual conflict that the believer must face is Satan. So the conflict of Ephesians 6 does not come from within but from without the believer. Paul gave instructions earlier in Ephesians as to how the internal enemy of the flesh was to be dealt with. These instructions were given specifically in 4:22-24, where we were told to put off the things related to the old nature and to put on those things becoming to the new nature. If we have done what Paul said to do, we can treat self, or the flesh, as a conquered foe. However, we must remember that the desires of the old nature continually seek our attention so we must always be on our guard concerning the flesh.

Having been faithful in overcoming the internal foe, we now can turn our attention toward overcoming the external foe. If, however, we have not come to grips with the problem of self, we are in no position to maintain victory over Satan. The Old Testament Israelites serve as a national parallel to this individual problem. After the Israelites were delivered from Egypt, they wandered in the desert, being preoccupied with themselves and murmuring against God. During the years of wandering they were ineffective for God because they refused to take Him at His word and go into Canaan and conquer the land. The older generation died in the wilderness because of their disobedience, but the new generation believed God, left the desert behind them and entered the land God had promised to them. There they engaged in warfare against God's and their common enemies, for even though God had promised them the land they had to act on faith and take it. They were able to effectively stand against their enemies only as they overcame preoccupation with themselves.

So, too, Satan has no need to attack us as long as we are preoccupied with self. However, when we take God at His word and walk by faith, we can be sure that we will be exposed to and experience the attacks of Satan. Of course, the believer can avoid much spiritual conflict by remaining in a spiritual desert even as Israel remained in the desert rather than believing God and engaging in warfare. But if the believer fails to move out for the Lord he will never know the joy of spiritual victory the Lord desires him to know. There may be conflict but it will be the conflict of the believer's will with God's will, not the spiritual conflict that is referred to in Ephesians 6.

The warfare described in Ephesians 6:10-20 is a warfare in which we join the Lord in holding the position of victory that He has already secured. We need not yield to fear concerning Satan for Christ has been victorious over him and our need is to claim our position of victory in Christ.

Binding the Strong Man

Matthew 12:28-30 gives us a lesson in spiritual warfare. The Lord Jesus Christ was accused of casting out demons by the power of Satan, but He answered, "If I cast out devils [demons] by the Spirit of God, then the kingdom of God is come unto you. Or how else can one enter into a strong man's house, and spoil his goods, except he first bind the strong man? and then he will spoil his house. He that is not with me is against me; and he that gathereth not with me scattereth abroad." The Lord Jesus was telling the Pharisees that the reason He was able to cast out demons was because He had power over Satan himself. Jesus' statement "He that is not with me is against me" (v. 30) refers to our refusing to take our position with Christ in binding Satan. After Jesus Christ died for our sin He was buried, rose from the dead and ascended to the Heavenly Father. He won the victory over Satan and provided salvation for the entire world. Those of us who trust in Him as Saviour become part of His mystical Body, the Church. Those who have not yet believed are in a sense bound by Satan because they have been blinded by him (II Cor. 4:3,4). Our responsibility as believers is to pray for these who are blinded by Satan, for in this way we engage in spiritual warfare and stand with Christ in overcoming Satan; that is, in binding the strong man (Matt. 12:29).

Notice that there is no neutral position—people are either for Christ or against Him (Matt. 12:30). It is impossible to maintain a middle-of-the-road position concerning one's relationship with Jesus Christ.

Even as God promised the land of Canaan to Joshua and the Israelites but required them to personally take the land, so Christ has gained the victory over Satan but requires us to take our position with Him in praying for those who are bound by him. By prayer, we loose them from Satan's power and gather them for Christ.

After the Israelites had been in the land a few years, they still had not possessed the land. Joshua said to them, "How long are ye slack to go to possess the land, which the Lord God of your fathers hath given you?" (Josh. 18:3). So, too, the Lord must wonder why some believers today are so hesitant to identify themselves with Him in victory over Satan and to engage in spiritual warfare to see others come to Christ.

Our warfare is not primarily with other persons but with Satan. Ephesians 6:11 says that we're to stand "against the wiles of the devil," and verse 12 reminds us that we are not in conflict against "flesh and blood." The real enemy is not visible; he is a mighty but unseen foe. However, he expresses himself through that which is visible, whether it be people or circumstances. He presents temptations to believers, hoping they will yield to them and discredit Christ. We are warring not only against Satan, but also against his hosts, for verse 12 says we're warring against "principalities, against powers, against the rulers of the darkness of this world, against spiritual wickedness in high places." Man-made weapons are of no advantage in this spiritual warfare. Man-made weapons are weapons of the flesh, but II Corinthians 10:3-5 reminds us, "For though we walk in the flesh, we do not war after the flesh: (for the weapons of our warfare are not carnal, but mighty through God to the pulling down of strong holds;) casting down imaginations, and every high thing that exalteth itself against the knowledge of God, and bringing into captivity every thought to the obedience of Christ."

The hosts of Satan are fallen angels who do his bidding. Although Satan is not omnipresent, his will is carried out on a universal scale through his emissaries. He is their commander in chief. This host of fallen angels are referred to as principalities and powers in Ephesians 6:12. This indicates that the messengers of Satan are a well-organized army divided into ranks and divisions. "Principalities" is literally "rulers," and "powers" is literally "authorities." Thus, principalities and powers refer to the supremacy of rule and authority in the satanic realm. The words "rulers of the darkness of this world" is literally "the world rulers of this darkness." No wonder it is said that our warfare is "against spiritual wickedness in high places" (v. 12).

The Greek word translated "high places" in Ephesians 6:12 is the same word that is translated "heavenly places" in 1:3,20; 2:6 and 3:10. Although the heavenly realm is referred to in both instances, a different sphere of heaven is intended. From II Corinthians 12:2 we learn that there are three heavens, for Paul referred to a person—probably himself—who was "caught up to the third heaven." The third heaven is the place of God's special abode, the second is the stellar heaven, and the first is the atmospheric heaven, which is closest to earth.

Although principalities and powers are in a heavenly realm, the believer's position with Christ is higher than these, for Ephesians 1:20,21 tells us that the Father set Christ "at his own right hand in the heavenly places, far above all principality, and power, and might, and dominion, and every name that is named, not only in this world, but also in that which is to come." It is the third heaven that Christ referred to as "my Father's house" (John 14:2), and it is there that Christ is seated at the right hand of the Father. It is here that we have our spiritual position with Christ; therefore, *in Him* we too are situated above these satanic forces in spiritual authority. This is our position by faith.

Satan's Dwelling Place

There was a time when Satan—then known as "Lucifer"—lived in the third heaven with God. Isaiah 14:12-14 refers to Satan's fall from the third heaven: "How art thou fallen from heaven, O Lucifer, son of the morning! how art thou cut down to the ground, which didst weaken the nations! For thou hast said in thine heart, I will ascend into heaven, I will exalt my throne above the stars of God: I will sit also upon the mount of the congregation, in the sides of the north: I will ascend above the heights of the clouds; I will be like the most High." Ezekiel 28:14,15 reveals that Lucifer was created without sin: "Thou art the anointed cherub that covereth; and I have set thee so: thou wast upon the holy mountain of God; thou hast walked up and down in the midst of the stones of fire. Thou wast perfect in thy ways from the day that thou wast created, till iniquity was found in thee."

Satan does not dwell in the third heaven although he has access to it to accuse those who have faith in God (see Job 1:6-12; 2:1-7). Having been thrown out of the third heaven, the place of God's abode, Satan now has domain in the first and second heavens—the atmospheric and stellar heavens. He is known as the "prince of the power of the air" (Eph. 2:2).

During the coming Tribulation, Satan and his angels will also be thrown out of the first and second heavens onto the earth. Referring to the battle of Michael and his angels against Satan and his angels, Revelation 12:9 says, "And the great dragon was cast out, that old serpent, called the Devil, and Satan, which deceiveth the whole world: he was cast out into the earth, and his angels were cast out with him." Viewing this time prophetically, the Apostle John said, "And I heard a loud voice saying in heaven, Now is come salvation, and strength, and the kingdom of our God, and the power of his Christ: for the accuser of our brethren is cast down, which accused them before our God day and night" (v. 10). Observe how Satan is overcome when he is thrown down to the earth: "They overcame him by the blood of the Lamb, and by the word of their testimony; and they loved not their lives unto the death" (v. 11). Because Christ fully judged Satan when He shed His blood on the cross, Satan has no power against the benefits of Christ's death or against the Word of God. When Satan and his angels are thrown out of heaven onto the earth, Satan's full fury will be seen "because he knoweth that he hath but a short time" (v. 12). Since these events will take place during the Tribulation, the Church of Jesus Christ will not be on earth, having been raptured before the Tribulation began. This is why verse 12 says, "Therefore rejoice, ye heavens, and ye that dwell in them." These words are said to the Church, who is dwelling in heaven with Christ while the Tribulation is raging on earth.

Know the Enemy

One of the most basic matters in warfare is to know the enemy you are fighting. We cannot expect to be successful in spiritual warfare against Satan if we do not know who he is and what his tactics are.

Even a casual acquaintance with Scripture reveals that Satan is much more than an influence; he is a person, and as such, he speaks, he plans, he deceives, he hates, he fights. Yet some people refuse to believe that the Devil is a real person, maintaining that he is only the influence of evil, or a symbol of evil. Even this misconception is a tribute to Satan's success in deceiving unbelievers. One of his best methods of concealing his activities is to influence people to think that he does not exist. A false optimism appears wherever Satan is not recognized as the key enemy working in human affairs. Satan has been so successful in hiding himself that some people even think they can bring in the millennium by their own good efforts. However, before a millennium of peace is known by the world it will be necessary for Jesus Christ to personally return and confine Satan to the bottomless pit (20:3).

The only way to overcome Satan is to confront him with the finished work of Calvary by which Christ gained the victory over him. Satan knows that he is ultimately a defeated foe because of what Christ accomplished on the cross. We have seen that during the Tribulation believers will overcome Satan by the blood of the Lamb and by their testimony (12:11). This is the same basis for our victory over Satan now, for we cannot be victorious over him on our own—it is only as we claim our position in Christ that we will experience victory.

The Bible has much to say about Satan. The titles it gives to Satan explain his activities. He is called the "prince of the power of the air" (Eph. 2:2), referring to Satan's exercise of power in the atmospheric and stellar heavens. He is also called "the prince of this world" (John 12:31), which reveals that Satan claims the throne of this world. Satan's power over the world is revealed in I John 5:19: "We know that we are of God, and the whole world lies in the power of the evil one" (NASB).

Satan is referred to as "the god of this world" (II Cor. 4:4), which reveals that he claims and accepts the worship of the world. Where the gospel has not been preached, it is common to find the people worshiping Satan and demons out of fear.

He is also referred to as "the accuser of our brethren" (Rev. 12:10), and the first two chapters of Job reveal how he does this. Satan seeks to bring about the ruin of God's children by these accusations. Satan first entices the people of God to sin; then he accuses them before God of the sin they have committed. However, we need have no fear for Jesus Christ stands as our Advocate before the Father: "My little children, these things write I unto you, that ye sin not. And if any man sin, we have an advocate with the Father, Jesus Christ the righteous" (I John 2:1). The Lord Jesus Christ pleads our case as does a lawyer, and the basis for his plea is what He accomplished for us on the cross. The following verse says, "And he is the propitiation [satisfaction] for our sins: and not for our's only, but also for the sins of the whole world."

When we sin we need to confess our sin to God, who has promised to forgive when we confess it: "If we confess our sins, he is faithful and just to forgive us our sins, and to cleanse us from all unrighteousness" (I John 1:9). God's forgiveness is based on the fact that Christ has already paid the penalty for our sin. Thus, when we confess our sin, we are restored to fellowship with the Heavenly Father.

THE BELIEVER'S FOES AND THEIR METHODS 267

Satan's Methods

When writing to the Corinthians regarding Satan, Paul reminded them, "For we are not ignorant of his devices" (II Cor. 2:11). However, it seems today that believers are frequently ignorant of the methods Satan uses, so let us look at several of them.

From II Corinthians 4:4 we learn that Satan blinds the minds of unbelievers: "In whom the god of this world hath blinded the minds of them which believe not, lest the light of the glorious gospel of Christ, who is the image of God, should shine unto them." Satan wants to keep people from seeing their need to receive Christ as Saviour. Our responsibility in this spiritual warfare is to cooperate with Christ, by prayer, in binding Satan so he will not be able to keep in bondage those he has blinded.

Another tactic of Satan is seen from II Corinthians 11:13-15: "For such are false apostles, deceitful workers, transforming themselves into the apostles of Christ. And no marvel; for Satan himself is transformed into an angel of light. Therefore it is no great thing if his ministers also be transformed as the ministers of righteousness; whose end shall be according to their works." There are many in pulpits today who do not preach the gospel of the grace of Christ; rather, they teach a gospel of works. It sounds reasonable because people like to think they must work for anything that is worth having. Through such teaching Satan has transformed himself into an angel of light that he might keep unbelievers from the kingdom of God.

From Ephesians 2:2 we see that Satan energizes men to disobedience: "Wherein in time past ye walked according to the course of this world, according to the prince of the power of the air, the spirit that now worketh in the children of disobedience."

The main tactic of Satan is to deceive the world. This is evident from Revelation 12:9, where he is referred to as "that old serpent, called the Devil, and Satan, which deceiveth the whole world." Referring to the Antichrist, who will appear during the coming Tribulation, II Thessalonians 2:9 says, "Even him, whose coming is after the working of Satan with all power and signs and lying wonders." By his "lying wonders" he will deceive the world during the Tribulation.

Paul referred to those who were caught in Satan's trap when he told Timothy, "With gentleness correcting those who are in opposition; if perhaps God may grant them repentance, leading to the knowledge of the truth, and they may come to their senses and escape from the snare of the devil, having been held captive by him to do his will" (II Tim. 2:25,26, NASB).

Satan also originates false doctrine to mislead mankind. The Bible says, "Now the Spirit speaketh expressly, that in the latter times some shall depart from the faith, giving heed to seducing spirits, and doctrines of devils [demons]" (I Tim. 4:1). Satan encourages all doctrine that is contrary to the Scriptures because it detracts from Jesus Christ. Liberal theology that denies the deity of Christ, His atoning work on the cross, and His personal return, is inspired by Satan himself.

The power of Satan is closely associated with his methods. Hebrews 2:14 indicates that before Christ's death on the cross, Satan had the "power of death." However, it is evident that even during Old Testament times Satan's power was restricted by God. When Satan wanted to bring affliction on Job, God said, "Behold, all that he hath is in thy power; only upon himself put not forth thine hand" (Job 1:12). Later, God permitted Satan to go further in his testing of Job, but told Satan, "Behold, he is in thine hand; but save his life" (2:6). From these verses we see that Satan was not able to exercise his power beyond the boundaries which God had prescribed.

The believer is able to be victorious over Satan because of his position in Christ and of the effectiveness of his weapons. Since we are seated "together in heavenly places in Christ Jesus" (Eph. 2:6), no one is able to touch us without touching Christ Himself. Paul reminded believers, "For the weapons of our warfare are not carnal, but mighty through God to the pulling down of strong holds" (II Cor. 10:4).

Our position in Christ makes it impossible for Satan to gain the victory over us as long as we remain in our position by faith. Christ has all power over principalities and powers; thus, the believer benefits from this power as he, by faith, utilizes the authority of Christ. Someone has said that the believer is a Christ-enclosed person; that is, Satan cannot touch him apart from touching Christ Himself.

Satan knows where he is defeated. He is too experienced to waste time and strength against walls that he knows are impregnable. So we need not fear Satan's attack as long as we are entrenched in our position in Christ. However, because Satan is cunning, he will attempt to draw us out of our position and cause us to rely on our own strength to defeat him, rather than on the strength we have in Christ.

Ephesians 6:11 refers to the "wiles" of Satan. The word translated "wiles" is the word from which "methods" is derived. As used in Bible times, it referred to cunning arts, deceit, craft, trickery. Satan uses subtle methods to allure us out of our stronghold in Christ. If Satan is able to get the believer to doubt, or even to entertain discouragement (both come from Satan), he has greater hopes of succeeding in his schemes. The moment the believer no longer relies on his faith position in Christ he falls under Satan's power. We need to heed Christ's words, "Watch ye therefore, and pray always" (Luke 21:36).

Paul did not view the Christian life as being easy, and he encouraged Timothy: "Fight the good fight of faith" (I Tim. 6:12). It is in this fight of faith that the believer needs to utilize the armor mentioned in Ephesians 6, which will be discussed in the following chapter. In the spiritual conflict it is important that we not be overconfident and think we can defeat Satan on our own. The Bible instructs believers, "Humble yourselves therefore under the mighty hand of God, that he may exalt you in due time: Casting all your care upon him; for he careth for you. Be sober, be vigilant; because your adversary the devil, as a roaring lion, walketh about, seeking whom he may devour: whom resist stedfast in the faith, knowing that the same afflictions are accomplished in your brethren that are in the world" (I Pet. 5:6-9). First Peter 4:7 says, "The end of all things is at hand: be ye therefore sober, and watch unto prayer."

It is encouraging to remember that the weakest believer who lives on the basis of his faith position in Christ is as safe as the most mature believer because both are within the same impregnable fortress. Such a believer can say with David,

"The Lord is my rock, and my fortress, and my deliverer; the God of my rock; in him will I trust: he is my shield, and the horn of my salvation, my high tower, and my refuge, my saviour; thou savest me from violence. I will call on the Lord, who is worthy to be praised: so shall I be saved from mine enemies" (II Sam. 22:2-4).

It should also be realized that the most advanced believer is weak and helpless the moment he ceases to rely on his position in Christ. It is not necessary for one to constantly think about his position in Christ, but it must be the basis for all that he is and does. It is necessary, therefore, for the believer to come to the point in his life where he recognizes this truth and lives accordingly from that time forward.

Ephesians 6:16 refers to the believer's being able "to quench all the fiery darts of the wicked [one]." These darts are the temptations by which Satan attacks the believer. However, when we are under the attack of some temptation, we should remember the truth of I Corinthians 10:12,13: "Wherefore let him that thinketh he standeth take heed lest he fall. There hath no temptation taken you but such as is common to man: but God is faithful, who will not suffer you to be tempted above that ye are able; but will with the temptation also make a way to escape, that ye may be able to bear it."

When we are under attack by Satan, we will find the Scriptures to be of particular encouragement, for they remind us of God's faithfulness in the time of testing. Several years ago when I was preparing for an overseas trip to take care of important Broadcast business, several told me of their fear that I might not return. The same fear had bothered me to the extent I realized I was doubting God's goodness and sovereignty in my life. After boarding the plane I turned to Psalm 91, which was of tremendous comfort to me at that time. As I read this psalm I was reassured of my position as a believer, and the attack of Satan was warded off. The peace that surpasses all understanding guarded my soul as I traveled, and I was reassured of the wonderful presence of God. Verses 1 and 2 of this great psalm say, "He that dwelleth in the secret place of the most High shall abide under the shadow of the Almighty. I will say of the Lord, He is my refuge and my fortress: my God; in him will I trust"

In this psalm God tells the believer, "Because he hath set his love upon me, therefore will I deliver him: I will set him on high, because he hath known my name. He shall call upon me, and I will answer him: I will be with him in trouble; I will deliver him, and honour him. With long life will I satisfy him, and shew him my salvation" (vv. 14-16). How wonderful and reassuring is God's Word when we are experiencing the fiery darts of the Wicked One!

Chapter 26

The Armor Provided
(Eph. 6:11; 13-17)

Ephesians 6:11 tells us, "Put on the whole armour of God, that ye may be able to stand against the wiles of the devil." Verse 13 says, "Wherefore take unto you the whole armour of God, that ye may be able to withstand in the evil day, and having done all, to stand." The words "whole armour" occur in both verses. Every piece of the spiritual armor is needed because of the nature of the conflict as described in verses 11 and 12. We are fighting against the "wiles of the devil" and "we wrestle not against flesh and blood, but against principalities, against powers, against the rulers of the darkness of this world, against spiritual wickedness in high places."

The whole armor of God that the believer is to take upon himself enables him to ward off the attacks of Satan. The provisions for living the abundant life are really centered in the second and third Persons of the Godhead—the Lord Jesus Christ and the Holy Spirit. Since the Holy Spirit's ministry is to reveal to the believer the things of Christ (John 16:14,15), the attention of the believer is to be focused especially on the Person of Christ. When this is so, it indicates the believer has been sensitive to the ministry of the Spirit, who seeks to direct attention to Jesus Christ. The Book of Ephesians emphasizes the Lord Jesus Christ, but it presupposes the ministry of the indwelling Holy Spirit.

Having been raised to sit in heavenly places "in Christ" (Eph. 2:6), we need to appropriate what Christ has provided that we might live abundantly. Jesus Christ has made available to us everything we need to enable us to victoriously stand against the Enemy. However, our position

272

must be occupied by faith; that is, our trust must be in Christ to do and provide what He has said.

Notice that Ephesians 6:11,13,14 uses the word "stand" in telling of our conflict with the Enemy. We are not to run but to stand. Too many seem to think that they can somehow outrun the foe, or they think that if they can at least stay a few steps ahead of him, they will be able to live abundantly. However, we are not called to a spiritual marathon; we are called to take a firm stand until the foe is doing the running. This is why James 4:7 says, "Submit yourselves therefore to God. Resist the devil, and he will flee from you." Notice that before we can successfully resist Satan we must submit ourselves to God.

First Peter 5:9 also reveals that the believer's position is not one of fleeing but resisting: "Whom [Satan] resist stedfast in the faith." As has been indicated, we withstand Satan now in the same way that believers will withstand him during the Tribulation: "They overcame him by the blood of the Lamb, and by the word of their testimony; and they loved not their lives unto the death" (Rev. 12:11).

As we take our position in Christ, we will be "strong in the Lord, and in the power of his might" (Eph. 6:10). This submitting to God involves the reckoning and yielding of Romans 6:11-13.

Notice that we are to "take" the whole armor of God (Eph. 6:13). God has already provided the armor; our need is to appropriate what He has made available. Just as God promised the land of Canaan to the Israelites but still required them to actually take the land (Josh. 1:3), so God has promised victory for believers but requires us to take up the armor and stand victorious.

Concerning verse 13 and the significance of the words "take unto you," a Greek scholar, Kenneth S. Wuest, has written: " 'Take unto you' is *analambano*, 'to take up' in order to use. . . . The verb is aorist imperative, which construction issues a command given with military snap and curtness, a command to be obeyed at once, and once for all. Thus, the Christian is to take up and put on all the armor of God as a once-for-all act and keep that armor on during the entire course of his life, not relaxing the discipline necessary for the constant use of such protection" (*Word Studies in the Greek New Testament*, p. 142).

Thus we see that the armor is not to be put on and taken off periodically but to be put on and left on. The armor is actually an attitude of faith; therefore, it is something that is put on by an act of the will and left on. As we mature in the Christian life, we will discover areas in our lives where our faith is not as strong as it should be; that is, the armor is weak in a certain place. At such a time, our responsibility is to go to the Word of God to study His promises concerning our area of weakness, so that our faith will be strengthened. The putting on of the armor once for all is well illustrated by the words of Romans 12:1,2: "I beseech you therefore, brethren, by the mercies of God, that ye present your bodies a living sacrifice, holy, acceptable unto God, which is your reasonable service. And be not conformed to this world: but be ye transformed by the renewing of your mind, that ye may prove what is that good, and acceptable, and perfect, will of God." There is to be a once-for-all presenting of the body to God, followed by a maturing attitude of heart and mind as we grow in the knowledge of Him.

Notice the parallel between Ephesians 6:11, "Put on the whole armour of God," and Romans 13:14, "Put ye on the Lord Jesus Christ." God's provision for victory is in the Person of the Lord Jesus Christ and through the Word of God.

In putting on the Lord Jesus Christ, we need to remember that the living Word (Jesus Christ) is revealed through the written Word (the Bible). In His prayer for His own, Jesus prayed, "Sanctify them through thy truth: thy word is truth" (John 17:17). We put on the Lord Jesus Christ as we study the Word of God and obey what it says.

The believer's armor, then, is not physical protective equipment but is Jesus Christ Himself. Putting on Christ is similar to what we are told in Ephesians 4:24: "Put on the new man." This new man is Christ formed in the believer. Paul was greatly concerned that this be true of every believer, and he told the Galatians: "I travail in birth again until Christ be formed in you" (4:19). Christ was being formed in Paul's life, and this was why he could say, "I am crucified with

Christ: nevertheless I live; yet not I, but Christ liveth in me" (2:20).

As we have seen from Ephesians 6:11-13 the emphasis is on the whole armor; it is not sufficient to take on only part of the armor. The Enemy strikes the believer at his most vulnerable point so it is imperative that he have the full armor. Just as some people are susceptible to certain diseases, some believers are susceptible to certain attacks of Satan. However, the only assurance of effectiveness against all attacks is to take on the whole armor. The whole armor includes the girdle of truth and the breastplate of righteousness (v. 14); shoes (v. 15); the shield of faith (v. 16); the helmet of salvation and the sword of the Spirit (v. 17).

Observe that the whole armor is for the whole body. God has provided the armor primarily to protect the most precious thing He has on earth—the mystical Body of His Son, which we are.

The armor is defensive in its entirety. Even the sword of the Spirit is mentioned here for defense against Satan's attacks, just as Jesus used the Word when attacked by Satan (Matt. 4:4,7,10). Although the Word of God is used offensively at other times, here the emphasis is on its defensive use.

As has been mentioned, the armor has been given so that we may be able to stand our ground against Satan. But the victory is not a once-for-all victory. Having stood our ground victoriously, Satan will attack us from a different angle or wait for a time when we do not have our armor in its proper place. Satan is not easily discouraged so we must watch his persistent attacks and not become lax after we have experienced a victory. We must keep right on standing in our victorious position. Peter says that the Devil is going about "as a roaring lion . . . seeking whom he may devour" (I Pet. 5:8). He is looking for someone who is off guard. Our responsibility is to "resist stedfast in the faith" (v. 9).

As we resist by faith, we may be confident that God will keep us in victory. Paul said, "But thanks be to God, which giveth us the victory through our Lord Jesus Christ. Therefore, my beloved brethren, be ye stedfast, unmoveable, always abounding in the work of the Lord, for as much as ye know that your labour is not in vain in the Lord" (I Cor. 15:57,58).

We are to stand against the wiles of the Devil and then go forward in service for Christ. Although Satan may roar as a lion, the noise he makes need have no terror for us. Since Satan realizes his time is limited he becomes more vicious in his attacks, but he is unable to harm the believer who is totally submitted to Christ. Satan is the one who must run and leave his position of control in the field of battle, for Satan is a defeated foe (Heb. 2:14).

There is no need for the believer to fear that Satan will attack him as if in the dark. Under the attack of the Enemy we can say with David, "Yea, though I walk through the valley of the shadow of death, I will fear no evil: for thou art with me; thy rod and thy staff they comfort me. Thou preparest a table before me in the presence of mine enemies: thou anointest mine head with oil; my cup runneth over" (Ps. 23:4,5).

The key words for believers are "watch" and "pray." We are to watch for Satan's attacks which we will discern as we study the Word of God. We are also to pray for wisdom and enablement in resisting the attacks of Satan. By watching the Word and praying in the Spirit we can remain in the fortress that allows us to stand victorious against Satan.

Having put Christ on as the armor, we do not need to fearfully look around to see if Satan is lurking someplace to attack us. Satan is not able to affect us without first affecting Christ, so our need is to keep "looking unto Jesus the author and finisher of our faith" (Heb. 12:2). When we take our eyes off Christ we leave ourselves open for attack.

Remember Peter who wanted to walk out on the water to meet the Lord? The Lord invited him to come, and the Bible says, "And when Peter was come down out of the ship, he walked on the water, to go to Jesus. But when he saw the wind boisterous, he was afraid; and beginning to sink, he cried, saying, Lord, save me. And immediately Jesus stretched forth his hand, and caught him, and said unto him, O thou of little faith, wherefore didst thou doubt?" (Matt. 14:29-31). Peter began to sink after he took his eyes off Jesus and began looking around him at the circumstances. So also, we leave ourselves open for attack from Satan when we take our eyes off Jesus. The Lord Jesus is concerned that Satan will not take advantage of the believer. At one time, Jesus told Peter, "Satan hath desired to have you, that he may sift you as wheat: but I have prayed for thee, that thy faith fail not" (Luke 22:31,32). Even Satan recognized that God makes a hedge around His own, for Satan said to God about Job: "Hast not thou made an hedge about him, and about his house, and about all that he hath on every side? thou hast blessed the work of his hands, and his substance is increased in the land" (Job 1:10).

Read some of the psalms and notice how the psalmist had confidence in God in face of the enemy. The psalmist said, "I will lift up my eyes to the mountains; from whence shall my help come? My help comes from the Lord, who made heaven and earth" (121:1,2, NASB). The psalmist took comfort in the fact that his God had made the heaven and the earth; therefore, God would certainly be able to deliver him from any difficulty he faced. Thus, he went on to say, "He will not allow your foot to slip; He who keeps you will not slumber. Behold, He who keeps Israel will neither slumber nor sleep. The Lord is your keeper; the Lord is your shade on your right hand. The sun will not smite you by day, nor the moon by night. The Lord will protect you from all evil; He will keep your soul. The Lord will guard your going out and your coming in from this time forth and forever" (vv. 3-8, NASB).

After the Lord had delivered David from his enemies, David wrote: "I love Thee, O Lord, my strength. The Lord is my rock and my fortress and my deliverer, my God, my rock, in whom I take refuge; my shield and the horn of my salvation, my stronghold. I call upon the Lord, who is worthy to be praised, and I am saved from my enemies" (18:1-3, NASB).

In another psalm, David said, "The steps of a man are established by the Lord; and He delights in his way. When he falls, he shall not be hurled headlong; because the Lord is the One who holds his hand" (37:23,24, NASB). These verses from the various psalms show the confidence David had in God. And we can have this same confidence as we "take . . . the whole armour of God" (Eph. 6:13).

Chapter 27

The Armor Described
(Eph. 6:14-17)

Having told believers to "put on" (Eph. 6:11) and "take" (v. 13) the whole armor of God, Paul then described the armor in verses 14-17.

Girdle of Truth

The first part of armor mentioned is the girdle of truth: "Stand therefore, having your loins girt about with truth" (v. 14).

Concerning truth, Jesus Christ said, "I am the way, the truth, and the life" (John 14:6). Since Jesus Christ is the personification of truth, to put on the girdle of truth is to "put . . . on the Lord Jesus Christ" (Rom. 13:14). Because He is God, Jesus Christ is the embodiment of all truth.

Not only is Jesus Christ the truth, but the Word of God is also truth. Concerning His own, Jesus asked the Father: "Sanctify them through thy truth: thy word is truth" (John 17:17). Christ is the Living Word and the Bible is the written Word, and these together form the believer's girdle of truth.

If we want to be protected against the attacks of the Evil One, we must know Jesus Christ as Saviour and be faithful students of the Word of God. The written Word directs our attention to the Living Word. The better we really know the Scriptures, the more we will want to please God in everything we do.

The psalmist said, "Thy word have I hid in mine heart, that I might not sin against thee" (119:11). This shows us the effect of the Word in a believer's life. Hebrews 4:12 says, "For the word of God is quick [living], and powerful, and sharper than any twoedged sword, piercing even to the dividing asunder of soul and spirit, and of the joints and marrow, and is a discerner of the thoughts and intents of the heart."

The Living Word and the written Word are the power of God. Our desire should be the same as Paul's, which was to know Jesus Christ "and the power of his resurrection" (Phil. 3:10). The power of God is referred to in several Scriptures. Paul said, "For I am not ashamed of the gospel of Christ: for it is the power of God unto salvation to every one that believeth; to the Jew first, and also to the Greek" (Rom. 1:16). First Corinthians 1:24 says, "But unto them which are called, both Jews and Greeks, Christ the power of God, and the wisdom of God." Paul wrote: "But in all things approving ourselves as the ministers of God . . . by the word of truth, by the power of God, by the armour of righteousness on the right hand and on the left" (II Cor. 6:4-7).

To have our "loins girt about with truth" is to have the Living and the written Word controlling our lives. The believer who loves the truth and lives it will have strong spiritual life. Such a person will not be "carried about with every wind of doctrine, by the sleight of men, and cunning craftiness, whereby they lie in wait to deceive" (Eph. 4:14). As Paul wrote to believers about the spiritual armor, he was writing from prison and was perhaps even at that time chained to a Roman soldier. The soldier's belt was not just an adornment; rather, it was to keep various parts of his clothing tightly in place so that he could have total freedom of movement in battle. For the believer to be girded with truth means that he is to have the Living and written Word in his heart and thus be able to meet the onslaughts of Satan.

Breastplate of Righteousness

The second part of the armor to which Paul referred was the "breastplate of righteousness" (Eph. 6:14). The breastplate was worn by the Roman soldier on the upper part of his body and covered both his front and his back. As such, it provided protection for the vital organs of his body.

To Paul, this literal breastplate represented a spiritual breastplate that each believer should use. This spiritual breastplate is an aspect of Christ's protection for the believer against the schemes of the Devil. Just as the literal breastplate protected the soldier's heart, so the spiritual breastplate protects the believer's heart. The Scriptures view the heart as the seat of the emotions, and Satan attacks the believer's emotions to draw his affections and desires away from Christ to the things of this world. The believer is protected from such attacks only as he, by faith, relies on the righteousness of Christ as his breastplate.

We need to remember that our right standing with God is only because of the righteousness of Jesus Christ. The Bible says, "But of him are ye in Christ Jesus, who of God is made unto us wisdom, and righteousness, and sanctification, and redemption" (I Cor. 1:30). Jesus Christ is made "righteousness" to the believer.

That our standing before God is based on His righteousness, not ours, is also seen from Romans 4:5: "But to him that worketh not, but believeth on him that justifieth the ungodly, his faith is counted for righteousness." It is this imputed righteousness of Christ—righteousness placed on our account when we receive Him as Saviour—that cannot be attacked by Satan. This righteousness alone is wound-proof—the darts of Satan cannot pierce it because it is the righteousness of Christ placed to our account. Regardless of Satan's accusations against us before God, we need not fear losing our position in Christ because we are accepted by God because of Christ's righteousness, not because of our own. However, we can be sure that Satan will attack us on the basis of our behavior, and will tempt us to believe that we have lost our standing with God. But Satan's attacks will not be effective if we stand by faith on what the written Word says and let it assure us of our position before God.

If we fail in the Christian life—and we will fail at times—our position in Christ does not change. The reason for this is that our position is not based on the good we have done, or even on our obedience—it is based on what Christ has done. It is for this reason that Satan's accusations, although at times well-grounded because of our behavior, cannot move us from God's presence because we stand there in Christ's righteousness. Christ is our advocate before the Father, and He pleads our case righteously as mentioned in

I John 2:1,2: "My little children, these things write I unto you, that ye sin not. And if any man sin, we have an advocate with the Father, Jesus Christ the righteous: and he is the propitiation for our sins: and not for our's only, but also for the sins of the whole world."

Many believers do not realize that Christ's righteousness is the basis of their security. Those who do not understand this become introspective and discouraged in their Christian life, and lay themselves open to Satan's attacks. Satan is always looking for opportunities to attack a believer. When Satan sees one who has sinned and who is greatly depressed because of his sin, Satan will take advantage of that believer and will bring him even further discouragement. Some become so depressed they even believe they have committed the unpardonable sin, not realizing that the Christian cannot commit such a sin, for all his sins were pardoned when he received Christ as Saviour.

We should once and for all put on the breastplate of righteousness; that is, by faith we should rely on our position in Christ. But it is not enough to know the doctrine; the doctrine must be put into practice. Ephesians 4:24 tells us: "And that ye put on the new man, which after God is created in righteousness and true holiness." We are also told: "For we are his workmanship, created in Christ Jesus unto good works, which God hath before ordained that we should walk in them" (2:10). We must not forget that we were created new for the purpose of good works, so those of us who know Christ should do good and bring glory to Him.

One of Satan's master tricks for those who know of their safety in Christ is to cause them to think that they have no obligation to do good. It is not pleasing to the Lord if we live a worldly, indifferent Christian life, and then put our conscience to sleep by saying something like: "Before God, I am righteous in Christ. What else do I need?" Paul's words answer this type of thinking: "What shall we say then? Shall we continue in sin, that grace may abound? God forbid" (Rom. 6:1,2). Since our standing is righteous in Christ, our practice should be right-doing. Christ is our righteousness for salvation, and He is also our life for our daily right living.

Our position in Christ should be reflected in the way we live. This was the evident desire of Paul's life, as seen from his words: "According to my earnest expectation and my hope, that in nothing I shall be ashamed, but that with all boldness, as always, so now also Christ shall be magnified in my body, whether it be by life, or by death. For to me to live is Christ, and to die is gain" (Phil. 1:20,21). This is why he also said: "I am crucified with Christ: nevertheless I live; yet not I, but Christ liveth in me" (Gal. 2:20). Christ is our righteousness as far as our standing before God is concerned, and He also lives in us to produce His righteousness in our daily lives.

Let us be careful about presuming upon the grace of God. If we are not concerned about glorifying Christ in our daily walk, we may force God to set us aside and to severely chasten us to bring us to our spiritual senses. Paul gave instructions to the Corinthian church concerning what to do about an incorrigible individual. Paul said for them "to deliver such an one unto Satan for the destruction of the flesh, that the spirit may be saved in the day of the Lord Jesus" (I Cor. 5:5). Paul also referred to those believers who will not be rewarded when they stand before the Lord: "If any man's work shall be burned, he shall suffer loss: but he himself shall be saved; yet so as by fire" (3:15). Such an individual, although a believer, has not allowed Christ to work in and through his life so there is no reward for him at the Judgment Seat of Christ (see also II Cor. 5:10).

So let us put on the breastplate of righteousness both as to our position in Christ and as to our practice in our daily walk, and thereby we will defeat Satan.

Shod Feet

The third piece of armor Paul mentioned in Ephesians 6 has to do with the believer's feet: "And your feet shod with the preparation of the gospel of peace" (v. 15). This verse is usually interpreted to mean that the believer is to be prepared to preach the gospel of peace. Romans 10:15 is often cited as a parallel passage: "How beautiful are the feet of them that preach the gospel of peace, and bring glad tidings of good things!"

However, it is my opinion that Ephesians 6:15 refers to having the "message of peace" in our hearts rather than "preaching" the message of peace. This is more in keeping with the context. In the spiritual warfare, Satan is out to destroy the peace in our hearts. He causes us to doubt and fret so that we are in turmoil of soul, thus part of the armor is to give us a settled walk that is peaceful. Ephesians 2:14 tells us that Christ "is our peace."

Many other Scriptures speak of peace. John 14:27 records the words of Jesus: "Peace I leave with you, my peace I give unto you: not as the world giveth, give I unto you. Let not your heart be troubled, neither let it be afraid." Jesus also said, "These things I have spoken unto you, that in me ye might have peace. In the world ye shall have tribulation: but be of good cheer; I have overcome the world" (16:33). Thus, we see that Christ is peace itself. When we possess Him we have true peace, for turmoil of soul disappears.

There are two kinds of peace spoken of in the New Testament—peace *with* God and the peace *of* God. Romans 5:1 refers to peace *with* God: "Therefore being justified by faith, we have peace with God through our Lord Jesus Christ." This kind of peace comes when we turn from our sin and receive Jesus Christ as Saviour. At that moment of decision we become children of God. Because Christ has paid the penalty for our sin, the moment we receive Him as Saviour we are at peace with God. Second Corinthians 5:18 tells us that God has "reconciled us to himself by Jesus Christ." Peace with God is also referred to in Acts 10:36: "The word which God sent unto the children of Israel, preaching peace by Jesus Christ." Christ has thus secured our peace with God inasmuch as this peace is obtained by receiving Him as Saviour. It is a permanent and settled relationship of peace with God that Satan's darts cannot disturb.

The Scriptures also refer to the peace *of* God. Philippians 4:6,7 refers to this kind of peace: "Be careful for nothing; but in every thing by prayer and supplication with thanksgiving let your requests be made known unto God. And the peace of God, which passeth all understanding, shall keep your hearts and minds through Christ Jesus."

Whereas peace with God is a judicial peace in that we are made right with God by receiving Christ as Saviour, the peace of God is an experiential peace. The life of believers is in great contrast to the life of unbelievers. Isaiah said, "But the wicked are like the troubled sea, when it cannot rest, whose waters cast up mire and dirt. There is no peace, saith my God, to the wicked" (57:20,21). Since unbelievers are not at peace with God it is not possible for them to experience the peace of God.

Consider the kind of peace God has. Nothing is able to upset or disturb Him. It is this kind of peace we can experience as we trust Him completely for everything.

Jesus wants His people to have this peace. On the Isle of Patmos, when John was given a revelation of Jesus Christ, John said, "When I saw him, I fell at his feet as dead. And he laid his right hand upon me, saying unto me, Fear not; I am the first and the last: I am he that liveth, and was dead; and, behold, I am alive for evermore, Amen; and have the keys of hell and of death" (Rev. 1:17,18). Jesus also said of Himself: "I am Alpha and Omega, the beginning and the ending . . . which is, and which was, and which is to come, the Almighty" (1:8). As we read these words concerning Christ we see His omnipotence and realize nothing or no one is able to defeat His program. He is allowing certain things to happen on earth now that go against His desires, but eventually Jesus Christ Himself will return to earth to establish His kingdom. He is not frustrated by the events that are now happening. Neither should the believer be frustrated by them, even though he is not able to understand them. If we could only see the future as God sees it, we would have no questions, but God has intended that we walk by faith instead of by sight.

We will experience the peace of God as we realize the security we have in Him. Jesus said, "My sheep hear my voice, and I know them, and they follow me: and I give unto them eternal life; and they shall never perish, neither shall any man pluck them out of my hand. My Father, which gave them me, is greater than all; and no man is able to pluck them out of my Father's hand" (John 10:27-29). So when Paul told believers that their feet should be "shod with the preparation of the gospel of peace" he was referring to the peace with God and peace of God that is possible for everyone who knows Christ as Saviour. Christ died so that we could have peace with God and its resulting peace of God, and through the Holy Spirit this peace is maintained in our hearts.

The question might be asked concerning Ephesians 6:15: Why are the feet mentioned in connection with this peace? The significance lies in the fact that feet are symbolic of our daily walk, or life. The Lord Jesus Christ is presented here as God's provision of peace for daily living. In the process of daily living, there are many circumstances that give rise to fear. In fact, fear is one of the chief characteristics of the last days. Describing these last days, Jesus said, "Men's hearts failing them for fear, and for looking after those things which are coming on the earth: for the powers of heaven shall be shaken" (Luke 21:26). The problems of fear and anxiety plague people the world over, and much study has been given to these subjects. However, the person who has peace through Jesus Christ does not need to fear or to be anxious. Although we do not understand how events will turn out, we are to put all of our care on God, because He cares for us (I Pet. 5:7).

The word in Ephesians 6:15 translated "preparation" means "readiness." However, concerning this word, M. R. Vincent points out that "in Hellenistic Greek it was sometimes used in the sense of the *establishment* or *firm foundation*, which would suit this passage: *firm-footing*" (*Word Studies in the New Testament*, p. 867). So with this solid footing of peace, we can publish the gospel of peace in a world of conflict and evil.

With this deep-seated peace, we can face the foe on every side with true confidence. The psalmist must have experienced this confidence, for he wrote: "It is vain for you to rise up early, to sit up late, to eat the bread of sorrows: for so he giveth his beloved sleep" (127:2). The psalmist also wrote: "Great peace have they which love thy law: and nothing shall offend them" (119:165).

We need to learn to live a day at a time; we should claim for each day God's victory over tension and worry. We should commit the problems of the future to the Lord, because only He knows what the future holds. Jesus spoke of the necessity of believers to have total reliance on Him each day. He said, "Take no thought for your life, what ye shall eat, or what ye shall drink; nor yet for your body, what ye shall put on. Is not the life more than meat, and the body more than raiment?" (Matt. 6:25). Jesus did not mean that we were to make no plans for the future, but we are not to worry about the future over which we have no control.

Jesus further said, "Therefore take no thought, saying, What shall we eat? or, What shall we drink? or, Wherewithal shall we be clothed? (For after all these things do the Gentiles seek:) for your heavenly Father knoweth that ye have need of all these things. But seek ye first the kingdom of God, and his righteousness; and all these things shall be added unto you. Take therefore no thought for the morrow: for the morrow shall take thought for the things of itself. Sufficient unto the day is the evil thereof" (vv. 31-34). To take "thought for the morrow" (v. 34) is to worry about the future, which Jesus says the believer should not do.

David saw the need of trusting the Lord for everything, thus he wrote: "Cast thy burden upon the Lord, and he shall sustain thee: he shall never suffer the righteous to be moved" (Ps. 55:22).

Shield of Faith

The fourth part of the armor for the believer is the "shield of faith." The Bible says, "Above all, taking the shield of faith, wherewith ye shall be able to quench all the fiery darts of the wicked" (Eph. 6:16). "The wicked" is literally "the wicked one" and refers to Satan. Notice the two "alls" in this verse: "Above all" and "all the fiery darts."

"Above all" shows the shield of faith to be of greatest importance. The shield was protection for the entire body. The believer's spiritual shield also protects every aspect of his being.

The shield of faith refers to the Lord Jesus Christ who is God's provision for our protection. It is through faith in Jesus Christ that we are completely protected against the attacks of Satan. The basis of our overcoming in the spiritual warfare is our faith in Christ. The Bible says, "For whatsoever is born of God overcometh the world: and this is the victory that overcometh the world, even our faith. Who is he that overcometh the world, but he that believeth that Jesus is the Son of God?" (I John 5:4,5). We are overcomers because of our faith in Jesus Christ who is "the author and finisher of our faith" (Heb. 12:2).

There is an incident in the Old Testament that provides an interesting parallel to the believer's shield of faith mentioned in Ephesians 6:16. Abraham, then known as "Abram," led 318 of his servants into battle against four kings and their armies in order to rescue Lot, Abraham's nephew. Against such odds, Abraham's victory over the kings was possible only by God's enablement. Abraham and his servants won the victory, and on their return the king of Sodom suggested they keep the spoil of victory. However, Abraham said to him, "I will not take from a thread even to a shoelatchet, and that I will not take any thing that is thine, lest thou shouldest say, I have made Abram rich" (Gen. 14:23). After this victory, Abraham was in great danger of the enemy returning, and he needed protection. This God promised him as seen in Genesis 15:1: "Fear not, Abram: I am thy shield, and thy exceeding great reward." Notice that God did not tell Abraham to "take thy shield" but told him "I am thy shield." God was thereby promising to be Abraham's protector because of Abraham's faith in God.

The psalmist spoke of the Lord as his shield: "Our soul waiteth for the Lord: he is our help and our shield" (33:20). "Thou art my hiding place and my shield: I hope in thy word" (119:114). Proverbs 30:5 says, "Every word of God is pure: he is a shield unto them that put their trust in him."

Although Job did not refer to God as his shield, it is apparent that Job knew this truth experientially, for in his intense suffering he was able to say, "Though he slay me, yet will I trust in him" (Job 13:15). Job also said of God: "He knoweth the way that I take: when he hath tried me, I shall come forth as gold" (23:10).

We must remember that the shield of faith is not something which the believer carries with him. It would be futile for the believer to carry a shield hoping to detect from which direction Satan would throw one of his darts. Satan attacks when we least expect him to, and we would never be able to effectively withstand his attacks if it depended on our intelligence or ability.

The only kind of shield of faith that is effective for us is one which protects us from all sides at the same time. This is exactly what Christ is to the believer. As we have seen throughout the Book of Ephesians, we are "in" Christ. Colossians 3:3 tells believers: "Your life is hid with Christ in God."

The believer is not viewed as hiding behind Christ or just being on the side of Christ, but "in Christ" (Eph. 1:1). Although Old Testament believers were not "in Christ" in the sense that New Testament believers are, the psalmist recognized that the Lord surrounded him: "Thou hast beset me behind and before, and laid thine hand upon me" (139:5).

Notice from Ephesians 6:16 that the believer is expected, by the shield of faith, to quench *all* of Satan's darts: "Taking the shield of faith, wherewith ye shall be able to quench all the fiery darts of the wicked [one]." Observe that it is not just "the fiery darts" but "all the fiery darts." We do this as we exercise our faith in Jesus Christ. God never provides just partial protection for His own; when we trust Him to do what He has said He will do, we have complete protection.

Note that this is a shield of faith. As we appropriate by faith what God has promised, we are "taking the shield of faith." For instance, Romans 6:14 tells us: "For sin shall not have dominion over you: for ye are not under the law, but under grace." As we place our faith, or trust, in this and other truths revealed in Romans 6, we will experience victory over sin in our daily life. Faith itself is a gift from God and comes by the Word of God, for we are told in Romans 10:17: "So then faith cometh by hearing, and hearing by the word of God." As we study the Scriptures we will grow in faith because we will know what God has done and said.

By means of the shield of faith we are to "quench all the fiery darts of the wicked" (Eph. 6:16). Charles B. Williams translates this verse: "Take on the shield which faith provides, for with it you will be able to put out all the fire-tipped arrows shot by the evil one." Let us consider some of the fire-tipped arrows that need to be put out. Satan's arrows, or darts, are his means of attempting to defeat us. He works through various aspects of our lives in attempting to do this.

Satan can attack us by encouraging us to be proud. Proverbs 16:18 warns: "Pride goeth before destruction, and

an haughty spirit before a fall." Satan can also attack through
the desires of the body. For instance, sexual desire is of God,
but Satan may encourage the Christian to satisfy this desire
in an illegitimate manner.

When we are tempted to do wrong, we must remember
that such a temptation does not originate with the Lord. The
Bible says, "Let no man say when he is tempted, I am
tempted of God: for God cannot be tempted with evil,
neither tempteth he any man: but every man is tempted,
when he is drawn away of his own lust, and enticed. Then
when lust hath conceived, it bringeth forth sin: and sin, when
it is finished, bringeth forth death" (James 1:15).

If we are relying on Christ, Satan's fire-tipped arrows will
be put out before they can do their damage. But if we do not
rely on Christ to be our strength when temptations come, we
will be vulnerable to Satan's attacks and will experience
serious frustration in the Christian life.

One of Satan's methods is to attack the believer's thought
life. Satan encourages doubts and anxiety which make the
believer less effective for the Lord. Realizing that the mind is
a spiritual battleground, Paul said, "We are destroying
speculations and every lofty thing raised up against the
knowledge of God, and we are taking every thought captive
to the obedience of Christ" (II Cor. 10:5, NASB). In times of
severe stress, Satan especially likes to implant doubt in the
Christian's mind concerning God's faithfulness, or concerning
the authority or reliability of His promises.

Satan also attacks the believer when he sins and suggests
to him that God does not really forgive his sin, or at least
that God is holding against him a sin he has committed in the
past. The promises of the Word of God are extremely
important at such a time. God says, "I have blotted out, as a
thick cloud, thy transgressions, and, as a cloud, thy sins:
return unto me; for I have redeemed thee" (Isa. 44:22).
Isaiah 38:17 records Hezekiah's statements to God: "Behold,
for peace I had great bitterness: but thou hast in love to my
soul delivered it from the pit of corruption: for thou hast
cast all my sins behind thy back." The New Testament states
concerning those who are in right relationship with Him:
"Their sins and iniquities will I remember no more" (Heb.
10:17).

The basis for such forgiveness is what Christ accomplished when He died on the cross for us. He fully satisfied the Heavenly Father's righteous demands for our sins. Therefore, we are delivered from condemnation by receiving Christ as Saviour. Knowing these truths, we should be faithful in going to the Scriptures to read them again when Satan attacks in this area.

When we go through trying experiences, such as losing our possessions or losing a loved one through death, we need to remember that the Lord has not forsaken us. Although Satan will encourage us to think that God has forgotten us, Hebrews 13:5 assures: "I will never leave thee, nor forsake thee." The Apostle Paul was able to be victorious in adverse circumstances because he had learned to trust Christ regardless of the circumstances. Thus, Paul was able to say, "Not that I speak from want; for I have learned to be content in whatever circumstances I am. I know how to get along with humble means, and I also know how to live in prosperity; in any and every circumstance I have learned the secret of being filled and going hungry, both of having abundance and suffering need. I can do all things through Him who strengthens me" (Phil. 4:11-13, NASB).

Strange things happen to us in God's perfect plan to shape us for eternity. When we become preoccupied in seeking to know why these things are so, Satan is given an opportunity to shoot his arrows of discouragement and doubt at us. Even though we do not understand all that is being allowed in our lives, rather than asking "Why?" we should take the shield of faith by trusting Christ and His Word completely.

When adversity comes into our lives, we need to remember Romans 8:28: "We know that all things work together for good to them that love God, to them who are the called according to his purpose." As believers we can know this truth with certainty even though we cannot understand what God is specifically trying to accomplish in our lives. When we are certain—because of our faith in God—that things are working together for our ultimate good and His glory, we will have a different attitude about difficult circumstances. As verse 31,32 says, "What shall we then say to these things? If God be for us, who can be against us? He that spared not his own Son, but delivered him up for us all, how shall he not with him also freely give us all things?" So when testing comes we need to read such passages as this to remind ourselves that God has a purpose for what He is doing and that He has not made a mistake in our lives.

Concerning suffering, James said, "Take, my brethren, the prophets, who have spoken in the name of the Lord, for an example of suffering affliction, and of patience" (5:10). Paul said, "For I reckon that the sufferings of this present time are not worthy to be compared with the glory which shall be revealed in us" (Rom. 8:18). Although God allows adversity to come in order that we might become more spiritually mature, He does not allow more than we are able to endure. First Corinthians 10:13 says, "There hath no temptation taken you but such as is common to man: but God is faithful, who will not suffer you to be tempted above that ye are able; but will with the temptation also make a way to escape, that ye may be able to bear it." Our trials may seem more than we are able to bear, especially if we do not trust God completely in our suffering, but note especially that He also provides necessary grace so we can escape and bear them. If we are living by faith we will be able to say with Job, "When he hath tried me, I shall come forth as gold" (23:10).

In considering the difficult circumstances that come into our lives, we need to remember that the Lord never tests us for the purpose of causing us to fail. Referring to our incorruptible inheritance waiting in heaven for us, Peter said, "Wherein ye greatly rejoice, though now for a season, if need be, ye are in heaviness through manifold temptations: that the trial of your faith, being much more precious than of gold that perisheth, though it be tried with fire, might be found unto praise and honour and glory at the appearing of Jesus Christ" (I Pet. 1:6,7). The Lord's purpose in discipline is not to cause us to fail but to make us more spiritually mature so we can share in His holiness. The Bible says, "Now no chastening for the present seemeth to be joyous, but grievous: nevertheless afterward it yieldeth the peaceable fruit of righteousness unto them which are exercised thereby" (Heb. 12:11).

There are many other darts that Satan shoots at us; they may be in the form of encouraging us to lose our temper or to harbor resentment. We especially need to be careful when we are criticized because this often gives Satan an opportunity to fire one of his darts at us. The words of Jude are especially fitting for us to remember in this regard: "But ye, beloved, building up yourselves on your most holy faith, praying in the Holy Ghost, keep yourselves in the love of God, looking for the mercy of our Lord Jesus Christ unto eternal life" (vv. 20,21). Colossians 2:6,7 tells us: "As ye have therefore received Christ Jesus the Lord, so walk ye in him: rooted and built up in him, and stablished in the faith, as ye have been taught, abounding therein with thanksgiving."

We take the shield of faith, then, by trusting Christ and His Word completely, which in turn protects us from Satan's fire-tipped arrows.

Helmet of Salvation

The fifth part of armor for the believer is mentioned in Ephesians 6:17: "And take the helmet of salvation." The helmet was for protecting the head, which is the center of the intellectual life of the body. A head wound is a serious matter because the body does not function properly if the head is not functioning properly. The "helmet of salvation" refers to Jesus Christ and reveals that He is the protection for this part of the body.

The psalmist said, "The Lord is my light and my salvation" (27:1). To take the helmet of salvation is to recognize Jesus Christ as the very life of our salvation. Having received Christ, we have eternal life, for the Bible says: "And this is the record, that God hath given to us eternal life, and this life is in his Son. He that hath the Son hath life; and he that hath not the Son of God hath not life" (I John 5:11,12). We will have a great advantage over Satan if we realize that salvation is not just something that the Lord gives, but it is Christ Himself who is given to us.

One of Satan's key attacks in the area of salvation is to cause the believer to doubt his salvation. However, as we have seen, I John 5:11,12 assures an individual that if he has Jesus

Christ, he has eternal life. Satan also causes some to think they can lose eternal life, but Christ said, "I give unto them eternal life; and they shall never perish, neither shall any man pluck them out of my hand. My Father, which gave them me, is greater than all; and no man is able to pluck them out of my Father's hand" (John 10:28,29).

Because the head is the center of our thought processes, Satan will distort our thinking from what God wants it to be if he effectively gets to our minds. For instance, if Satan can cause us to doubt our salvation, he has struck at the basis of all our spiritual functions of life. If, however, we know we have salvation in Christ and are trusting completely in the efficacy of God's saving grace, we have the proper basis necessary for spiritual maturity. As we trust in Christ regarding our salvation, He is the helmet of salvation to us and Satan's attacks are nullified. All the processes of spiritual maturity and an effective life for the Lord depend on the knowledge of our salvation in Christ.

The Bible teaches that the person who places faith in Christ is secure in Him. Concerning Christ, it says, "Wherefore he is able also to save them to the uttermost that come unto God by him, seeing he ever liveth to make intercession for them" (Heb. 7:25). Of believers, I Peter 1:5 says, "Who are kept by the power of God through faith unto salvation ready to be revealed in the last time." Of Christ, I John 2:2 says, "And he is the propitiation [satisfaction] for our sins: and not for our's only, but also for the sins of the whole world." Since Christ has paid the penalty for sin, "as many as received him, to them gave he power to become the sons of God, even to them that believe on his name" (John 1:12). When the believer commits a sin, he does not lose his salvation; rather, he loses fellowship with God. However, this fellowship is restored when he confesses his sin. The Bible says, "If we walk in the light, as he is in the light, we have fellowship one with another, and the blood of Jesus Christ his Son cleanseth us from all sin. If we confess our sins, he is faithful and just to forgive us our sins, and to cleanse us from all unrighteousness" (I John 1:7,9).

Even a true concept of the vital doctrines of the Scriptures depends on an accurate comprehension of salvation being based on the finished work of Christ. To realize from the Scriptures that our salvation is complete in Christ and Him alone, requires that one also believes in the deity of Christ, His virgin birth, His substitutionary death, and His burial and resurrection. If we deny any of these related truths, we deny the efficacy, or effectiveness, of Christ's work on the cross. For instance, if Christ was not born of a virgin, then He would also have had a sin nature and the benefits of His death could not be applied to others. So to believe in salvation "by grace . . . through faith" (Eph. 2:8) presupposes correct beliefs concerning other doctrines. Those who do not believe the Scriptures concerning these other doctrines will teach salvation by works rather than grace because they do not believe that Christ has paid the full penalty for sin.

Satan concentrates many of his attacks at the believer's hope of salvation because if he can succeed in getting us to doubt our salvation he has laid the basis to lead us into error. Thus we see how vital the helmet of salvation is to every believer. Our trust must be in Christ not only for salvation but also for His ability to carry our salvation through to the end.

Sword of the Spirit

The sixth and final part of the armor to be taken by the believer is "the sword of the Spirit, which is the word of God" (Eph. 6:17). The sword of the Spirit is not an instrument to be placed in the believer's hand; it, too, refers to the protection given by the Lord Jesus Christ, even as the other pieces of the armor refer to an aspect of Christ's protection. Notice what the sword of the Spirit is—"the word of God." The Gospel of John refers to Jesus Christ as the "Word," especially in 1:1-14. This Gospel begins: "In the beginning was the Word, and the Word was with God, and the Word was God" (v. 1). This passage concludes: "And the Word was made flesh, and dwelt among us, (and we beheld his glory, the glory as of the only begotten of the Father,) full of grace and truth" (v. 14). These verses reveal that the "Word" refers specifically to the Lord Jesus Christ who left heaven's glory to take upon Himself the form of a man and die on the cross for the sins of the world.

The Bible is also referred to as God's "Word" (note several verses in Psalm 119). As has been indicated previously, the difference is that Jesus Christ is the Living Word and the Bible is the written Word. The two are brought together in Hebrews 1:1,2: "God, who at sundry times and in divers manners spake in time past unto the fathers by the prophets, hath in these last days spoken unto us by his Son, whom he hath appointed heir of all things, by whom also he made the worlds." God gave the written Word through the prophets, and He gave the Living Word when He gave His only Son to come to earth.

Jesus told of the necessity of assimilating the Living and written Word, and His comments are recorded in the Gospel of John. Jesus said, "I am the living bread which came down from heaven: if any man eat of this bread, he shall live for ever: and the bread that I will give is my flesh, which I will give for the life of the world" (6:51). The Jews could not understand how Jesus could give them His flesh to eat. Jesus added: "Whoso eateth my flesh, and drinketh my blood, hath eternal life; and I will raise him up at the last day. For my flesh is meat indeed, and my blood is drink indeed. He that eateth my flesh, and drinketh my blood, dwelleth in me, and I in him. As the living Father hath sent me, and I live by the Father: so he that eateth me, even he shall live by me" (vv. 53-57).

Many turned back from following Jesus because of these words which they could not understand, but Jesus gave the clue to their meaning in verse 63: "It is the spirit that quickeneth [makes alive]; the flesh profiteth nothing: the words that I speak unto you, they are spirit, and they are life." Jesus did not intend for His flesh to be literally eaten; He was emphasizing the need for His message to be completely assimilated and obeyed. It was the same as if He would have told His followers that they needed to feed upon Him and His Word.

The Word is referred to as "milk" (I Pet. 2:2) and "meat" (Heb. 5:14). Thus, the Word is spiritual food for the believer. Jeremiah said, "Thy words were found, and I did eat them; and thy word was unto me the joy and rejoicing of mine heart: for I am called by thy name, O Lord God of hosts" (15:16). By this statement, Jeremiah was saying that he fed upon the message contained in the Word of God. The psalmist said, "How sweet are thy words unto my taste! yea, sweeter than honey to my mouth!" (119:103).

God's written Word came to us by inspiration: "All scripture is given by inspiration of God" (II Tim. 3:16). The Living Word came to us by incarnation: "The Word was made flesh, and dwelt among us" (John 1:14). The written Word (Bible) and Living Word (Christ) are inseparable. The written Word is the message of the Living Word. Those who love the Living Word also love the written Word for it tells about Him. To be careless about our relationship with the written Word is also to be careless about our relationship with the Living Word.

It is the ministry of the Holy Spirit to reveal Christ to the believer (John 16:15), and He does this by revealing to the believer the truths of the written Word. This is why the Bible is referred to as the "sword of the Spirit"; it is the method by which the Spirit works in our lives, making Christ real to us.

Hebrews 4:12 says, "For the word of God is quick [living], and powerful, and sharper than any twoedged sword, piercing even to the dividing asunder of soul and spirit, and of the joints and marrow, and is a discerner of the thoughts and intents of the heart." The power of His spoken word is seen in Genesis 1, for God spoke and the result was creation.

As part of the believer's armor (Eph. 6:17), the Word of God is to be used primarily as a defense against Satan's attacks. Christ Himself gave us an example of how to meet the attacks of Satan by the written Word (Matt. 4:1-11).

The degree to which we will be able to use the sword of the Spirit depends on the degree to which we allow it to penetrate our hearts; that is, to become real and living within us. This involves more than just memorizing the Scriptures; it requires that we respond to the Scriptures by putting the message of the Word of God into action in our lives. It is not enough to know the Scriptures, we must act on the basis of what they say. Even Satan knows what the Scriptures say, but he rejects the message, and even comes as an angel of light quoting it to deceive others. Just as Satan did with Eve, he can raise questions about something God has said and in that way plant doubts in a person's mind. There is no substitute for our knowing what the Scriptures teach and for doing what it requires. As we have seen concerning the believer's armor, it is particularly important that we know what the Scriptures say about our relationship to God.

Not only is the sword of the Spirit, the Bible, to be used defensively against the attacks of Satan, but we are also to use it offensively in seeking to win others to Christ. Jesus commanded: "Go ye into all the world, and preach the gospel to every creature" (Mark 16:15). We should always use the Scriptures when helping someone see his need of Christ. The Bible is the only authoritative Word of God so it is the basis we must use in telling others of their sin and their need to receive Christ as Saviour. Because the Bible is the only authoritative revelation from God, Paul urged Timothy: "Preach the word; be instant in season, out of season; reprove, rebuke, exhort with all longsuffering and doctrine" (II Tim. 4:2).

To be able to use the sword of the Spirit effectively either defensively or offensively calls for the greatest degree of spiritual devotion to Christ. Mere repetition of words does not make an efficient sword. But when the sword of the Spirit is spoken from a heart that is filled with the Spirit, there will be eternal benefits.

The sword must be ready at a moment's notice because Satan attacks without warning. He does not wait until we have our Bibles open and are reading God's Word before he attacks. He often waits for the opposite—when our minds are farthest from the Word. However, even though we may not have the Bible available to read at the moment it can be available if we have memorized portions of it. In times of need, the Spirit will bring to our attention the truths of God's Word if we have spent time thinking deeply on them in the past. It is one of the Holy Spirit's ministries to bring things to our memory: "But the Comforter, which is the Holy Ghost, whom the Father will send in my name, he shall teach you all things, and bring all things to your remembrance whatsoever I have said unto you" (John 14:26). In this way, the Word becomes a sword of the Spirit even though we may not have the Bible available to read. So it is important that we hide the Word in our hearts, even as David did (Ps. 119:11).

It is well to remember that, in witnessing, our responsibility is to set forth the Word; we do not need to defend it. On commenting about the lack of need to defend the Word, Spurgeon pointed out that one does not need to defend the Word any more than he needs to defend a lion; let the lion out of his cage and he will defend himself.

The Results Expected

If we put on "the whole armour of God" (Eph. 6:11), what results can we expect? In considering this, we should remember that the armor is available to all who know Christ and who will appropriate it by faith. No believer has an excuse for any vulnerable spot because the armor is available for full protection.

The results that can be expected when the entire armor is appropriated by faith center in the three occurrences of the word "able" in this passage (vv. 11,13,16). Verse 11 says, "Put on the whole armour of God, that ye may be able to stand against the wiles of the devil." From this verse we see that the appropriation of the entire armor enables us to stand against the Devil's craftiness. Even the weakest believer can overcome Satan by exercising faith in Christ for each aspect of his life. God desires that each believer have a victorious Christian life. With Paul, we can say, "Thanks be unto God, which always causeth us to triumph in Christ" (II Cor. 2:14). We can also echo his words: "Thanks be to God, which giveth us the victory through our Lord Jesus Christ" (I Cor. 15:57). And we can apply Paul's conclusion: "Therefore, my beloved brethren, be ye stedfast, unmoveable, always abounding in the work of the Lord, forasmuch as ye know that your labour is not in vain in the Lord" (v. 58).

So let us expect victory, not defeat. By faith we can conquer! Too many have been defeated simply because they have gone into the spiritual conflict anticipating failure. Let us not forget that we are "able."

The second occurrence of the word "able" is in Ephesians 6:13: "Wherefore take unto you the whole armour of God, that ye may be able to withstand in the evil day, and having done all, to stand." Another result of appropriating the spiritual armor by faith is that we will be able to stand victorious in the evil day. The word translated "withstand" can also be translated "resist," as it is in James 4:7: "Submit yourselves therefore to God. Resist the devil, and he will flee from you." This word is translated "resist" in I Peter 5:9 also: "Whom [Satan] resist stedfast in the faith, knowing that the same afflictions are accomplished in your brethren that are in the world." The armor enables the believer to effectively resist Satan and thus to stand victorious in the "evil day." The "evil day" probably refers to the time of severe temptations and trials.

The only way that we can successfully encounter and defeat Satan is when we are, by faith, entrenched in Christ. This is why James 4:7 first mentions that we are to submit ourselves to God before it mentions that we are to resist the Devil. When we submit to Christ and depend on Him as our fortress, He Himself will be our wall of defense.

The statement in I Peter 5:9 saying that we are to "resist stedfast in the faith" reminds us that we are to stand fast in faith's victorious position. It is evident that the spiritual conflict is a fight of faith. At the end of his life, Paul charged Timothy: "Fight the good fight of faith" (I Tim. 6:12). Of himself, Paul could say: "For I am now ready to be offered, and the time of my departure is at hand. I have fought a good fight [of faith], I have finished my course, I have kept the faith: henceforth there is laid up for me a crown of righteousness, which the Lord, the righteous judge, shall give me at that day: and not to me only, but unto all them also that love his appearing" (II Tim. 4:6-7).

Let us trust the Lord for every detail of our life. If we fail, let us confess our sin to Him and remember that He has promised to forgive when we confess it (I John 1:9). Let us "walk in the light, as he is in the light" (I John 1:7), and we will experience victory over Satan. As we study the Word of God we should let the light of His Word expose any sin and immediately confess it.

The third occurrence of the word "able" concerning the spiritual armor is found in Ephesians 6:16: "Above all, taking the shield of faith, wherewith ye shall be able to quench all the fiery darts of the wicked [one]. Thus we see another result that can be expected when we appropriate the armor by faith—we will be enabled to put out *all* the fire-tipped arrows of the Devil. This is possible by trusting in Jesus Christ who is the shield of faith for the believer. We have carefully examined the verses previously which reveal that Christ is our shield and life and that He lives in and through us (Gal. 2:20; Col. 3:3,4).

Christ is the shield that faith apprehends, and He stands between the believer and Satan so we need never fear. The Lord is with us at all times even as David realized (Ps. 23). As we put our trust in Him He will protect us on every side.

The truth we have seen from the six pieces of armor is that each one presents a different aspect of the way Jesus Christ is the protection for His own. Our responsibility is to place our confidence in Him for each step we take.

Chapter 28

Resources for Victory
(Eph. 6:18-20)

In the Book of Ephesians, prayer reaches the highest pinnacle of any place in the Bible. Two of Paul's prayers are recorded in this Book. The first prayer (1:15-21) was for the believers to have the spirit of wisdom and revelation in the knowledge of Christ. The second prayer (3:14-21) was for believers to have an experiential knowledge of Christ's indwelling work within believers.

In connection with the spiritual armor of believers, another reference is made to prayer: "Praying always with all prayer and supplication in the Spirit, and watching thereunto with all perseverance and supplication for all saints" (6:18). Here we see that in addition to taking on the entire armor of God, believers are to be constantly praying. Prayer is not regarded as part of the armor, but the believer who has on the armor is to persevere in prayer. Romans 13:14 tells us to "Put ... on the Lord Jesus Christ" and this is done by prayer, for Christ is made real to us through prayer.

In order for believers to stand victoriously in the conflict—even with the complete armor—there must be constant, earnest prayer. It is through prayer of faith that the believer's armor is first put on, and then becomes effective. Since prayer is associated here with warfare, the indication is that prayer itself is part of the battle. Daniel experienced the battle of prayer. He had been praying without answer, and then he said: "Behold, an hand touched me, which set me upon my knees and upon the palms of my hands. And he said unto me, O Daniel, a man greatly beloved, understand the words that I speak unto thee, and stand upright: for unto thee am I now sent. And when he had spoken this word unto

301

me, I stood trembling. Then said he unto me, Fear not, Daniel: for from the first day that thou didst set thine heart to understand, and to chasten thyself before thy God, thy words were heard, and I am come for thy words. But the prince of the kingdom of Persia withstood me one and twenty days: but, lo, Michael, one of the chief princes, came to help me; and I remained there with the kings of Persia" (10:10-13). This gives us an insight into the way principalities and powers seek to hinder answers to prayer.

Our Saviour also knew of the battle of prayer for He agonized in prayer. While He was in the Garden of Gethsemane, He thought about His coming death on the cross "and being in an agony he prayed more earnestly: and his sweat was as it were great drops of blood falling down to the ground" (Luke 22:44). The word translated "agony" refers to a conflict, fight or contest. Here it denotes severe emotional strain and anguish. Jesus was having an intense struggle in prayer because of the cross that loomed before Him.

Prayer is a conflict in itself, and it is vital in the spiritual warfare in which every believer is involved. Notice from Ephesians 6:18 that praying and watching should be done "with all perseverance." This doesn't mean that we defeat Satan by working and striving in prayer, for we have already seen that Satan is a defeated foe because of Christ's work on the cross. However, our agonizing in prayer has to do with our taking our position in Christ as the victorious one. We are to "fight the good fight of faith" (I Tim. 6:12) by means of prayer.

Someone has said, "Prayer is not trying to persuade God to join us in our service for Him. It is joining Him in His service. Prayer is a true Christian laying hold by faith on property which Satan controls but which rightly belongs to God, and holding on until Satan lets go."

Praying in the Spirit

Ephesians 6:17 tells of the "sword of the Spirit"; verse 18 tells of praying "in the Spirit." Just as human weapons are of no value in the spiritual warfare (II Cor. 10:4), prayer that is not in the Spirit is also of no value. A prayer that is lovely to listen to may not necessarily be "in the Spirit." Some believers may not know how to express themselves adequately in prayer before others, but they may be praying effectively in the Spirit.

Prayer is effectual when it has its origin with God. God sees the whole battlefield and knows the Devil's plans. God decides the place and part of every soldier in the conflict, and He directs the movements of the entire spiritual army. Since God sets forth definite objectives to be carried out in His eternal purpose, He must also implant in us our prayers for spiritual victory. God communicates to us through the Holy Spirit the prayers we are to pray. The Holy Spirit lays the proper burden on us and He motivates and gives us the throughts to pray. Romans 8:26 says, "Likewise the Spirit also helpeth our infirmities: for we know not what we should pray for as we ought: but the Spirit itself maketh intercession for us with groanings which cannot be uttered."

So it is God who gives the deep sense of urgency for prayer and also gives assurance of victory. We do not know where Satan has placed his snares and pitfalls, but if we are alert to the Holy Spirit He will stimulate prayer within us so we will be forewarned and fully ready with the provided armor. We should be sensitive to the Holy Spirit's work in our lives as He prompts us to prayer and gives assurance that our prayers will be answered. Even though we do not know what to pray for, the Holy Spirit will prompt us and will pray through us. The Father, through the Spirit, motivates us to pray for what we should (Rom. 8:26,27). Then we, in the Spirit, present our petitions back to the Father in the name of Christ. Someone has said, "Prayer in the Spirit must be Spirit-inspired, Spirit-inwrought, Spirit-taught, Spirit-directed and Spirit-energized." Even in prayer, we can expect God to work in us to give us the desire to pray and then to energize us as we pray (Phil. 2:13).

Praying Constantly

The words "praying always" (Eph. 6:18) suggest alertness as well as praying at all times under all conditions. This is unbroken communion with the Lord, not just set times of coming to Him in prayer. It is good to have definite times set aside to spend in prayer, but throughout the day we should be talking to the Lord as we go about various tasks.

Praying constantly in the Spirit has two significant implications: (1) It is an admission of our ignorance and impotency in spiritual conflict—we do not know what to do and we do not have the power, of ourselves, to do anything. Such prayer is heeding the words of Proverbs 3:5,6: "Trust in the Lord with all thine heart; and lean not unto thine own understanding. In all thy ways acknowledge him, and he shall direct thy paths." (2) It reveals to the Enemy that we are totally depending on God because we do not have supernatural wisdom and power. By means of prayer, we are "strong in the Lord, and in the power of his might" (Eph. 6:10).

The prayer warrior is a paradox: Toward Christ he shows conscious weakness and seeks strength and wisdom; toward Satan he shows strength in Christ and stands firm in the place of victory.

In ourselves we can do nothing, as is evident from Christ's words: "For without me ye can do nothing" (John 15:5). However, in Christ we can do all things, as Paul stated: "I can do all things through Christ which strengtheneth me" (Phil. 4:13). As we claim our position in Christ through prayer, He will always cause us to triumph (II Cor. 2:14).

Ephesians 6:18 instructs that we are to pray "with all prayer." This refers to every kind of prayer—public, private, long, short, audible, inaudible, asking, thanking. The Bible tells us: "Stop being worried about anything, but always, in prayer and entreaty, and with thanksgiving, keep on making your wants known to God. Then, through your union with Christ Jesus, the peace of God, that surpasses all human thought, will keep guard over your hearts and thoughts" (Phil. 4:6,7, Williams).

Persevering in Prayer

Satan fears the believer who knows how to prevail with God in prayer, for he knows that means the omnipotent power of God is being rallied against him. Because of this, Satan will use any device he can to keep us from praying. Sometimes he uses fatigue for if we wait until the end of the day to spend time in prayer with God we will frequently be too tired to pray. Or Satan will use lethargy and encourage us to delay talking to the Lord about our needs. Satan also uses doubt, discouragement and depression to take away our desire to pray. If these do not work, Satan may use problems at work or in the home to preoccupy our thinking and keep us from prayer. But we are to resist Satan in these attempts and are to be "praying always with all prayer and supplication in the Spirit, and watching thereunto with all perseverance and supplication for all saints" (Eph. 6:18). We are to be alert—"watching thereunto with all perseverance."

The best way the believer has of "watching" or keeping on the alert is through the study of the Scriptures. It is from the Scriptures that we learn to know God's mind, and from them we also learn how Satan may sidetrack us. We must always be on the alert and persevere in our watching.

Notice that we are to pray and watch "with all perseverance." That is, we are not to give up or become discouraged when answers to prayer are delayed. Perhaps you have been praying for something for a long time. Have you ever thought about the fact that God knows exactly when to answer that prayer? Our responsibility is to keep on praying and to trust God completely for an answer according to His will in His own time. If God has really laid something on our hearts that is His will to do, we should not pray and then wonder whether He will do it or not. We should pray and then watch how God is going to answer.

Praying for All Believers

Ephesians 6:18 tells us that we are to be praying and "watching thereunto with all perseverance and supplication for all saints." Prayer for all the saints is necessary because we are all in the spiritual conflict together. All believers are members of the Body of Christ and the Bible says, "Whether one member suffer, all the members suffer with it; or one member be honoured, all the members rejoice with it" (I Cor. 12:26). We need to work together as a team. And remember, individuals who excel in team sports may receive much attention, but much of their success depends on their team

working effectively together. Let us pray for each other in
the spiritual conflict so we will all stand victorious.

Paul was concerned that the Ephesians not only pray for
all saints but that they also pray for him in particular: "And
for me, that utterance may be given unto me, that I may
open my mouth boldly, to make known the mystery of the
gospel, for which I am an ambassador in bonds: that therein I
may speak boldly, as I ought to speak" (Eph. 6:19,20).

Satan had succeeded in getting Paul thrown into prison
but Satan had not succeeded in putting him out of the
spiritual conflict. Paul was still able to bind Satan by prayer
and he was still able to pray for other believers. Paul was
concerned that they pray for him so that he could speak
boldly when opportunity arose.

Do you pray for your pastor? He is in the forefront of
the battle because he has been called of God to lead a
congregation. As a leader, he becomes a special target of
Satan's most vicious attacks. If Satan is able to discredit a
leader, he is able to discredit Christianity in the minds of
many people. No pastor is above the need of prayer. He
needs to be supported by prayer so he will be strengthened to
utter the Word of God in boldness. Of course, when things
are not going well in a church it is easy for the people to
complain about the pastor. Few accept seriously the means
of prayer that God has provided for changing their pastors
into preachers of power—or giving the prayer warrior a better
attitude if that is the problem.

Paul was concerned that he might have the message of
God to give when opportunity arose; thus, he wanted
believers to pray "that utterance may be given to him."
Another translation of this verse is: "And for me that a
message may be given me when I open my lips, so that I may
boldly make known the open secret of the good news"
(Williams). Paul was concerned not only that he have a
message from God when opportunity arose to give it, but also
that he might be able to "speak boldly."

The need today is for the gospel to be given out boldly,
not apologetically. Satan blinds the minds of men to the
gospel (II Cor. 4:4), so the gospel must be stated boldly in
the power of the Holy Spirit if it is going to have an effect.
Some have become utterly confused even as to what the

gospel really is. They equate the gospel to a message of social action. Whenever people come into a personal relationship with Jesus Christ the effects will be felt by society around them, but the gospel is not social action itself. The gospel is the good news that Jesus Christ has paid the penalty for sin and that anyone can have forgiveness of sin and eternal life by receiving Him as Saviour. Our need then is to speak the gospel distinctly and boldly so others will know what the Word of God teaches concerning sin and salvation. Let us pray that there will be a scriptural understanding of the gospel, and that it will be preached boldly in its purity as God's grace to fallen man and available to all who believe.

From Ephesians 6:10-20 it is obvious that we who know Christ have the responsibility to take our victorious position in Christ against Satan. By prayer we must bind the power of Satan to loose those who are bound. We have been endued with power and authority in Christ Jesus, and as we claim our position in Him we will be able to stand victorious against Satan.

Conclusion

As Paul concluded his letter to the Ephesians, he said, "But that ye also may know my affairs, and how I do, Tychicus, a beloved brother and faithful minister in the Lord, shall make known to you all things: whom I have sent unto you for the same purpose, that ye might know our affairs, and that he might comfort your hearts" (Eph. 6:21,22). Paul's tenderness toward the Ephesian believers is seen in that he sent Tychicus to comfort them because of their concern over his well-being.

Paul ended his letter with the benediction: "Peace be to the brethren, and love with faith, from God the Father and the Lord Jesus Christ. Grace be with all them that love our Lord Jesus Christ in sincerity. Amen" (vv. 23,24).

Paul began his letter with the words "grace" and "peace" (1:2), and he concluded it with the same words invoking God's blessing on those who have entered into the transforming truths of this short epistle. The peace to which Paul referred is available to all who will enter into the victories, and grace is always available to those who claim it. May those of us who know Christ return often to the Book of Ephesians to be reminded of our position in Him and then may we live accordingly, for this is living abundantly.